The Complete Idiot's Reference Card

The Children's Book Genres

Here's a quick reference to approximate age levels and lengths for different book formats. Use these as guides, not rules:

- **Board books**   10+ pages, very few words, 0- to 3-year-olds
- **Picture books**   24 to 48 pages (most are 32 pages), 500 to 1,500 words, 3- to 6-year-olds
- **Easy readers with chapters or "early chapter books"**   48 to 64 pages, 1,000 to 5,000 words, approximately 6- to 8-year-olds
- **Young middle-grade**   48 to 80 pages, 3,000 to 20,000 words, longer if nonfiction, fewer illustrations and more difficult vocabulary than easy reader or early chapter books, 7- to 9-year-olds
- **True middle-grade**   80 to 160 pages, 10,000 to 40,000 words or occasionally more, 8- to 12-year-olds
- **Older middle-grade or transitional**   A bit longer, 20,000 to 50,000 words, 10- to 14-year-olds
- **Young adult (or YA)**   Up to 300 pages, up to 75,000 words, 12 and older

What to Include with a Submission

Your story, of course, is the most important element of your submission. Before you mail it off, make sure it is as polished as you can make it. It should …

- Be typed, double-spaced, on one side only of standard white paper. Computer printouts qualify as typed; use a printer that produces clear, crisp documents.
- Include your name, address, and phone number on each page. You can do this as a header or a footer.
- NOT reveal to your prospective editor what you had for breakfast. In other words, no coffee rings or jelly smears.

When you're ready to put your manuscript in the mail, your package should include …

- A brief cover letter
- A SASE with sufficient postage
- Your manuscript with your name and address on it

Most of the time you'll want to package everything in a 9" × 12" envelope so it lies flat. Be sure to put enough postage on your package, and send it first-class mail.

ALPHA

What Not to Include with a Submission

- ➤ A resumé
- ➤ A marketing plan
- ➤ Illustrations (unless you are an illustrator)
- ➤ Plush toys
- ➤ Food and other goodies
- ➤ Cassette tapes or floppy disks

Some Key People at a Publisher

- ➤ **Acquisitions editor**   The person who "acquires" your manuscript and offers you a contract.
- ➤ **Art director**   The person who oversees designers and works with illustrators.
- ➤ **Copy editor**   The person who checks your book for such things as grammar, spelling, and house style.
- ➤ **Designer**   The person who conceptualizes the art and layout of your book and who hires the illustrators.
- ➤ **Development or project editor**   The person who follows your book from manuscript to finished form and works with all aspects of the production of the book. At children's publishers, often the same person as the acquisitions editor.
- ➤ **Managing editor**   The person who keeps track of schedules at a publishing company.
- ➤ **Production manager**   The publisher's contact with printers, companies that do scanning, and so on.
- ➤ **Publicist**   The person responsible for planning and implementing any publicity regarding the publication of your book and who sends your book to the major reviewers.
- ➤ **Sales representative**   The person who shows your book to bookstores and wholesalers.
- ➤ **Subsidiary rights manager**   The person responsible for licensing your book to other companies and getting income from audio cassettes, book clubs, magazines, and so on.

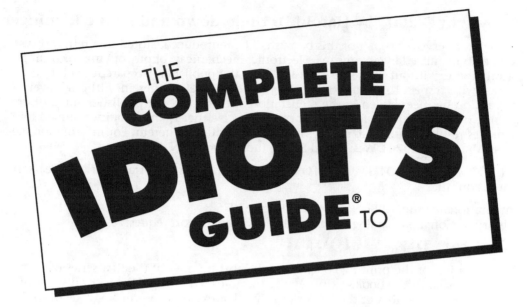

THE COMPLETE IDIOT'S GUIDE® TO

Publishing Children's Books

by Harold D. Underdown and Lynne Rominger

ALPHA

A Pearson Education Company

Publisher
Marie Butler-Knight

Product Manager
Phil Kitchel

Managing Editor
Jennifer Chisholm

Senior Acquisitions Editor
Renee Wilmeth

Development Editor
Deborah S. Romaine

Technical Reviewer
Alison James

Production Editors
Billy Fields
JoAnna Kremer

Copy Editor
Faren Bachelis

Illustrator
Jody P. Schaeffer

Cover Designers
Mike Freeland
Kevin Spear

Book Designers
Scott Cook and Amy Adams of DesignLab

Indexer
Lisa Wilson

Layout/Proofreading
Svetlana Dominguez
Lizbeth Patterson

Contents at a Glance

Contents

Foreword

In this honest and precise book on writing for children, Harold and Lynne have managed to cram in almost everything about writing for children there is to know.

Almost everything.

What they have left out are these three things: joy, gathering, and ducks.

I know this is an odd list. But read on a bit and see what I mean.

Joy. Too many writers talk about the difficulties of writing. How it takes blood and bile. How it is enormously difficult and lonely. How no one in his or her right mind would plan to make a living at it.

But I always want to come down on the side of joy.

Think of it: You will be writing down stories, poems, anecdotes, and information that might change lives.

I always told my children that they should leave the world a little better than they found it. Some might say it's an easy task, given in what awful shape the world is now. But I believe they have taken that mother line to heart. They are good, moral adults, and in their work do make a difference to the world.

Well, I am not modest about it. I get enough letters from children whose lives I *have* changed with my fictions and my poetry to know that it happens. On a small scale—certainly. One reader at a time—absolutely.

Art can work miracles.

Story can.

Now about **gathering**, here is what I mean.

My son Adam, his wife Betsy, and their little daughter Alison live in Minneapolis. When I travel there, I know I will visit with family. Have good meals. See friends. Indulge in amusing conversations. Lots of fun music. (Adam is in two bands.)

What it doesn't mean is writing.

I can still accomplish daily things like keeping up with e-mail and phone calls.

But I do no writing.

Still, I consider these kind of trips "gathering days." Good writing is made up of details. So on these hours away from the computer, away from actual writing, I become a collector of details. Some I collect actively, most passively.

The sweet talc smell of the baby's neck, under the chin. The way my son flicks his long hair away from his daughter's grabby hand. How John, who plays backup guitar in Adam's Irish band, sweats in large discontinuous swatches on his T-shirt. The silhouette of my daughter-in-law holding Alison and how they pat one another on the back simultaneously. The damp Minnesota heat that leaves moist patches, like tears, under my eyes. The exact arch of a catalpa tree leaning over the street.

It may look as if a writer uses such stuff to keep her away from the actual hard work of writing. And in fact many authors will tell outsiders just that. But do not be fooled. It is actually all grist to the mill.

For example, while I am speeding through the latest Dick Francis novel, I am also noting how he keeps his story moving, how the arc of his telling forces the reader to keep going. Reading the latest issue of *Cricket* or Richard Peck's Newbery Award novel I am taking in what is considered the best writing today. Working crossword puzzles, I am discovering new words. Watching TV, I am practicing dialogue. Listening to local gossip, I invest in character.

I never turn off my writer's head. Conversations are stuffed in there, the chalky sweet smell of paper-white roses, the sharp fishiness of herring fillets, the rough crumble of unharled stone, the way a rose bush points its wayward fingers upward in its search for some new purchase, how the ruined towers of a castle take on extra life against a grey sky, the feel of my granddaughter's small wriggly hand in mind.

All this and more will be returned to me when I need it in a scene or a poem or as a central metaphor for a story.

I didn't know that when I began writing. I thought any time away from the typewriter was wasted time. Then my husband and I spent nine months camping in Europe and the Middle East and I started throwing images of what I had seen into my stories. That's when I understood how important gathering days are for writers.

Finally, there are those **ducks.**

Often I feel as if my writing time is slowly being nibbled away by ducks. Other writers have made similar complaints. Life, we all say, simply gets in the way.

But then on reading a biography about Emily Dickinson, where she's shown making tea cakes and writing letters, helping in the house and playing with her nephew, etc., I realize that we writers still must live in the real world. That means cakes, letters, bills, clogged toilets, etc. That means reading other people's books, watching TV, doing crossword puzzles, chatting on the phone. That means taking children to school, to the orthodontist, to choir practice, to basketball games. That means working till 3, till 5, till 8, till midnight. That means vacuuming the living room of cat hairs, dog hairs, husband's hairs. That means running to the grocery store, the paint store, the shoe store. That means going to the doctor, the dentist, the hair salon.

What that means is life.

Besides, without life, what's there to write about?

—Jane Yolen

Jane Yolen is the award-winning author of more than 200 books for children, young adults, and adults. Ms. Yolen's best-known title, the critically acclaimed *Owl Moon* (Putnam/Philomel), illustrated by John Schoenherr, won the prestigious Caldecott Medal for 1988. Among Jane Yolen's many other awards are the Catholic Library Association's 1992 Regina Medal for her work in children's literature and the University of Minnesota's Kerlan Award for the body of her work. She has also received numerous state awards, including New York's "Charlotte," Nebraska's "Golden Sower," and New Jersey's "Garden State Children's Book Award."

Introduction

Harold attends children's writer's conferences, and he runs a personal Web site on the world of children's publishing, and over and over again people ask him about how to get started, where the publishers are, how to get feedback on a manuscript, and about other problems with which writers struggle as they try to establish themselves. It's hard to find all the basic information about this cozy but mystifying world. And that, quite simply, is why we wrote this book—to bring together all that information. What you have in your hands is, we hope, a resource that lays out all the basics and points writers in the correct direction to learn more.

Different people, of course, may have different ideas about what the basics are, or need different kinds of information at different times. So we've written dozens of definitions of publishing terms and taken a philosophical look at how your motives can affect your writing. We've dissected the parts of a book and sketched a mini-history of children's publishing. We provide help in understanding contracts and sample letters to accompany manuscripts. And we've included many places to go for more information.

We love being involved in children's books, but know from personal experience that there's a lot to keep up with. We hope this book helps you to do that, and to spend more time writing and less time trying to figure it all out.

How to Use This Book

The world of children's book publishing can be confusing and complicated to those unfamiliar with its traditions and procedures. We've organized this book into five parts to unravel the complexities for you, guiding you through the maze to your ultimate goal: publication.

Part 1, "Where to Begin?" provides suggestions and information about moving your ideas from your imagination onto paper—the first steps of their journey to publication.

Part 2, "Finding Out What's Possible," explores the many faces of children's publishing. From board books for toddlers to historical novels for young adult readers, the kinds of children's books have different audiences, approaches, needs—and, of course, publishers.

Part 3, "Out into the World," gives you guidance in getting your manuscript from your desk to the right company, and to the right editor at that company.

Part 4, "Working with a Publisher," explains what happens after you sign on the dotted line. If you think your work ended when the publisher accepted your book, these chapters are especially for you!

Part 5, "My Book Is Published! Now What?" discusses the many events that move your book up the sales chain. From publicity appearances to reading for school children, there are many opportunities for you to increase your book's presence in the marketplace.

We've also created a glossary of terms used in children's publishing, a resource list of books, magazines, organizations, and Web sites, and sample letters and guidelines. You'll find all these in the appendixes.

Extras

Sidebar boxes throughout the book highlight interesting information and important details.

Vocabulary List

These boxes explain terms and lingo common in the children's publishing industry.

Class Rules

These boxes provide warnings and cautions.

Can You Keep a Secret?

In these boxes, you'll find suggestions, tips, and resources to help you present yourself as a pro.

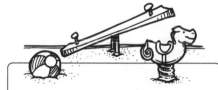

Stories from the Playground

These anecdotes from, and profiles of, children's authors and publishers give you an inside view of the children's publishing world.

Acknowledgments

From Harold D. Underdown: Harold is always telling writers that a book is a team effort. This one was no different. It wouldn't have happened without the help of dozens of people. Renee Wilmeth contacted me to start it off and helped me shape the outline, Lynne Rominger came on board to help make it happen—and to add her own expertise, particularly in the marketing area. Debbie Romaine was an editor's editor (quite literally). Finishing this while I was working full-time was tough, but Debbie made it possible.

Many others contributed their expertise and experience in e-mails and phone conversations, some of which I've quoted directly, others of which contributed to the thinking that shaped the book. They include Jennifer Armstrong, Bruce Balan, Susan Campbell Bartoletti, Miriam Bat-Ami, Carmen Bernier-Grand, Larry Dane Brimner, Evelyn Coleman, Elizabeth Devereaux, Muriel L. Dubois, Lisa Rowe Fraustino, Sandy Ferguson Fuller, Charles Ghigna, James Cross Giblin, Lois Grambling, Megan Halsey, Tony Johnston, Elaine Landau, Grace Lin, Diane Mayr, Stephen Mooser, Josephine Nobisso, Jules Older, Larry Pringle, Dana Rau, Pam Muñoz Ryan, Aaron Shepard, Alexandra Siy, Donna Spurlock, Ginger Wadsworth, Jan Wahl, Rozanne Lanczak Williams, Carolyn Yoder, and Jane Yolen. If I talked with you and you're not on this list, blame my record-keeping, not my lack of gratitude.

I interviewed a number of people by phone or e-mail and appreciate the time they took to deal with my sometimes lengthy lists of questions. So my special thanks to Emma Dryden, Bernette Ford, Jennifer Greene, Regina Griffin, Kate Jackson, Margaret K. McElderry, George Nicholson, and Paula Quint—and also to colleagues at Charlesbridge and ipicturebooks.com, for putting up with my sometimes distracted air while working on the book.

My family and friends have been remarkably tolerant of my absence from their lives over the last several months and of my aura of pre-occupation on the rare occasions when I came to the surface.

My thanks above all to my wife, Ann Rubin, who not only encouraged me to take on this project when it first was offered, but never once expressed regret at having done so, and even continued to encourage me. As an artist, not a publishing insider, she also brought perspective into what was truly important on the many occasions when I got lost in the details. Most of all, her confidence that what I might want to say was worthwhile kept me going. This book would not have happened without her.

From Lynne Rominger: First, Lynne would like to thank God. I can do nothing in this world without His Grace. Next in line: Harold Underdown, of course. It was a pleasure working on this book with such a professional, knowledgeable, and interesting children's book super editor! You are an inspiration to me, Harold. Another round of thanks go out to Sheree Bykofsky, my agent, Renee Wilmeth, the acquisitions editor of this book, and Jennifer Basye Sander, my mentor. All women deserve my gratitude for nurturing my writing career. And Debbie Romaine receives a huge thank you; you are a miracle worker, Debbie. Now, how can I possibly write a book without thanking my family? Nick, Sophia, Faith, and Hope—you are the most patient and loving children in the world. I promise to read to you all often and hope you grow up to love books. Finally, my undying adoration and thanks go out to my soul mate and the eternal love of my life, Pashko Gjonaj. There was not a moment while writing this book that you were not in my mind and my heart, your love leading me to the next paragraph and the next page. I am wired backward without you but forward with your arms around me. I love you so much I could just burst. With you, I am complete.

Special Thanks to the Technical Reviewer

The Complete Idiot's Guide to Publishing Children's Books was reviewed by an expert who double-checked the accuracy of what you'll learn here, to help us ensure that this book gives you everything you need to know about writing your story, getting your children's story into the hands of a publisher, working with a publisher, and building a career. Special thanks are extended to Alison James.

Ms. James is an author of novels and picture books, a translator, and a founder and organizer of the Kindling Words conference and Writers Colony.

Trademarks

All terms mentioned in this book that are known to be or are suspected of being trademarks or service marks have been appropriately capitalized. Alpha Books and Pearson Education, Inc., cannot attest to the accuracy of this information. Use of a term in this book should not be regarded as affecting the validity of any trademark or service mark.

Part 1

Where to Begin?

If you're not a part of it, children's publishing can be a confusing world. In this part of the book, we're giving you the basics so you can get started with what you want to do: write books for children.

We kick off with ways to get started writing, show you how to find the best, most popular, and most recent children's books, and take a look at how your motives for writing can affect your writing itself. Then we take you from your immediate world—your office space and how to get organized—to the big world of publishing and what's been happening there recently. Finally, we give you a detailed guided tour of a book, so you can call each part by its right name.

That's a lot to cover, so hold on to your hat, and turn the page!

Chapter 1

Adults Rule the World

In This Chapter

➤ What this book is all about

➤ Some basics about children's books

➤ The importance of taking yourself seriously

➤ An introduction to the challenges of writing for children

➤ A quiz—what do you want to know?

Welcome to a wonderful and challenging world, the world of children's books. We gave this chapter a title that pushes against the subject of this book just to remind you (and us) of a strange paradox at the heart of children's publishing. We are at work creating books for children, but everyone involved in producing and then buying them, with rare exceptions, is an adult. Even if in your mind you are writing for a child you know well—your own child, or the child you once were—for your work to become a book it must go through the hands of many adults.

Getting Started

So you want to write a children's book. Maybe you already have. Maybe you've sent it out to a few publishers and it's come back to you. Or maybe you've been writing for a few years, and had some success, but want to push on ahead. Wherever you are, you're beginning, though what you're beginning may be your whole career or just a stage in it. In either case, we think this book is for you. Getting started is hard, so we've filled this book with information, advice, resources, and stories of success and failure.

Piercing the Static

Harold describes the thousands of manuscripts that children's publishers receive every year as static, making it almost impossible for the few good ones to be noticed. You've got to pierce that static. To do that, you need four things:

➤ You need to work hard on your writing and keep striving to improve it.

➤ You need to learn as much as you can about the publishing world.

➤ You need to be persistent, over years if necessary.

➤ You need some luck.

That's a tall order. Many people never do get published. We aim to help you get through the static so you can have a chance of being among those who do.

No One Best Way

You may be looking for the best way to get your children's book published. If so, we want you to know up front that there isn't one. There are as many ways as there are people, and that can be both frightening and freeing. It's frightening, because you'll have to figure out some things for yourself. It's freeing, because it allows you to be yourself. The good news is that in this book you'll learn about options you might not have considered—types of writing to try, ways to approach publishers, kinds of publishers to investigate—and you'll learn how to chart your own path. Keep going down that path! If you don't, you won't reach the end of it.

It Takes Time

We hope you'll come to understand the value of patience. As you'll see in some of the stories we tell, writing for children is not the simple task that some outsiders assume. It's more like becoming a brain surgeon, in some ways. It takes years and years, in which you learn many things and practice your technique and gradually get better.

So don't be too hard on yourself, and don't look over your shoulder to compare yourself to others. Deal with the challenges in front of you, whatever they may be, and after that you can worry about the next ones. As you learn and grow, and improve, you may not even notice your progress, but a day may come when you look up and find that you're on the top of that hill that only a short while earlier had looked like it was unclimbable.

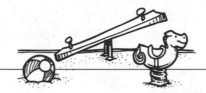

Stories from the Playground

It can take longer than you might expect to feel that you have arrived. So said Simms Taback, illustrator, in his acceptance speech for the Caldecott Medal, the most prestigious award for illustrators (his speech was published in the July/August 2000 issue of *The Horn Book Magazine*): "What's really wonderful about getting this award is that I feel like a relative newcomer to the world of illustration, as if I have only just arrived as a practitioner of this craft. But actually, I have been illustrating for 40 years." He goes on to cite missteps and bad luck that kept him from feeling that he had ever "made it."

Lots to Learn—Start Here

There is a lot to learn. Children's book publishing is a big business. There are many kinds of publishers, and many kinds of books, and right ways and wrong ways to do even such a simple thing as write a cover letter to go with a manuscript. This is a world unto itself, and you need to know the jargon and the shared assumptions of the people in it if you are going to have a better chance of succeeding.

Books and Publishers

Writing itself is hard enough. But if you are to go from a neatly typed manuscript to an actual book, you need to make sense of the children's publishing industry. You need to figure out what you have written and what publisher might be interested in it.

Picture Books and Chapter Books

There are many kinds of children's books, and we'll go into them in the chapters in Part 2, "Finding Out What's Possible," but to start with you need to understand a basic distinction. *Picture books* are books in which the pictures and words tell the story together. Often they have pictures on every page, and are read to children by the adults in their lives. *Chapter books,* on the other hand, have chapters. They may also have pictures, but they aren't as important. The words tell the story. And these books are usually meant to be read by children or teenagers themselves.

Both of these basic types get divided up into smaller categories. Do you have to know exactly what you've written? No, and sometimes a publisher will have a different idea about what you've written than you do. But it helps to know the basics, because some publishers only publish one type or the other. So you'll need to learn about them, too.

So Many Publishers!

At first glance, it may seem like there are hundreds of publishers all over the country. Or it can seem like there are only five, and they're all in New York. It's tricky to sort them all out, especially since in the last decade publishers have bought out other publishers in what seems like a never-ending dance of mergers and acquisitions. Actually, though five or six very large publishers may seem to dominate the market, there are many other publishers around the United States and Canada, and we are going to help you find them.

Kinds of Publishers

Different publishers, and sometimes different divisions of the same company, create very different kinds of books. A company selling books to libraries takes a different approach than one that sells its books in bookstores, or one that puts its books in racks in drugstores. Depending on what you want to write, you've got to find the right match. *Trade* publishers aim for the bookstores for the most part, though some also sell to schools and libraries. *Mass market* publishers target a wider audience, and find it in supermarkets and other general retail stores. Beyond books, magazines and electronic publishing beckon, too.

We'll have a lot more to say about these different markets later in the book.

Putting Away Childish Things

As you read this book, and as you start to have contact with publishers, writers, and librarians, you'll find that children's publishing isn't all fluffy kittens and sad-eyed puppies. It may not be quite so cutthroat as some businesses, but we've both heard it said that "it's a bunny-eat-bunny-world." Be prepared for this.

Take It Seriously

Begin by taking what you are about to do seriously. This is not a hobby or a pastime, or something you can succeed in by writing only during your summer vacations. On the other hand, you don't have to define success by making money from your writing. As many will tell you, it's unlikely you'll ever be able to quit your day job. Writing for children is not easy and takes time, space, and dedication. As we'll detail in Chapter 5, "The Piggy Bank and the Notebook," it's important to set up a space, set aside writing time, and remember that you need and deserve this.

Art and Commerce

Remember, too, that at the end of the process, at least if you want to get published, is a book or magazine or something similar that someone (actually thousands of someones) will have to decide to buy. You're an artist, but you're not creating one idiosyncratic work that needs to find only one buyer, or that you might even be keeping for yourself. Book publishing lies in an interesting middle area between art and commerce, between pure self-expression and the manufacture of millions of such useful but generic items as pencils and bars of soap. There's room for creativity, but you need to find an audience (your market), and a publisher will help you do that.

Can You Keep a Secret?

How big is children's publishing? Estimates suggest about $2 billion in sales annually, with six publishers—Random House, Penguin Putnam, Golden Books, HarperCollins, Scholastic, and Simon & Schuster—accounting for about half. This is 4,000 to 5,000 books published each year, half by the big guys. But hundreds (maybe thousands) of smaller companies publish books, too, right down to individuals who publish their own books.

"When You Grow Up, Will You Write for Adults?"

Once you reach the point of identifying yourself as a writer for children, it won't be long before you run into the condescension of those who assume that they, too, could write wonderful children's books, if they could just find the time. Or those who exclaim that it's just wonderful that you've taken up such a hobby.

Sadly, many people don't understand that writing for children is as significant, challenging, and absorbing as any other form of writing, from investigative journalism to spoken word poetics. The attitude of these benighted souls seems to be that children aren't as mature or intelligent as adults, and so it must be easier to write for them. Don't slide unaware into becoming one of the people who believes this. You are doing serious writing, writing that actually is harder than writing for adults. After all, you aren't writing for someone just like you, though perhaps you are writing for the child you used to be. It can be tricky to write for this "other": after all, adults writing for other adults can use their own reactions as guides to how their audiences will react. You can't do that. Be proud of what you are doing.

What This Book Can Do for You

Just how are we going to help you deal with the issues we've been discussing, as well as teach you what you need to learn? What follows is a discussion of what we realistically can and cannot do for you.

The Whole Picture

We've worked hard to give you a comprehensive overview of this field. We aren't just giving you information about children's book publishers—we look at magazines and electronic publishing too. We get you started with tips on getting your manuscript to the right publishing companies, follow up with guidance on revision and contract negotiation, and help you complete the process through marketing and self-promotion. We've included a little of everything, though of course we'll be happy to hear from you if there's something you think we've left out and you want to suggest for the next edition—we provide contact information in Appendix B, "Resources."

No Magic Formula

Looking for guidance on writing? We give you help on getting started writing, on examining your motives for writing, and on getting feedback. But we don't tell you *how* to write. There are so many different kinds of children's books, and we're covering so much other information, that a how-to-write section would have become a series of oversimplified formulas. You could use them, and end up with formulaic stories, but there's nothing an editor dislikes more than formulaic stories. Fortunately, there are already many great books that explain how to write different kinds of children's books. We've listed many of them in Appendix B.

X Marks the Spot

The many books, Web sites, and other sources for more help that we identify in the appendixes and throughout make this book a treasure map to the many places you can go for more information. You could find those places yourself, of course. But there are hundreds of books on publishing and on children's books, and as many Web sites. We've checked them out and organized them and made some judgments on which ones are worthwhile, so that you don't have to take the time out from your writing to do a lot of digging.

How Others Did It

A book full of advice and information would be pretty dry and hard to understand without real-life stories. We don't include these just for the human interest, though that would be enough of a reason. We include them because there's no better way to learn how to move forward in children's publishing than to hear how others have done it. Or failed to do it, as the case may be. We've got stories and tips from extremely successful authors, and from authors just getting started, from authors who've succeeded in many areas, and from others who've specialized. And when it's called for, we've got stories from publishing insiders too, so you can begin to get to know the people with whom you may be working.

Class Rules

Children's author Jules Older notes three mistakes many writers make starting out:

1. Thinking cute, instead of thinking big.
2. Failing to be funny.
3. Writing for a previous generation, instead of today's.

A Vade Mecum

In a way, this is a most old-fashioned kind of a book, a "vade mecum." This is a reference manual, a book that "goes with me." We don't expect you to read it from cover to cover, though we've set it up so that you could if you wanted to. We think you're more likely to read some of it, put it on your shelf, pull it down to look something up, look through it again a year or two from now, and perhaps find that a section that hadn't seemed relevant at first has become critically important. We hope this book will go with you as you learn and move ahead with your career.

Know the Forest, Not the Trees

Though we've packed it full of specific information, we hope this book will most of all help you begin to get to know the forest of children's book publishing. The strange ecosystem that is children's publishing changes slowly, even though individual trees may come and go. From the trees in this book—individual publishers, editors, types of books—you'll begin to put together an understanding of how the forest works, so that when you venture into new and uncharted parts of it you'll be less likely to get lost and go hungry. You'll know where to look for food and how to watch out for danger. You'll know how to survive, even if you don't recognize all the trees.

No Guarantees

One thing we can't offer you in this book is a guarantee. There are thousands of aspiring authors out there, and we know from talking to some of them that you can follow the "rules" (or even find creative ways to bend them) and work for years and still not get published. If all you want is to get published by a well-known publisher, in fact, you might want to give up now. That desire isn't going to be enough to get you there. You have to like what you are doing, and stick to it, have some talent, and, even then, understand that you might not make it. If the journey is worth it in itself, we're here to help you choose your supplies and maybe even be one of your traveling companions. But if the trip's only worth it if you arrive at your destination, you might want to think twice.

Above all, be inspired by the example of a J. K. Rowling, but don't be disappointed if a career like hers doesn't evolve for you. With the amazing worldwide sales of millions of copies that the Harry Potter books have achieved, she did what no other author, whether for adults or for children, has ever done. Ever! Don't measure your success, or lack of it, against hers—or against the success of any other author. Your personal best is what matters.

Enough of preamble! On with the book!

The Least You Need to Know

➤ You're starting out on a long and interesting road. Don't try to rush it.

➤ Getting a children's book published takes persistence.

➤ Understand the difference between picture and chapter books and between trade and mass market.

➤ Take yourself seriously, and take writing for children seriously.

➤ Use this book as a reference manual and a starting point—we don't have all the answers, but we'll help you find them.

Chapter 2

I Don't Know What to Say! And What Comes Next

In This Chapter

➤ How to find a direction

➤ How to use a journal to explore your interests

➤ Why writing must be practiced and how to do it

➤ What you need to do to write and how to create the time and space

➤ What to do when you think you're finished

There are few things as terrifying as a piece of blank paper staring up at you. Hungry polar bears in a snowstorm or ghosts in a bedding shop come to mind. The empty whiteness of it is terrifying, as Melville said about the eerie whiteness of Moby Dick.

We're going to suggest ways to fill that page: how to discover what you want to write, if you're unsure, and how to practice your writing and imagining skills, in much the same way you might practice skiing or hitting a golf ball. These are limbering-up exercises—we won't tell you how to write them, but we'll get into the specific formats and types of children's books in Chapters 7, "What's in a Book? A Guided Tour," and 8, "Animal, Vegetable, or Mineral? Book Formats and Age Levels." In this chapter, you'll also learn how to create the conditions you need to write without distractions, and how to keep working on your writing until it's truly ready.

You Are What You Read

Do you have the writing bug, but you just don't know what to write? Take a few minutes to ask yourself what you like to read. When I say, "Go," I'd like you to get up, go over to your bookshelves, and take a careful look at them. Which books sit there, never opened? Which ones have cracked bindings, well-thumbed pages, and little notes in the margins? Can you see certain kinds of books you usually read, or are your favorites fiction, nonfiction, light, heavy—all over the map? Then come back here and think about what you've seen. OK, go!

Back already? So, what did you notice? Do you read lots of fiction? Nonfiction? Do you really love detective novels but never read those serious novels you think you should?

In your reading, as in your writing, rule one is to write what you want to write, not what you think you should. "Shoulds" clog the mind and get in the way of the clear thinking you need to do your best writing, so run away from them.

Let's say you've noticed that you really like to read books that present science to a general audience, such as Lewis Thomas does for adults. Well, you can do the same thing for children, provided you do your research, of course, and truly understand the scientific principles covered. Almost any kind of book you like as an adult points to a similar kind for children:

➤ Like romance novels? So do teenagers.

➤ Enjoy science fiction? Children do, too.

➤ Biographies grab you? Libraries grab them.

➤ Prefer magazines? So do many children.

Rest assured, you'll find something to write. But don't be too hasty and start by writing a specific type of book for a specific audience. First you need to explore ways of generating raw material, get in some practice, and set up the habits and schedule that will keep you going.

Can You Keep a Secret?

Your ninth-grade English teacher may have instilled in you a deep respect (and fear?) for the classics, but that doesn't mean that you have to go out and try to write one, at least not yet. Creativity is hard enough; do like the pros do and write what you like to write, not what your family says you should.

Dear Diary

Just about everybody has kept a diary at some time or another. If you haven't, don't feel bad, because most diaries cover mundane events, or, if written by a teenager, feelings that are very important to the diarist but probably to no one else. Now that you are writing, however, you should seriously consider keeping a diary that goes by a grander name—a *journal*.

A journal can be many things. You can use it to write about whatever is on your mind at the time. You can use it to record things you've observed that interest you, from the changing of the cloud patterns in the sky to the changing of emotions in the teenagers sitting next to you in the bus. You can use it to note ideas, remember sentences that come to you, transcribe snippets of dialogue, or to do pen portraits of interesting characters. You can use it to explore your feelings about writing, or your reactions to books you've read. More practically, you can keep track of when you write, for how long, and how effectively, so that you can figure out your best writing times.

Vocabulary List

The word **journal** is related to the French word for day, *jour*. As that implies, a journal is a blank book to write in daily. Your journal should be as much a part of your life as a cup of coffee in the morning or the evening news.

If you're going to get the most out of your journal, you need to use it regularly. It's good to keep it with you so you can jot something down whenever you want to, but don't stop there. Make an appointment with yourself to write in your journal every day. Try to make it be the same time. If you can't, make sure that you find times when you won't be interrupted.

Writing every day can be difficult to maintain, especially without a structure. Don't feel bad that you aren't inspired; give yourself a break and give yourself a structure. Take a month to explore your feelings about your parents and your siblings, or to note down some key memories from a particular year of your childhood. Or give yourself a theme of the day:

➤ Monday for family.

➤ Tuesday for friends.

➤ Wednesday for writing.

➤ Thursday for the natural world.

➤ Friday for planning.

➤ Saturday for fun.

➤ Sunday for spirituality.

Choose whatever topics are most important to you. What matters is that you make your journal your own, and that you be as honest with yourself in it as you can be. Make a point of reading back through it from time to time. Gradually, ideas and areas of interest will start to emerge and become clearer. Also, with the added practice of writing in a journal, your writing will benefit.

Practice Makes Perfect

A journal isn't the only way you can practice your writing. There are many ways in which you can work not only on improving the quality of your writing but also on your fluency. Getting words down on paper so that you can go back and revise later is a challenge to every writer, so the more easily and rapidly you can write, the better.

Writing exercises will also help you get started on a particular project. No writer starts a manuscript without a considerable amount of what is called "prewriting," meaning brainstorming, outlining, and the like. Jennifer Armstrong, a published author of fiction and nonfiction, observes:

> I spend a lot of time on preparation. Lots of notes, lots of outlining, lots of character sketching. (This of course all depends on what I'm writing.) Not until I really know where the book is going do I begin writing prose.

Our schools often leave us with the idea that the best way to write, and the way that the *good* writers write, is to sit and let the story flow out. That doesn't happen very often. There's a lot that comes beforehand, and as you'll see a little later in this chapter, there's a lot that comes after.

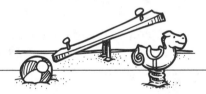

Stories from the Playground

When exploring writing for children, don't limit yourself to books aimed at children's writers. Natalie Goldberg's *Writing Down the Bones* and *Wild Mind: Living the Writer's Life* are great sources of inspiration and practical exercises. Ignore the New Age vocabulary if it bothers you. Or check out Jessica Wilbur's *Totally Private and Personal: Journaling Ideas for Girls and Young Women*. In spite of the title, it's great for people of any age and either gender. Take the time to browse through the general writing section in your local bookstore for books like these.

As you'll discover when you spend a little time exploring the titles about writing in a good bookstore, there are many ways to work on your writing. Here are a few.

Let It Flow

Writing without stopping to edit yourself or rethinking is difficult to do, but you can learn to do it. Give yourself five minutes to write, without stopping, without going back and correcting a word or a spelling. If you can't think of anything to write, just write "I can't think of anything to write," and keep going. Use a pen, a pencil, a typewriter, or a computer. The tool doesn't matter, so long as you feel comfortable with it. Do this every day, in your journal or not, as you choose.

After you've had some practice with this technique, try varying it. Give yourself a topic to start off with, or a writing prompt (a sentence to complete), and see where it leads you. Write "I love to write children's books because …" or maybe "I'm scared to write children's books because …." After some use of this technique, you may find that your conscious mind lets go a little, and you start writing things that surprise you. Like speakers practicing speaking off-the-cuff on impromptu subjects, this free, sustained writing can loosen you up and raise the overall quality of your writing. You'll still be revising, but from a higher level. Our thanks to Natalie Goldberg for these ideas.

Visualization

Clear, concise description is a joy, and difficult to achieve, whether you are writing about a dark and stormy night or a new scientific discovery. Practicing visualization can help you improve your skills at description.

Settle on a scene you'd like to visualize, perhaps from your childhood, perhaps more recent, but not one that's right in front of you. Close your eyes, and conjure it up. Take some time to bring as much of it to your mind's eye as possible. If it's a room, imagine yourself walking around in it, looking under things, behind things, maybe even out the window. If you imagine yourself outside, walk around there, too. Settle on the limits of your scene. After you've looked your fill, listen. What sounds belong in your scene? What do you smell? What do you feel: the temperature of the air, the textures of the objects around you? If there's something edible, what do you taste?

After you feel you've fully placed yourself in your chosen scene, open your eyes and write. Describe it as fully and evocatively as you can. Don't edit! As with the previous exercise, just keep writing. After you have finished—and you could go on for pages and pages—you can go back and edit. You might use this to help you imagine a setting for a story, or you might just use it for practice. But try it again, with a different place. With practice, your ability to picture places familiar and unfamiliar will improve, and so will your ability to describe them.

Memories

Many writers for children draw on childhood experiences and memories as the raw material of their writing. Even if that is not your intention, even if you plan to write only about American history or biology or sports, being in touch with your own childhood and the feelings that you had then can only improve your ability to connect with your audience.

Can You Keep a Secret?

Looking for some guidance on writing specific kinds of children's books? You won't find it here, because that would be a whole other book, and because there are already many wonderful books that provide just that help. What books, you say? You'll find a carefully selected list of them in Appendix B, "Resources."

Think about an important milestone in your childhood, maybe the moment when you first succeeded in tying your own shoelaces, or the moment when you walked up to the chalkboard and wrote the right answer to a difficult math problem, or the moment when you said something clever at lunch and you noticed that cute boy (or girl) smiling. Visualize it. Write about it. Or remember the time you got lost in the big department store, or the time you had a fight with the playground bully, or the time you saw the girl (or the boy) you had a crush on dancing with someone else at the school dance, and obviously enjoying herself. Visualize that and write about it.

You might take some time exploring as many memories as you can bring up from a particular time in your life, or following a thread of memories about your pesky kid sister from your earliest one to the day you left for college. Set yourself your own memory explorations. Try different emphases: for one, you might concentrate on recalling how the breakfast table and your family around it looked; for another, you might focus on the story of what happened when you dug a hole to China in the back yard. Find the threads that interest you and follow them!

You may then develop something from your memory explorations. One or more of them could become the basis for a scene in a novel, or for an entire picture-book story. Or these explorations might help you understand what interests you in the world around you and find ways to present information to excite the child, you, and—we hope—your audience.

Get a Feel for It

Do you think you're ready to write that story? Maybe you already have. Whether you have or not, here's one final exercise that will help you get a feel for the form of a children's book.

Choose a favorite children's book and head to your typewriter or word processor. And all you have to do is to type it up, breaking the paragraphs where they break in the book. If it's a picture book, do the whole thing. If it's a novel, do a chapter or part of it.

Spontaneity or Results?

Now you're all ready to be creative. So wait for inspiration to strike, and then get to work. You may be waiting a long time. Writers—accomplished writers—learn early to just start writing. Writing is work: flashes of insight followed by the labor of translating that insight into words, and then revision (tips follow). Just like any other job, if you plan to succeed and turn in the goods, you need to put your nose to the grindstone.

But unlike those lucky people in 9-to-5 jobs, writers don't have supervisors breathing down their necks to get the job done—especially unpublished writers without deadlines. Your first book will result entirely from your own willpower. And even after you've got a book contract or established yourself as a full-time children's book author, you still won't have anyone hovering over you with a whip each morning, yelling, "Write!" You also won't have anyone telling you that your break ran too long. In one word, the profession you've chosen takes *dedication*. You need to look at your writing as you would any other job and set up a schedule.

Sitting behind a computer day-in and day-out in your bathrobe, barely showered, slaving away on a manuscript that might sell to a publisher or might not, isn't super glam. Believe us. It's easy to procrastinate. We, too, have had those times when washing the dog seems more urgent than writing. To succeed in the solitude of writing, we offer these tips:

➤ Set a schedule and stick to it. Say to yourself, "I'm going to write every day from this time to that time," and do it. If you can only manage 15 minutes, that's OK. Just make it every day. Post your schedule on the refrigerator, and ask your family to respect it.

➤ Remove distractions, including children. Many, many parents hope to juggle the needs of their writing and of their children. But writing is a job. Any established writer will tell you that you can't concentrate on children and writing at the same time.

➤ After you establish a schedule, every so often give yourself a change of scenery. When you write full-time from home, you'll find yourself turning into Howard Hughes if you don't get out of the house sometimes. So take a notepad and pen to your local coffeehouse or library and write there. Stick to your schedule, just write somewhere other than home.

Class Rules

We're emphasizing the importance of setting up time to write, but don't leave out time to goof off, as Barbara Seuling notes in *How to Write a Children's Book and Get It Published*. If you feel guilty about doing things other than writing, sooner or later writing will become a drag. Give yourself writing time, yes, but give yourself nonwriting time, too.

Can You Keep a Secret?

Jennifer Basye Sander, an author of more than 20 books and the mother of two small boys, hires a baby-sitter for several hours a day while she writes. Coauthor Lynne either has her mother care for her four small ones while she writes, or she writes in the early morning or late evening hours while they sleep.

➤ Let your neighbors and friends know you're working, not watching old movies. If you don't, you may find yourself the block baby-sitter or errand runner. Be firm and practice saying, "I'm sorry, but I'm working, I can't pick up your dry cleaning for you or baby-sit your son."

➤ Let the answering machine pick up the phone, and don't answer the door. You aren't home, you're writing.

Other than these few tips, there really isn't much more we can say about time management. You just need to do it—write! If you want it (the finished book) badly enough, you'll do it.

Do It Again!

Remember when you were in school you'd sit down and write an essay straight through from start to finish and hand it in? Professional writers don't work like that. You spend a good amount of time first getting ready to write—researching, brainstorming, outlining—you write, and then you revise. And it's no exaggeration to say that most writing is revision. Because a lot of that happens after you start working with an editor, we go into the different parts of that process in Chapter 21, "Make It Better." But of course, you'll also want to revise on your own.

You can go too far with revision. There's a point where more revision is just avoiding the dreaded time when you show your work to someone else. How do you know when you've reached that point? You'll have to learn your own work habits, but watch out for revisions that don't change much. Are you changing a word here and there on each round, just tinkering? Or are you switching back and forth between two approaches? Both of these are clues that you're really done with the piece, for now, and that it's time to send it out. At least it's time to get some good feedback on it, as we will show you how to do in Chapter 4, "Why Write a Children's Book—and Why Not?"

The Least You Need to Know

➤ Knowing what you like to read will help guide you in discovering what you might like to write.

➤ Systematic use of a journal can help you grow as a writer.

➤ Creativity exercises will help you explore your interests and improve your writing.

➤ Set a schedule for yourself.

➤ Revise, revise, revise—but know when to stop.

Chapter 3

Survey Course: The World of Children's Literature

In This Chapter

➤ Why your audience is so important

➤ Find out where to learn about the different areas of children's literature

➤ Learn about which children's books are most respected by librarians and other adults

➤ Discover good ways to learn what children like to read

Crucial to writing for children is acquiring an understanding and knowledge of what children want to read, have read, and continue to read. You need to immerse yourself in the world of children's literature. Just as it's not enough to think you have a good idea for a business and then plunge yourself and your money into it, it's not enough to think you have a good idea for a children's book. What would you do in the case of a business? You'd research your prospects. Check out the competition. Look at how a similar business might have thrived in the past. The same goes in children's writing. You need to immerse yourself.

In this chapter, we'll navigate you through your possibilities. We'll give you the map to the world of children's literature—from classics to cool new books—and also touch on why understanding your audience is crucial in writing for kids.

Try It, You'll Like It

Remember how Mom used to nudge you into exploring new foods? "Try it. You'll like it," she'd say, as she'd thrust avocados or a new casserole on your plate. And as you grew up, you found many new favorites by listening to her, right? Well, children's

Vocabulary List

When you write, you write in the hopes other people will read your work. Your readers become your **audience.** It remains important to know who your audience is—especially in children's writing, where you are not a member of your audience, and where there are big differences in reading ability and maturity. Your audience will ultimately determine your style and tone.

Class Rules

Don't assume that books you loved as a child are in fact classics or would be loved by children today. New classics come along, and old ones retire. We tend to believe that "the classics" are a fixed pantheon, but in fact every generation adds and subtracts to suit new tastes, conditions, and assumptions about what is good for children.

literature is kind of like trying foods. There is no one right way to write or one group for which you're writing. Instead you'll find varied reading levels, age groups, styles of writing, and audiences. As a result, the tone you use in a book for a witty and worldly sixth-grade boy probably isn't the same tone you'd employ in a picture book for a toddler. Case in point: *Island of the Blue Dolphins* (an historical novel by Scott O'Dell) and *Goodnight Moon* (a picture book by Margaret Wise Brown) are both considered classics of children's literature, but clearly the *audience* for each is vastly different.

To really get a feeling for what book ideas work for a toddler, 10-year-old, or early teen, you must get to know the various books out there and how the publishers differentiate the genres. Don't rely on your memories of the books you read as a child. Publishing is different today and is changing all the time.

How do you do that? Find out what critics and librarians deem the best of the best in books for kids. Where do you start? You started out thinking, "Hey, I want to write a children's book, and I have an idea!" No one told you you'd need a B.A. in English and a Ph.D. in children's literature. Relax. We're not suggesting a four-year course of study, just a crash course in finding your way to the reading rainbow.

The Classics

Who can forget his favorite bedtime story? For Lynne, it was *Rapunzel.* Her own toddler twins love *On the Day You Were Born,* while her preschooler enjoys *Madeline.* There are many titles that endure the test of time and generations of readings: *Make Way for Ducklings, Curious George, Charlotte's Web.* Even more recent books, from picture books like Dr. Seuss's *Oh, the Places You'll Go,* Liz Rosenberg's *Monster Mama,* and Chris Van Allsburg's *The Polar Express* to novels by Judy Blume, Virginia Hamilton, or Lloyd Alexander, now rank as classics.

Although you may rattle off the titles of adult classics—such as *The Great Gatsby, Great Expectations,* or *The Odyssey*—titles throughout the many age levels and audiences in the children's arena may prove more elusive. We could list every title in every category for you, but that's another book entirely (we list some examples of such books in Appendix B, "Resources," and in Chapter 10, "Apples and Oranges: Kinds of Publishers and What They Do," we go over the categories). Slogging through reference books isn't much fun, so how do you find out who's who in classic children's literature? You go to the experts in your own backyard.

Ask a Librarian

So you spilled your grape juice (that you weren't supposed to have in the library anyway) in the stacks while in college and got kicked out of the library by the research librarian. Get over it, and go ask a your local children's librarian to show you around the world of classic children's literature. Children's librarians are experts on the classics and the very latest new books, and chances are they'll enjoy sharing their expertise with you. Follow these steps to ensure you receive some good take-home reading material:

➤ First make sure you hold an active library card. You'll want to check out titles to read and study.

➤ Call the library and ask wheter a children's resource specialist or a librarian specializing in children's literature exists at the location. If you receive a yes, ask to speak to that person. If not, find out who handles the children's books.

➤ If your local branch doesn't have a children's area, find out about a branch or a main library that does. Call there.

➤ After you have the librarian on the phone, explain that you are researching children's literature and, when convenient, would like the librarian to give you an overview of classics, as well as pull several examples within different categories and age levels for you to check out and read. Make the appointment and keep it.

If your local library doesn't have much of a children's collection, or is too far away for easy access, your local school is an alternative resource. If your children attend school, you have a very good reason to find out what books the kids are reading at what level and to ask about other recommended books. Even if you have no children in school, state curriculum guides may be available to you from your state department of education—you may find them on-line or be able to purchase them. In addition to learning about specific titles you might want to read, you can learn from educators when they start using novels, what skills they teach in which grades, and so on. This can be useful background knowledge.

21

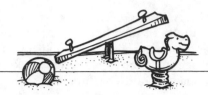

Stories from the Playground

We're telling you to consult experts, children, best-seller lists, and "Best of" lists in this chapter, but personal experience tells us that all of this should lead in one direction: developing your own taste. When Harold was getting started in children's publishing, which wasn't as long ago as you might think, he read Alison Lurie's *Don't Tell the Grown-Ups: The Subversive Power of Children's Literature*. This had a big influence on him in developing his own tastes, exactly because the book confirmed some of his own vague notions of what he loved.

I Can Count to 100

Newspapers, magazines, and even television shows often put together "best of" lists that you can consult for guidance. For example, *School Library Journal,* one of the nation's most respected reviewers of children's book publishing, got together a panel of experts as the millennium approached to determine the "100 Significant Books" of the twentieth century. According to Karen Breen, Kathleen Odean, Zena Sutherland, and Ellen Fader in their article in the January 2000 issue of *School Library Journal,* the list "[represented] the history of children's trade-book publishing from the moment Peter Rabbit first hopped onto the scene, in 1902, up to the present … and [included] books with literary and artistic merit, as well as books that are perennially popular with young readers, books that have blazed new trails, and books that have exerted a lasting influence on the world of children's book publishing." We highly recommend poring over each title and discovering more about each author in your quest for knowledge about the classics. Here are a few you might not know:

➤ *Tuck Everlasting,* by Natalie Babbitt

➤ *Freight Train,* by Donald Crews

➤ *And Then What Happened, Paul Revere?,* by Jean Fritz

➤ *Shapes and Things,* by Tana Hoban

➤ *Chicka Chicka Boom Boom,* by Bill Martin Jr. and John Archimbault

➤ *The Alfred Summer,* by Jan Slepian

Hot! Do Touch That!

Beyond immersing yourself in the classics, you also need to know what's hot now—what kids are reading and parents are buying for their kids today—besides Harry Potter, please! After all, there are at least 4,000 new children's books published every year in the United States and Canada, though no one knows exactly how many. So though old standbys retain steady sales year after year, the new kids on the block are also worth examining as trends emerge. Moreover, you'll discover the pulse of kids' immediate reading preferences. It may seem like an overwhelming endeavor as you explore all the new titles bursting forth from the publishers ("Just how am I going to read everything?" Answer: "Don't try to"), but there remain ways to streamline your mission. Follow the leader as we return to the library.

Back to the Library

Start again with a live source. Perhaps when you return all those classics that you checked out, you should ask the librarian to show you the hot titles of today. If the books are really hot, there may be a waiting list at the library for specific titles. Join the list—but at least you get an idea of what kids are enjoying nowadays. You might also ask for "Children's Choices," a list created by the International Reading Association and the Children's Books Council, which the library might have on hand.

Here a Bookseller, There a Bookseller

Another great way to get up on the latest and greatest books for kids is by visiting the children's department at your local bookstore. Just by virtue of filling the shelves, employees in this department will know what's selling. They see what children and young adults pluck from the rack—and they may have noticed that these self-selected titles are quite different from what parents and grandparents are buying. Bookstore staff also typically perform story times at the stores and gain a good idea of those picture books that keep little ones' interests.

Can You Keep a Secret?

What books do children themselves like? You could poll everyone under the age of 18 in your neighborhood. Or for a wider perspective, get your hands on the annual IRA/CBC Children's Choices list. You can find the list released in 2000 on-line at http://www.cbcbooks.org/choices/2000list.htm. Children in schools all over the United States vote for this list annually.

Lynne recently ran reconnaissance in the children's department of a major superstore and asked the department supervisor a few questions. The fearless coauthor, disguised as an average reader, asked first for hot young reader choices—books to give an elementary school student to read. The employee immediately said, "Anything with a timeless theme—like friendship or conflict—how about *The Wind in the Willows* by

Can You Keep a Secret?

Another way to find out about what's hot in the bookstores is to consult the best-seller lists. Both *Publishers Weekly* and *The New York Times* produce children's best-sellers lists. Of course, in many cases the books on these lists are the ones with name recognition or big promotion budgets, but it doesn't hurt to learn about that side of things, too.

Class Rules

Children's honesty is expressed by their bodies. If you're reading a picture book to a toddler, and she starts to squirm, she's not interested. Now you need to find out why. Try different books and see which she prefers. You can do the same thing with older children; just be sure you listen to their body language, not what they tell you afterward.

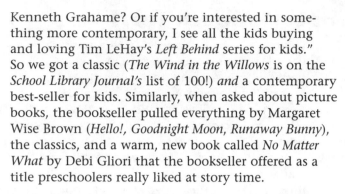

Kenneth Grahame? Or if you're interested in something more contemporary, I see all the kids buying and loving Tim LeHay's *Left Behind* series for kids." So we got a classic (*The Wind in the Willows* is on the *School Library Journal's* list of 100!) *and* a contemporary best-seller for kids. Similarly, when asked about picture books, the bookseller pulled everything by Margaret Wise Brown (*Hello!, Goodnight Moon, Runaway Bunny*), the classics, and a warm, new book called *No Matter What* by Debi Gliori that the bookseller offered as a title preschoolers really liked at story time.

Booksellers also meet with sales representatives from all the book publishers, who provide overviews of all the new titles launching each season. Pick the brain of a bookseller; you'll probably find yourself wading through piles of really wonderful new literature and classic stuff, too. Incidentally, Lynne bought *No Matter What*—to the delight of her twins, who ask for a reading nightly now.

Stop, Look, and Listen: Talk to Children

One of the really great things about children remains their forthright natures. Most children tend to be honest and direct. If they feel comfortable with you, they'll call 'em like they see 'em—though they do like to make adults happy, so don't telegraph the answers you want to hear when discussing books with them. One of your greatest assets in discovering wonderful children's literature, when you take the right approach, is a child. Ask the kids of your uncles, cousins, neighbors, and friends what they like to read—and ask your own kids, too. Don't suggest possible titles, and don't settle for what they read in school. Ask them what they read when they can choose the book. Children's tastes can outweigh any marketing plans. It's been said that the initial popularity of the Harry Potter series can be traced to word-of-mouth through kids, not to what the publisher did. Go, kid power!

If you're able to gather up a group and talk about certain books, do it. Perhaps a teacher you know will welcome you as a guest storyteller, or you might even become a regular volunteer. Bring a stack of various picture books and read for half an hour to first graders. Read the books beforehand, so you can keep your eyes on the children and not on the page. Gauge their interest and reaction to the materials. Be careful of your delivery. You don't want to bore the kids with a monotone reading, but you also don't want to slant their reaction by giving an animated show either. See if the story and the illustrations deliver the goods. This experience will help you gauge reactions if you ever try out your writing on children, a tricky thing to do that we discuss in more detail in Chapter 12, "Is It Ready to Hand In?"

After all, you want to write for children, so get to know what they find amusing, interesting, or fascinating.

The Least You Need to Know

➤ Recognize that there are various styles of writing for children. There is a difference between what a toddler enjoys to read and what a teen enjoys, but they are both categorized as children's literature.

➤ Study myriad works—from classic picture books to contemporary young adult novels. You can't write for kids if you don't know what they read.

➤ Get help on your quest for kids' literature by asking a librarian, bookseller, or child to lead you toward what's out there and what's selling.

➤ Start to develop a sense of what children like, and how it's different from what adults want them to like.

Chapter 4

Why Write a Children's Book— and Why Not?

In This Chapter

➤ Why a desire for money and fame can let you down

➤ How your wishes for children can affect the way you write

➤ Why (and why not) self-expression can be a good way into writing for children

➤ How likely you are to succeed

➤ How some other writers have succeeded

We all have reasons for doing what we do, whether that's becoming a parent or having another slice of cake. That's good—if we didn't have reasons, we wouldn't do it. But when we don't understand our own motives, they can affect what we do in unexpected and possibly damaging ways. And that's bad.

This happens with children's books, too. The motives and reasons that lead writers to write children's books are as varied and different as people are, of course, but those who have been in the business for a while will tell you that they all boil down to one or a combination of a few. Some writers want fame or money. Others want to teach children something or to make them feel good about themselves. Still others write as a means of self-expression.

In this chapter, we'll look at motives and disentangle the effect they can have. You'll learn how your motives can affect the writing you do, for better and for worse, and how they can affect your ability to stay in the field for the long haul. We'll also show you how your motives can help you succeed.

I Want Money, But I'll Settle for Fame

If you judge by what you read in the newspapers and see on television, authors can expect million-dollar advances and national book tours, not to mention appearance on Charlie Rose and other television shows. Children's books don't get quite so much attention, or at least they didn't until J. K. Rowling's Harry Potter books, a staggeringly successful fantasy series set in a British school of magic, each of which sold millions of copies. Reading about them, it's tempting to see this as an opportunity. Because children aren't as good at reading as adults, and their books aren't as long (*Harry Potter and the Goblet of Fire* excepted, of course), it must be easier to write for them. This must be a path to fame and fortune!

Class Rules

Trends are a will-o'-the-wisp. Chase one, and by the time you've got a manuscript done and maybe even approved, a new trend has popped up. Stories based on current events go stale even faster. Because it takes two years to do a good job with a picture book, your hot item will have cooled off by the time it's on the market.

If that's what you're hoping, wake up and smell the hot chocolate. Like the 100-foot waves in the *Perfect Storm*, several factors came together to create this once-in-a-century phenomenon. No other book has ever sold as well. It may sound like we're going out on a limb, but we also believe that in the next 50 years, no other children's book, either on its own or in a series, will be as successful as the Harry Potter series.

What's the harm of trying to emulate this kind of success, if it gets you motivated to write? The danger is that if a desire for fame and fortune is what drives you, you can end up chasing the trends and the "hot" areas of the market. A few years ago, for example, you might have tried to write a scary/funny series à la the "Goosebumps" series—but by the time you finished it, the market had moved on. Or it might lead you into writing about things that don't interest you to the detriment of your writing. Ask any published authors and they'll tell you that it's better to write what you like to write, or you won't be able to stick to it.

It's also true that in a more modest way, money *can* motivate you, if only to keep you at your writing. Writing can be a full-time job. This takes dedication, the ability to juggle multiple writing projects, and not least the will to face down the fear that sometime soon—tomorrow, next week, next year—you will run out of inspiration and out of income. Jennifer Armstrong, a successful full-time writer of fiction and nonfiction, comments:

> I don't know that I believe in inspiration, frankly. Either you want to write or you don't, but there won't be a beam of light coming through the window and into your ear.

> I always have multiple projects underway, so there's always something that has to be done. Deadlines are powerful motivators, as are mortgage payments and

other bills. I've seldom known that whip not to work. I may be among a small group of writers for children and young adults who actually do make a living at this. I have to get my work done. That's all there is to it.

She has arrived at this point after several years of work, of course, and many successful writers never do make writing a full-time job, but it is a possibility, with persistence and discipline. Appearing on *Oprah*'s book club may be out of reach, but if you want to write, you can eventually earn a living at it.

I Want to Be the Teacher

You love the way that children ask questions. Or maybe you are disturbed by the way in which children are raised today, or by the influence of the media. You feel that you have something to teach children. This is a worthy motive, but how will it affect your writing? Your desire to teach can powerfully affect your writing, whether it's fiction or nonfiction.

> **Vocabulary List**
>
> A story in which the moral or message the author wants to convey overwhelms the plot is called **pedantic** by editors. It's a story that teaches, but in a narrow way.

Writing fiction, in picture book or novel form, is one way to teach. If something bad happens to a child who acts in a certain way, the author hopes that this will teach the reader a lesson. This can be done effectively, and not so effectively. When a story is overwhelmed by its message, editors dismiss it as *pedantic,* and reject it immediately. Here's an example of a pedantic story:

Mary Who Didn't Listen

by P. Dan "Tick" Underdown

Once upon a time there was a little girl named Mary. She was like most little girls her age, which was six. She liked ice cream, she liked to play, and she liked to take care of her kitty. But in one way, Mary was not like other little girls. She never listened to her parents.

One day, Mary was playing "Treasure Chase" on the Zinblendo console for the TV. A fire truck went past, blowing its siren and making a big racket. Mary's kitty was scared and hid under the sofa. But Mary didn't hear the siren, she was so caught up in getting the next Gold Treasure. Mary played for hours. She was a very inattentive little girl. When her mother called her to supper, she didn't hear her. Her mother called her again, and still Mary didn't hear. Mary's supper was getting cold, and her father had to come upstairs and unplug the TV to get Mary to pay attention. Her mother and father were angry and said to her, "You are becoming Mary Who Doesn't Listen!"

The next day in school, Mary was drawing a picture of her kitty in her notebook when her teacher called on her. But Mary didn't hear her. Mrs. Maestra had to walk to her desk and

Part 1 ➤ Where to Begin?

close Mary's notebook before Mary would look up. Mrs. Maestra said, "You are Mary Who Doesn't Listen!"

And so it went on. Mary was so lost in her own little world that she never heard what anyone said to her, and she truly was Mary Who Didn't Listen.

But one day, Mary and all her friends were going to go to Playland, look at the kitties and puppies in the pet shop next door, and then have ice cream, to celebrate the end of school. While she waited for her friends to come, Mary started playing her favorite game on the Zinblendo upstairs.

When Sally's mother called for Mary to come get in the van, Mary didn't hear her. Sally and her mother and all Sally's friends called, but Mary didn't hear them. Mary's mother and father did, but they didn't say anything because they knew that their little girl needed to learn a lesson. Soon Sally's mother gave up, and she drove all the girls to Playland, leaving Mary behind.

Much later, Mary felt tired and stopped playing her game. Then she looked up. It was starting to get dark, and she realized that she had missed the trip to Playland. She was very upset, and she ran downstairs and said to her parents, "I'm going to listen from now on so I don't miss anything ever again!"

And do you know what? She did just that. She became Mary Who Did Listen, and she was a much happier little girl. So if you don't listen, watch out, because you might miss something.

What's wrong with this story? We know nothing about Mary beyond her problem, which is that she doesn't listen, and nothing happens to her but an experience that teaches a lesson. Even worse, P. Dan "Tick" keeps hitting us over the head with the "bad" behavior the child has. There is no humor and little dialogue. Few children will want to read it again.

If you want to teach children through your writing, don't despair. There are ways you can do it and be effective. In fiction, use humor and exaggeration, as in the classic *Struwwelpeter* stories. These classic stories, originally published in Germany in 1848, each feature a child whose outrageously bad behavior leads to a rather gruesome end—one is eaten by a lion, one starves to death, and so on. Children old enough to recognize them as fantasies find them extremely funny, and take them no more seriously than the violence they see all the time in cartoons. At the same time, they get the point.

Today, we take a gentler approach, but the humor of bad examples and the lesson they teach is exactly what Nancy Carlson plays on in *How to Lose All Your Friends*. David Wisniewski pokes fun at grown-ups while finding new reasons for the "rules" they enforce in *The Secret Knowledge of Grown-Ups*. You get the idea: a story in which a child who doesn't clean up his bedroom ends up being trapped inside could have a similar effect.

For older children, dramatizing a situation instead of talking about rules, even humorously, can work. Do you want to teach children about the dangers of drugs?

Consider a novel in which one of the characters has a bad experience with drugs—but the author must let the experience develop naturally and refrain from commenting on it even through the mouth of another character. Trust your ability as a storyteller. If the story tells itself, and the consequences of a particular action are clear, the reader will get the point with no need to underline it during the story or repeat it at the end. Vicarious experience puts your message across.

On the other hand, you may wish to teach children information or understanding. Again, your mission could overwhelm your writing. Even nonfiction—particularly nonfiction!—must be interesting. A list of facts or an essay that reads like an entry from an encyclopedia is a good solid piece of factual material. But it's also writing that has been overwhelmed by the author focusing only on what he wanted to say, and not on how to say it.

Instead, present your material simply and clearly, with a narrative if possible. Consider a book like Eve Bunting's *Ducky,* about a load of plastic toys washed off a freighter that ultimately became an opportunity for scientists to learn about the currents of the Pacific Ocean. The story brings this event to life through the "eyes" of one plastic duck; compare this to newspaper stories from the time to gain some insight into one way in which events or information can be transformed. For older children, Laurence Pringle's *An Extraordinary Life* (which Harold worked on when he was at Orchard Books) reveals the life and migration of a Monarch butterfly, in story format. Again, there is plenty of information presented here, but it's woven skillfully into the story.

Does nonfiction have to be presented in a fictional form to be effective? No, but don't forget to make an effective presentation, and to use narrative form if it works, as Patricia Lauber does in *Volcano!* and Susan Campbell Bartoletti does in *Growing Up in Coal Country.*

So if you want to teach, you can, but don't lose track of the fact that you are a storyteller first, and a teacher second.

I Get to Be the Mommy

You like taking care of children. Maybe you are a parent. You want to write stories that will help children feel happy and especially happy with themselves. This, too, is a worthy motive, but if it leads to you removing all conflict and difficulty from a story, it's gone too far.

In his work at Charlesbridge, Harold saw many manuscripts submitted in which the author had worked very hard to remove anything painful or dangerous from the story. The following story shows this impulse in action.

The Happy Child

by Syrup E. Underdown

Billy was a happy child. He lived in a big house with his mommy, his daddy, his dog Spot, and his sisters and brothers. Every day when he woke up he smiled, because he knew he was going to have fun! He didn't care if it was a school day or a weekend day. He knew he would enjoy it.

One day, he woke up and smiled even wider than usual, because he was going fishing with his Grandpop. He got dressed and washed up. Then he went downstairs singing "I'm going fishing!" When he got downstairs he said, like he always did, "Good morning, Mom!" and, "Good morning, Dad!" He felt it truly was a good morning.

They smiled and said, "Good morning, Billy!"

Billy said, "Guess what? I'm going fishing with Grandpop! We're going to take Spot, and we're going to have lots of fun."

"I know, Billy, I'm sure you'll have lots of fun," said his mom.

Billy sat down at the table, unfolded his napkin, and ate his cereal. Just when he had finished, the doorbell rang. Billy jumped up and ran to the door. Just as he had hoped, it was his Grandpop! Billy called out, "Hi, Grandpop! I can hardly wait to go fishing."

"Hi, Billy, I'm sure we're going to have lots of fun," replied his Grandpop, smiling. When Grandpop smiled, Billy thought he smiled even more than most people because all the wrinkles on his cheerful face smiled too.

As soon as Grandpop had said hi to Billy's dad and Billy's mom (who was also Grandpop's daughter) and all of Billy's brothers and sisters, they grabbed the fishing tackle from the back porch, got Spot from the backyard, and drove off to the fishing hole.

They were sure they were going to have a great time. And they were right! Billy caught lots of fish and had a grand time with his Grandpop. He was one happy boy when he fell asleep that night, and dreamed of going fishing again ....

The End

What's the problem with this story? To start with, it isn't a story. Nothing happens. Billy accomplishes nothing, because there is no tension or problem. Syrup E. has worked so hard to make the writing safe and reassuring that it has lost the feel of real life.

What to do? It is more truly and deeply reassuring to a child to see a character realistically overcome a difficulty than to read a story about a world in which there are no difficulties, because, much as we would like to believe otherwise, children know quite well that life is about difficulties and overcoming them. How could they not? They are in the middle of the process of growing from being helpless infants to resourceful, self-confident adults (or so we hope) and as they do they experience many triumphs (and failures). We do them no favors if we sugarcoat the world for them. And your writing suffers.

Published authors know this, and you can find many wonderful examples of books that give true comfort to a child by showing a child dealing realistically with a real problem. For a child confronting death, for example, you can find picture books, such as Judith Viorst's *The Tenth Good Thing About Barney,* nonfiction, such as Janet Bode's *Death Is Hard to Live With,* or novels, such as Katherine Paterson's *Bridge to Terabithia*. Parents are there to take care of children, but for you as a writer the challenge is to tell the story.

Look What I Did!

An enduring motive for writers, particularly those who have been writing for some time, is self-expression, finding satisfaction through the use of words to get across their feelings and experiences. This approach is the one that is most likely to keep you going when you can't get published or you are published, but getting bad reviews. Your own satisfaction with the way you put words together needs no outside validation.

The danger of self-expression is that you can get so caught up in your own pursuit of writing that you lose track of your audience, and write pieces pleasing to you, but to no one else. So develop a thick skin, but don't close your ears completely to what people—critique group members, your editor, a reviewer, a thoughtful child reader—say about your work.

Self-expression can mean different things.

Personal Passions

Is there some area of knowledge about which you care deeply? In your passion for the subject, you'll find the motivation to get it across clearly, with the dramatic and exciting aspects of it that grab you right there to grab your reader.

Writing about it can lead you to learning even more about it, and from there to other things about which you want to learn. Harold talked with the noted nonfiction writer James Cross Giblin about his latest book, a biography of Adolf Hitler. Jim told him that he got interested in this grimly fascinating subject while writing his biography of Charles Lindbergh, the flawed American hero—his flaws most apparent in his open sympathy for the Nazis. So follow your desire for understanding, and pass on what you've learned.

Open to Inspiration

When asked what inspires him, published poet and picture book author Charles Ghigna replied:

> Nature, kids, animals, sports, travel, the weather, daily celebrations of life, and my own childhood memories. My son, Chip, and my wife, Debra, also inspire

many of my poems, as do my editors, neighbors, and friends. I often receive inspiration from reading newspapers, magazines and books. I guess one might say that everything inspires me!

A writer with this attitude—one that you can cultivate—will always be motivated, and always have fresh ideas. Give yourself time to notice what is around you, and time to think about where it could lead you.

The Inner Child

Jan Wahl, an experienced picture book author with more than 100 books to his credit, has this to say about writing for children:

> I don't try to write for editors or for librarians or for teachers—and, especially, I don't write for reviewers. I don't try to write for any specific child. I feel that's a big mistake.

Can You Keep a Secret?

No motive will carry you farther than your own internal motive of a desire to express yourself. Your own innate drive to learn, to be moved, and to find fresh language to express your passions is what will keep you going when dreams of fame or fortune succeed.

He's not concerned with how people are going to react, and he doesn't even feel that a child he knows, or a classroom of children, can give him a clue as to whether or not he is succeeding. To him, writing for children means something else:

> It means enjoying afresh, each day, those insights and glimpses of the universe I had as a child. A writer can't ask anything more than this—what is it? That everything seems new.

However you do it—by following your own interests, by keeping yourself open, or by listening to your inner child—express yourself. No one else has exactly your point of view or your way of putting things. Expressing oneself, and getting better and better at doing so, is a strong motive for a writer. Hold onto it, develop it, and you'll find satisfaction, even if you never get published.

I Got a Star

Success is possible, though it can take many years. What does success mean? What "success" is varies from writer to writer, but you may be surprised to hear that for most writers, it's not fame, or money (though a steady income is a good thing) that matters.

As coauthor Harold knows, Miriam Bat-Ami recently won a prestigious award for *Two Suns,* a historical fiction book about a detention camp for European refugees in upstate New York during the Second World War. Her success did not come out of nowhere. In the early 1990s, Harold published a picture book and a short novel of hers. A few years later, with another publisher, she published a novel. *Two Suns* came from a third publisher, six years after her first book. She tells us she needed that time, not only to work on the book but also to find the right publisher and the right editor for it. What does she most appreciate about her success? You might be surprised to hear:

> Success is fun because I get to see a plus figure on my royalty statement. Seeing a negative one is very depressing, as is seeing negative reviews.

> But there are things you can see with books that may not be the "successful" ones and those you remember. I do like seeing a teenager at a table next to mine reading my book and seeming so concentrated on it. … Success is having someone come up to my son and say she wants to borrow another copy of my book to lend a friend. "Hey," I think, "she can buy it, but, hey, she likes it enough to ask for another copy." So I lend it out. But real success has to do with self-respect, and successfully working with an editor to tell the story I want to tell, and those are connected to my sense of myself as a writer.

The Chance of Getting There

No matter what your motives, you want to know what chance you have of getting published. The odds don't look good when you consider that there are usually thousands of manuscripts going through the doors of a typical publisher in a year, only a few of which are accepted for publication. But consider that maybe 90 percent of those submissions are just not very good, or are completely wrong for that publisher. Writers who keep working at their writing, and who find the right publishers, have a chance of getting there. They'll still have to compete with the others who have what it takes, but with the help of this book you can get into that group.

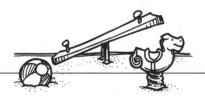

Stories from the Playground

Sneed Collard, a well-known writer of nonfiction for children, says: "Writing is a LONG road. I've been writing for 18 years now and only in the last five have I begun to understand what I'm doing. If you're not willing to put in the years and continue to grow, this field isn't for you. If you are willing to keep learning and growing, however, children's book writing can be an enormously satisfying ride."

And Stephen Mooser, president of the Society of Children's Book Writers and Illustrators (SCBWI), says this about the path to success:

> In my years with the SCBWI I have seen hundreds of people sell their first book. None of these books, however, came easy. They studied the market, they studied published children's books, they wrote and rewrote and wrote again. They were persistent and they succeeded, even if it took 10 years. There is a lot of competition and you have to give it your best. I've published 60 books, but probably had that many rejected.

There aren't any guarantees. You'll need persistence (possibly years of it), some talent, and a little luck, luck that you may be able to create, to have a chance of getting there. Do you have those prerequisites? You won't know until you try, so get to it.

The Least You Need to Know

➤ You probably won't become rich or famous by writing children's books, but you might be able to make a full-time job out of it.

➤ If you want to teach through your writing, find ways to dramatize your lessons or to present information in a narrative or other engaging form.

➤ To help children feel better about themselves, show children living in the real world and triumphing, not cocooned in a safe fantasy.

➤ Self-expression as a motive can lead to self-indulgence, but it's also an ever-expanding reason to keep writing.

➤ Success is not assured, but the journey is worth it if you find writing itself satisfying.

The Piggy Bank and the Notebook

Now we're getting to the nitty-gritty of the business of being a writer. Although it may seem romantic to say to others at a cocktail party over canapés and Chardonnay, "Well, I'm a writer of children's books," actually hard work, organizational skills, tenacity, tools, and self-initiative (oh, and perhaps little monetary reward, too) go with the title you bestowed upon yourself at the bar. So buck up and learn what you'll need to get started and compete in this "playground" of publishing.

In this chapter, we'll offer you the tools—both technological and traditional—that you'll require to succeed in writing (especially after you earn a book contract) and also some organizational and time management tips. Moreover, we'll go over the truth about money. In other words, we'll give you the lowdown on what to expect in your piggy bank.

School Supplies

Remember when the teacher sent you home on the first day of school with a list of required supplies? Come on, that cubbyhole and pencil box didn't miraculously sprout painting smocks and #2 yellow pencils. In school, you went about the business of learning—which necessitated supplies and tools (such as a ruler for math class and pencils for writing). Today, as you embark upon a career as a children's book author, you'll also need certain tools and supplies.

So what do you really need—at minimum—to get started? Actually, not too much. In fact, you probably already possess many of the items in the following list:

➤ A telephone. This is a business, after all. You will find that you use the telephone often and for long periods as a writer—even as a writer of children's books. You'll make calls to colleagues, editors, contacts, and sources for research.

➤ A computer with word processing capabilities and a printer. An editor won't accept your manuscript scribbled out in pencil. If you can afford to own a computer, buy one. Otherwise, you can rent time on a computer at stores such as Kinko's.

➤ If you have a computer, make sure you also have a way to back up your files—by saving them to a disk, to a back-up tape, or sending them to sites on the Internet—so that if something goes wrong with your computer you won't have to retype all your work.

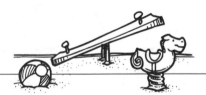

Stories from the Playground

Nowadays, just about everyone writes on computers using word processing programs that do the duty of typewriters and more. If you're on a budget, and you're using a computer for writing only, you don't have to have the latest PC or Mac computer equipped with the latest version of Word. When Harold was freelancing a few years back, he relied on a three-year-old computer and a word processor called Word Express, which did everything he needed it to and didn't cost as much as the name brands. You don't need to buy new. A two-year-old, refurbished computer from a local store for under $500 will suit you just fine.

➤ Internet access, either from home or by the hour at a public library or a retail store that rents computers. You may be thinking, "I'm going to write a children's book. I just need my imagination! Why do I need the Internet?" First, you can a lot of research on-line. Second, you'll find fabulous and helpful information for writers there.

➤ Electronic mail, known more familiarly as e-mail. Nowadays, you can't communicate with an editor without e-mail. Your trusted coauthors of this book, Harold and Lynne, communicated with each other by e-mail almost daily during the writing of this book and sent chapters as *attachments* to the publisher.

➤ Standard desk supplies. Think paper (for the printer, notes, outlines, scratch), pens, pencils, files, a stapler, paper clips, and anything else you use to keep life organized.

➤ A filing cabinet. We'll get to organizing it and what types of files you'll find yourself making a little later in this chapter.

➤ Access to a fax machine. You probably don't need to own a fax machine, but do know where you can fax from in your neighborhood. Or, if you have a modem on your computer, in many cases you'll be able to set it up to fax directly from your word processing program.

That's it! Given these items, you can compete and do business in the world of publishing.

Really Cool Toys

We just gave you the basic tools to get going on your writing endeavors. But there remain a few other helpful items that may prove especially useful as your career develops.

Vocabulary List

When you send an entire document—such as your manuscript for your book, which you have saved either to your hard drive or to a disk—you will attach it to an e-mail message. These documents, sent with the electronic message (or e-mail), are called **attachments.**

Can You Keep a Secret?

Here are three of the many useful World Wide Web sites you can find:

➤ Harold Underdown's Web location at www. underdown.org for articles and useful links.

➤ Aaron Shepard's personal site at www.aaronshep.com/ index.html, to see what one author has done with his Web site.

➤ The Society of Children's Book Writers and Illustrators at www.scbwi.org.

➤ Camera. Who knows when inspiration will strike? A picture may indeed be worth a thousand words.

➤ Dedicated phone line (second phone line). When you spend time researching on-line, you won't miss calls if you have a dedicated line. Moreover, you can run your business of writing through this line and keep work and home separate.

➤ Laptop computer. Coauthor Lynne swears by this item. "We had a fire in our home while I was in the midst of writing several articles and a book. Luckily, I had a laptop because my desktop was destroyed." Within one day, Lynne was back on-line in a hotel room, plugged into her editors by e-mail, and she could continue to write and meet her deadlines.

➤ Business cards. Establish yourself as a writer. Don't invest in anything fancy, but do print up cards (perhaps on your own computer) with your name, phone, fax, home office address, and e-mail address. You'll be glad you have them when you can pull one out to pass to another writer, an editor, or anyone else you make as a contact in the publishing world.

A Place for Everything

It's all about a system, really. You need to find the system that works best for you. But regardless, don't delude yourself into thinking that disorganization is your system. Everything put neatly away in filing cabinets and desk drawers isn't necessary if you can find what you want in the umpteen stacks scattered around your workspace. And when you are writing, you don't need to have an empty desk. But to thrive as a writer, you'll need to take your supplies and set them up before you begin writing.

Many writers also can't break the momentum after they begin. If they stop writing, for example, to find a sharpened pencil—yikes!—they can't get back to it for hours, days, or months. So it really is best to consider several organizational ideas before writing. Just like a pilot observes a preflight checklist, you should observe a pre-write checklist to be sure you have the items you need. Have reference books, computer supplies, sharpened pencils, your notes, your files, extra paper, candy, or anything else you might need at hand, so that you don't have to break the flow.

Here a Book, There a Book, Everywhere a Book, Book!

You can't avoid it. You'll need to fill a shelf in your writing area with reference books. Reference books every writer should possess include the following.

➤ Dictionary. Get a comprehensive one. Don't pick up the 200-pager at the 99¢ clearance center or even a pocket paperback edition. We highly recommend a quality, sturdy, hardbound, heavy dictionary: *Webster's Third New International* or the more portable *Webster's Collegiate* are publishing standards.

➤ *Chicago Manual of Style.* This is the bible of editors and publishers everywhere. There's (almost) too much information. But, then again, you never know when you'll need to know when to capitalize something or how a book is laid out, right?

➤ *Roget's Thesaurus.* Don't depend upon your word-processing program to do the work of a real book. Just like the dictionary, invest in a good, hardbound *Roget's* today and never fumble for a synonym, antonym, or perfect word again.

➤ *Bartlett's Familiar Quotations.* So many reasons to possess this title! Quotations can provide springboards for ideas. You may choose to sprinkle one or two within your book.

➤ Any grammar book. Hey, when you have to know whether you've split an infinitive, a good grammar book will move dangling modifiers.

➤ This book, of course.

➤ Strunk and White's *Elements of Style.*

Now, do you have your reference books handy? If so, check it off.

Puss and Booting Up

Do you have …

➤ Paper for your printer?

➤ Ink or toner in the cartridge of your printer?

➤ A disk on which to save your work?

Even in our technological age where paper seems obsolete when we move documents via e-mail, you just may want to proof your work the old-fashioned way—on paper. Without any in the printer, you won't have the option. And, even if you do have the paper, if you don't have ink in the printer cartridge, you can't print. Finally, make sure you own plenty of clean floppy disks. Writer after writer can recall horror stories of entire works disappearing in the twitch of a computer. We said this before: it's always best to save all your work not only on the computer's hard drive but also on a disk you can take out of your work area as a back-up. If you can sound off an affirmative for the above three items, check 'em off.

Class Rules

Do you need everything we list here to succeed? No. You'll know what you need and what you don't. But don't sabotage yourself. There is a minimum. You need a quiet, distraction-free (and that means child-free) space in which to work, a work surface you don't have to clear off every time you want to use it, and a schedule your family and friends respect.

41

Red Rover, Red Rover, Send Research Right Over

Are your research, notes, and any other documents necessary for your writing present and within reach? You'll hate yourself if you sit down to write and can't find important facts pertinent to your story line. If they're handy, then good. Check it off the list and move on.

The Secret Files Garden

Part of maintaining your research is, of course, your file system. But how do you know what topics need their own files? You don't. You'll probably determine how to file things as you go along, but we'll offer you a few examples right now on some obvious (and not so obvious) choices.

Keep separate files for …

➤ Book ideas. As one idea develops after another and you gather stuff pertaining to a book or items that spawn plot ideas, you may want a completely separate file for each book on which you are working. Otherwise, you may just want to stuff ideas that you've jotted down into one file (or notebook, even).

➤ Research of topics. Coauthor Lynne currently is gathering pieces of information on the 50 states for a nonfiction children's book she hopes to write. Every time she comes across an item of information about a state pertinent to the premise of her book, she files it away in the folder with the tab "Fifty States." When she sits down to write the book, she'll need only to pull that file.

➤ People. You might choose to use experts in your writing or need to call upon experts for a project. Many writers keep files on people involved in a particular topic.

➤ Contracts. After you sign them for a book deal, keep them.

➤ Submission letters and proposals. Keep track of the submissions and proposals you've sent out. Maintain a separate file, perhaps even organized by months, with printed copies of your correspondence.

➤ Business expenses. Writing is a form of self-employment so keep a file for expenses such as telephone calls, printer cartridges, and any other item you may be able to write off if you have proof you used it in the course of your business.

There's a Time and a Space for Everything

Many years ago, Virginia Woolf wrote about the importance of having a room of one's own. She pointed out that in Britain, women had problems finding a space to call their own in which to write and the time to do it. Women weren't perceived as potential writers. Times change, but the situation for writers of children's books in North America today is not much different from what Woolf described.

Most of you are women, and if you're not, hey, you're a guy in a profession that is devalued partly because it's mostly an occupation of women. You probably have a hard time getting people to take you seriously—possibly even the people in your own family. And as a result, you have a hard time getting the space and time to write.

But you know what? You need that space. You need a desk, and good light, and room for the books you may need to refer to, and hours of time during which you don't need to worry about being interrupted or needed.

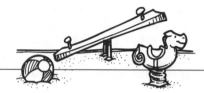

Stories from the Playground

Don't have time to write? Make time. Susan Campbell Bartoletti wrote and published several books while teaching full time: "In order to make time to write, I woke at 4 A.M. to write before school. (My dog wouldn't even get up with me!) With my sixth book contract, I left teaching to write full time.

"The morning hours still work best for me, and I have my best writing days when I'm at the computer by 4. I enjoy the early morning hours, while it's still dark outside. Ideas grow in the dark. It's the perfect time for creating, for taking that which is without form and void and separating darkness and light. I always feel as though I'm working toward the light."

After you have that time and space—and if you don't insist on it you won't get it!—you need to cultivate the discipline you must have if you are going to stick with writing for the long haul. You've got to have that "butt-in-chair" time if you are going to write in your journal, try some writing exercises, plan out a project, and actually write it. So like we said before, give yourself a schedule too. Maybe you can't get up every morning at 4 A.M. to write. How about two hours three nights a week while the rest of the family is watching television? Throw in Saturday afternoon and you've got 10 hours a week of solid writing time. You can get a lot done. Just do your best to resist the temptation to do laundry, or wash the dishes, or do any of those things that suddenly seem so tempting when a blank page is staring up at you.

Jack and the Bean Stock: Income

So with all this writing, you'll soon be rolling in the big bucks, right? Well, wrong. Most writers for children do not work full time at writing. Some hold down unrelated jobs. Others bring in money through related work we'll go into in Chapter 31, "Building a Career." Those who do write full time have reached this blissful state after what amounts to an apprenticeship of 5 to 10 years of learning. Please don't quit your day job yet! You should give serious thought to leaving a steady income in the hopes of supporting yourself—or goodness sakes, a family—on a writer's income.

Sad to say, you may never pay the bills from the royalties and advances from your book writing—even with several books on the market. Even if one or more books does well, income from book writing—any writing really—is sporadic. We hate to burst your bubble, but how many rich and famous children's book writers do you know or know of? If you want to write a children's book to get rich, forget it. Can you make a decent living as an author? Absolutely. Just understand that you'll need to keep your day job until things really start cooking.

The Least You Need to Know

➤ A writer today needs certain tools to compete in the publishing world and write. These are a computer, a phone, fax access, and on-line capabilities including e-mail.

➤ You'll want to organize your writing area and have necessary supplies, reference materials, and research readily available to you before you sit down to write.

➤ Set up a filing system now to keep all the tidbits of information and ideas easily accessible to you.

➤ No writer should be without a good dictionary and thesaurus.

➤ Self-starters succeed as writers; schedule time to write and stick to it.

➤ Don't think that you'll earn riches by writing children's books. In fact, keep your day job.

It's a BIG World

Once upon a time, children's book publishing was a genteel industry run by white-gloved ladies with backgrounds as librarians. Today everything is different. Such is the way many people see the changes in the business end of children's books.

That genteel business may be something of a myth, but there's no denying that the business *has* changed. In this chapter, you'll find out how. You'll learn about the decline of the library market and the rise of the consumer market, the growth of paperbacks, and the buyouts that have hit publishing just as much as other industries. You'll also get an assessment of just how much the Internet has affected the business, so far.

And why do you need to know this? Because you need to know who's buying the books. The business is not what it was.

The Golden Age

Publishers have been making books for children for about as long as there have been printing presses. Right through the nineteenth century, however, these were sidelines to their main business of publishing books for adults. In the United States, the first companies to create their own children's book divisions, with their own staff, did so after the First World War.

In the 1920s and 1930s, other publishers followed suit, hiring librarians to run their children's divisions. Why librarians? Because children's books were mostly sold to libraries back then, so if a company wanted to make sure that a book would appeal to the library market, it made sense to let someone with library training decide what books to publish. Librarians knew what they wanted. Solid informational books like Hendrik Willem Van Loon's *The History of the World,* which won the first Newbery Medal, and folktale collections with Arthur Rackham–style illustrations were in demand.

This was a fairly cozy little business, but a profitable one. More than one company had its literary but money-losing adult division kept alive by the steady sales of its children's books. In the 1940s, following pioneering research into what appealed to children, books got livelier: The bright colors in *Goodnight Moon* don't look exceptional today, but it was a groundbreaking book when it was first published. And not much of a success at first, either. Influential librarians didn't like it.

Looking back, these times can seem like a golden age. "Commercial" considerations didn't rule the business. Publishing quality books that conformed to a librarian's judgment of what was right for children was what publishers tried to do. This started to change as early as the 1950s, when Sputnik spurred investment in science education in the schools and in funding for nonfiction books for libraries.

Paperbacks: Fun and Cheap

The business really changed in the 1960s. Federal money from Lyndon Johnson's "Great Society" programs sparked a minor boom in children's publishing. All of a sudden, there were federal funds for schools and libraries to use to purchase books. Many more picture books, with more and more creative art, could be published. And publishers realized that Americans were not all white, and books that reflected our multiracial, multiethnic, multicultural society started to come out in increasing numbers. Ezra Jack Keats's *A Snowy Day,* a prize-winning book in 1963, was an early sign of the changes. This attractive and still popular book was one of the very first to matter-of-factly feature a black child, a boy named Peter, as he enjoyed a snowy day in his urban neighborhood.

The rise of the paperback, which began in the 1960s and continues to this day, was possibly a more significant if less obvious change. Until that time, quality publishers, the ones focusing on the library market, published only in hardcovers. Hardcover books were expensive, and so few families could buy them. But when books like *Charlotte's Web* and *Stuart Little* came out in an attractive, large paperback format, individuals bought them.

And the bookstore market began to change. Back then, there were no children's-only bookstores, and few large bookstores. Cheap, popular books like those published by Golden Books could be found in department stores and the like, but there were no inexpensive editions of the quality books sold to libraries. Those children's books took up a small section in most bookstores, and the booksellers expected to sell most of their books as gifts. When the "good" books started to be available in paperback, larger children's sections and children's-only bookstores started to appear, and gradually, bookstore sales became a larger part of the children's market.

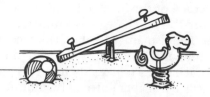

Stories from the Playground

Until 1967, if a parent or a teacher wanted to buy a children's book, it had to be a hard-cover or a low-quality paperback. But in that year, George Nicholson launched Dell Yearling, a trade paperback program. The first two titles, *Charlotte's Web* and *Stuart Little*, for which Dell paid Harper and Row an enormous advance for the time ($35,000), were not only huge successes, but didn't hurt Harper's hardcover sales. Harper was willing to say so in writing, other publishers made deals with Dell, and the rest is history. Paperbacks, including books published as originals, not reprints of books first published in hardcover, are becoming a larger and larger part of the children's book market.

Starting in 1975, Random House published its new inexpensive "pictureback" line of original picture book paperbacks, serious competition to Golden Books' inexpensive hardcover books. They sold well in bookstores. Improving technology also made paperback versions of hardcover picture books possible. At the same size, and same quality paper, but one-half to one-third of the price of a hardcover book, paperback picture books became more and more available. Today, almost every publisher publishes hardcovers and paperbacks, the paperback editions coming out a year or two after the hardcover, or less often at the same time. No longer do children's book publishers publish solely for the library market.

The Big Get Even Bigger

Other changes were taking place, too. In the 1970s, children's publishing was hit by the end of the federal funding that had supported its growth a decade earlier. Publishers laid off staff, and hunkered down for hard times. Jim Giblin points out that the photoessay, a nonfiction picture book illustrated with photographs, goes back to this time. With library-oriented nonfiction not selling as well, publishers found that the photoessay, which was more attractive, sold in bookstores.

Times got better in the 1980s. Though shortsighted tax revolts had further cut funding that libraries could use to buy books, the economy was good, and many parents had money to spend at the bookstores. And if they wanted to have books for their children, they had to spend money on them, because they could no longer count on finding them in the library. The business boomed—until the early 1990s, when sales went down and the buyouts, closures, and mergers began and continue to this day.

The 1990s were the decade of the merger. Some of the biggest deals were the merger of Penguin and Putnam, the purchase of Macmillan by Simon & Schuster, the merger of Random House and Bertelsmann's Bantam Doubleday Dell, HarperCollins's purchase of William Morrow, and Scholastic's acquisition of Grolier (Franklin Watts, Children's Press, and Orchard). The largest children's publishers today are part of media conglomerates, many of them owned by multinational corporations. We've come a long way from white-gloved library publishing.

Class Rules

It's hard to keep track of the constant change in publishing, but you need to try. Don't rely on out-of-date information. If you have a favorite market guide, buy a new one every year. Contact publishers to confirm addresses. Don't send submissions to "Harper & Row" or to "Macmillan Children's Books." Those names no longer exist.

Looking at the latest information available, from 1999, six big companies make half of the approximately $2 billion in annual sales in children's publishing:

➤ Random House

➤ Penguin Putnam

➤ Golden Books

➤ Simon & Schuster

➤ HarperCollins

➤ Scholastic

If you leave off Scholastic and Golden Books, which only publish for children, the four remaining companies are also the ones that are publishing the most best-selling books for adults. Truly, these companies are publishing giants, with thousands of employees, and are often part of even larger companies also owning cable channels, television stations, newspapers, and the like.

Who's Buying?

Because individual consumers call the tune, and large companies dominate the landscape, children's books just aren't what they used to be. That ain't necessarily a bad thing! There are books available now reflecting the experiences of all Americans, though not as many as there might be. There are books available in a dazzling array of art styles and techniques. There are many more affordable, but high-quality books available. It's a different world. Children's publishing, in a way, has grown up. It's more like publishing for adults, for better or worse. What does that mean?

Eye-Catching Books

Time was, thoughtful reviews in respected journals helped libraries choose which books to buy. They still do. But consumers are also buying those books now. And partly in an effort to get their attention, the art in children's picture books, and on the cover of children's novels and nonfiction, has become ever more eye-catching.

Some children's picture books have art that seems to have appeal primarily for adults, which makes sense—adults are the ones buying the books. Some of the more sophisticated novels for children are read by adults, too. The trade association of children's books publishers, the Children's Book Council, even publishes a booklet highlighting children's books for adults, under the title *NOT Just for Children Anymore!* with the hope of inspiring booksellers to carry them and promote them in this way.

TV, Movies, and Candy

If a consumer knows the name of an author, illustrator, or movie, he or she is more likely to buy a book with that name on it. So the byword of the 1990s was "brand"—a name that is known and respected and therefore likely to help sell a book and its associated merchandise too. Brand names may be those of a book or author, or be brought into the book from the outside. Do not be quick to exclaim in horror at this phenomenon! Licensing of this kind is not an entirely new phenomenon; Lewis Carroll of *Alice in Wonderland* fame licensed such products as a *Through the Looking Glass* biscuit tin.

Can You Keep a Secret?

Publishers actively market their children's books, even picture books, to adults. We've seen ads in *The New Yorker* for *Little Lit* (HarperCollins, 2000), free postcards in coffee bar racks for *Dr. Pompo's Nose* (Scholastic, 2000), and blurbs on the back cover of *Olivia* (Athenuem, 2000), by David Hockney and Mikhail Baryshnikov. Those aren't aimed at children.

Some publishers have been able to create children's book brand names:

➤ *Dr. Seuss* became a brand name because his books were so consistently good *and* easily recognizable.

➤ *Arthur* has become a brand name after the success of the TV series based on the book.

➤ *The Little House on the Prairie* has recently and quite deliberately been developed into a brand by HarperCollins. You can buy Little House picture books and Little House paper dolls, among other things.

➤ Celebrities from Shaquille O'Neal to Mary Chapin Carpenter may write or lend their name to children's books.

➤ Houghton Mifflin has hired writers and illustrators to create new *Curious George* books, to extend another "classic" brand name.

Publishers may also *license* a brand from another company. Licensing characters and the right to create books tied in to a movie (such as *Star Wars* or *Pocahontas*) or TV series has long been a way to associate a book with an already familiar brand name.

Vocabulary List

A **license** gives you the right to do something. In publishing, it gives you the right to publish a book or books, or to use a character or name or story created by someone else in a book (or some other product—a lunch-box manufacturer might license the right to make a Pokémon lunch box).

More recently, companies have looked to other sources. One early and successful example of this was *The M&M's Counting Book*. More recently we've seen Animal Crackers books, Cheerios books, Lionel trains books, and other books tied into popular consumer products and toys.

This is all part of a wider strategy publishers have of moving into the consumer market to replace lost library sales. At the same time that publishers have cut back on books intended for libraries, they have opened or expanded divisions that do brand-name publishing. As one example, look at Simon & Schuster, a large children's publisher owned by Viacom. Viacom also owns Nickelodeon, and Simon & Schuster has successfully published a large number of Nickelodeon-derived books. Other publishers are doing the same. Some other examples: Scholastic is publishing a line of *Teletubbies* tie-ins and is getting a "first look" at Warner Brothers' TV, movie, and Cartoon Network properties; Penguin Putnam has an agreement with DreamWorks to publish tie-ins to upcoming feature-length animated films.

Our Friend Harry Potter

Good old Harry! He's shown the world something that we already knew—that a good children's book is a good book for children *and* adults. He's reminded us of the power of the imagination—the first four books came out long before any movie or licensed product, leaving his millions of fans free to imagine him as they liked. He's reminded us of the power of word of mouth—the first book became a hit in England because children told their friends about it, and they told their friends, and so on.

But will Harry have a lasting impact? It's too soon to tell for sure, though we can predict confidently that hundreds of people are at work this moment, trying to be the next J. K. Rowling. And we can hope that after swallowing the heftier price tag on a Harry Potter book, adults will now be more willing to pay more than $16.95 for a children's book, allowing publishers to make longer, larger, or otherwise more expensive books. And we can expect that children's books will be a little more in the minds of the media, meaning more coverage that will keep this market healthy in years to come.

It's an Electronic World

Throughout children's publishing, people get excited about the "new media"—the new electronic ways to publish or present material, from CD-ROMs to *e-books* and more. Publishers see amazing opportunities or terrifying threats. Authors and illustrators fear exploitation. The pundits have a field day, and no week goes by without the announcement of a new alliance, format, or e-commerce Web site.

None of the wilder predictions have come close to coming true so far. This is a change to the business that's still mostly in the future.

Several years ago, some saw CD-ROMs as a real threat to traditional books, and even to illustrated books. Many companies invested in CD-ROM publishing, only to discover how difficult it is to make money in this area. Today, reference is the only area of publishing in which CD-ROMS have had a big impact. That's not surprising. A CD-ROM is for many people an improvement over a multivolume encyclopedia set. Publishers have yet to convince the ordinary consumer that an electronic book is preferable to a paper one.

There are two types of electronic books or e-books. Some can be read on personal computers (PC), perhaps from Internet sites, while others require special viewers. Though a few name-brand authors have already published e-books, and publishers are starting to release electronic editions, this is a very new area. Publishers are already at work in it, of course. Coauthor Harold is now working at one of the pioneers in this field, ipicturebooks.com, a company making illustrated children's books available in different electronic formats. Electronic children's books may not be bought much as individual titles, but parents may want to subscribe to them, and schools and libraries may be interested in getting access to on-line libraries of books, some not available in print at all.

Handheld e-book viewers may also have an impact fairly soon—in the textbook market. We've heard about four different models, ranging in price from $200 to $1,500. Readers then pay for books either by subscription or on a per-title basis. Though more convenient than a personal computer, few people are likely to buy these instead of a computer. Their market will instead be limited to people who can buy both an e-book reader and a PC—or to school districts interested in them as replacements for textbooks. And after a good number are in use, can the young adult novels for them be far behind?

Vocabulary List

A book that must be read in an electronic format instead of on paper is an **e-book.** These books can be set up for reading on personal computers or on special readers.

Can You Keep a Secret?

To see some of the latest developments in electronic publishing, visit these Web sites:

www.ipicturebooks.com

www.iuniverse.com

www.glassbook.com

www.backinprint.com

www.ipublish.com

www.ebookcity.com

www.netlibrary.com

On-demand publishing, in which single titles of books are printed when needed, is a different kind of electronic publishing, because it relies on electronic files of books and their use to create speedy printings of one book (or more) when needed. Academic and specialty publishers can use it to sell copies of their books in bookstores that can't otherwise carry them. This technology could also enable publishers to keep a novel or black and white nonfiction title technically "in print" indefinitely, even if not selling lots of copies. So far, this doesn't work for books with color, and prices tend to be high.

Developments keep coming thick and fast. For now, most publishers see electronic publishing as an opportunity to sell a book in another format, much like audiotapes or paperbacks, and not as a replacement for books themselves.

It's a brave new world in children's books, but also a big and diverse one. It's not the world we knew as children, but it's still a world in which dedicated and creative writers—and that means you—can find a place.

The Least You Need to Know

➤ Children's books used to be published mostly for sale to libraries, but that's not true anymore.

➤ Paperbacks are an increasingly common way to publish a children's book.

➤ Publishing companies are getting bigger and bigger and often are part of multinational corporations.

➤ Publishers are trying to sell more books to consumers, and so make them attractive to adults; they also license movies, TV shows, and products to make their books instantly familiar.

➤ Electronic publishing hasn't had a big effect on children's books yet, but it probably will in the future.

Chapter 7

What's in a Book?
A Guided Tour

In This Chapter

➤ What goes on the cover, jacket, and spine

➤ All the items listed in the front of the book

➤ The differences between dedications, forewords, and introductions and where you find them in the book

➤ What you'll find in the body of a picture book, a chapter book, and other types of books

➤ The material in the back of the book

A book, any book, is made of many parts, with names you need to know. In this chapter, we'll navigate you from cover to cover through the components of a children's book. You'll learn where everything from the copyright information to the glossary goes. Along the way, we'll also offer definitions used in the publishing world for specific areas of the book. Get ready because here comes your crash course in "the anatomy of a book."

It's a Cover-Up! The Cover, Jacket, and Spine

When you walk into any bookstore and pull a book from a shelf, you immediately see the cover—the front of the book, most likely covered by a jacket. You may have heard "don't judge a book by its cover," but most people do, or at least identify a particular book by its cover. To the publisher, the cover consists of three parts—the front, the back, and the spine. More about each part in a second. But first let's check out the whole cover.

Vocabulary List

When a book is produced with a hard, stiff outer cover, it is called a **hardcover** book. The covers are usually made of cardboard, over which is stretched cloth, treated paper, vinyl, or some other plastic.

When the cover of a book is pliable, the book is then called **softcover.** Pliable covers are usually made of thick but flexible paper or light cardboard coated with varnish or a synthetic resin or laminate.

Vocabulary List

The center panel of the binding of a book is called the **spine.** The spine hinges together the front and back cover to the pages and faces out when the book is shelved. The pages of the book all connect at the spine.

The book's cover may either be hard (called *hardcover*) or pliable (called *softcover* or paperback). What gets printed on the front cover depends upon whether the book is a hardcover or softcover.

Traditionally, hardcover books didn't have anything on the front and back covers, with the possible exception of a decorative design stamped on. Identifying elements are found, instead, on the *spine* of the book—the last and first name of the author, the publisher, and the title of the book.

But hardcovers come with jackets. According to *The Chicago Manual of Style, 14th Edition,* book jackets— nowadays glossy paper, as a protective wrapping for the hardcover—entered the publishing arena in the twentieth century. On the book jacket, you'll find identifying elements—the title, the author, the illustrator, the publisher, the *ISBN* (*International Standard Book Number*), the price, and on the flaps of the jacket, promotional blurbs about the book. Increasingly, children's picture books may also have printed covers that duplicate the eye-catching design of the jacket.

Let's take a look at the book jacket of the award-winning hardcover edition of *The Tombs of Atuan* by Ursula Le Guin. This book offers you a good example of what you'll see on a hardcover book jacket.

A softcover or paperback book does not have a jacket. The information you see on the front and spine of the jacket of the hardcover book is printed on the cover itself. Typically, you'll find some promotional information on the back, but not as much as that on the flaps of a jacket. Some publishers are also choosing to print promotional copy on the inside of the cover.

Let's take a look at the paperback cover for *The Tombs of Atuan.* The design is different, which is typical for a novel, and if you look at the back you'll also see that the ISBN is different.

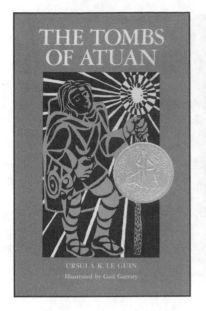

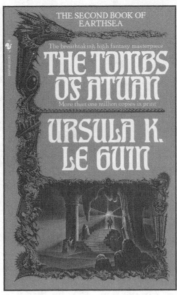

The hardcover jacket (left) and the paperback cover (right) of the same title may look different, though often for picture books they are the same.

Teacher Says, "Give It a Title"

When you first open a book, you see blank pages. These, including the one stuck down on the inside of the cover, are called endpapers. You can guess why! Publishers may gussy them up with maps or use fancy paper, but you don't need to worry much about them now.

Keep turning the pages. Soon, you should find the title page. The title page contains many things other than the full title. You'll find the author's full name (no initials unless the author goes by initials only), the illustrator, and the name and sometimes the location of the publisher. If the publisher has a logo, that appears here, too. The main point of this page, though, is the title.

Vocabulary List

ISBN is the acronym for **International Standard Book Number.** This number gives the book a unique ID for orders and distribution. The publisher assigns the ISBN based upon procedures set up by the R.R. Bowker Company and the International Standards Organization. You'll find the ISBN of your book in the bar code on the back of the jacket for a hardcover, on the back of a paperback cover, and on the copyright page.

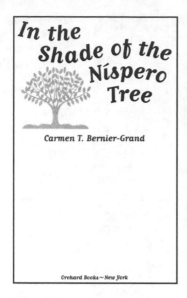

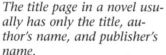

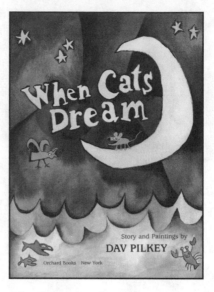

The title page in a novel usually has only the title, author's name, and publisher's name.

The title page of a picture book is usually more elaborate.

Legal and Other Details

The page directly after the title page is the copyright page and colophon (unless a publisher puts this material at the end of the book, for design reasons). Several kinds of information are printed here. Most important, the publisher states that it has copyrighted the text and illustrations in the names of the author and illustrator (see Chapter 20, "They Might Take My Idea! Copyright Basics," for more on copyright).

Can You Keep a Secret?

Many of the elements of a book's design go back to the nineteenth century or earlier, and have been retained even though they may not be needed in a book. Title pages, for example, were much more necessary when books were published unbound, possibly in installments, to be bound and given covers by the purchaser. "Half title" pages, on which nothing more than the title of the book appears, occasionally appear before the title page as another one of these traditional elements.

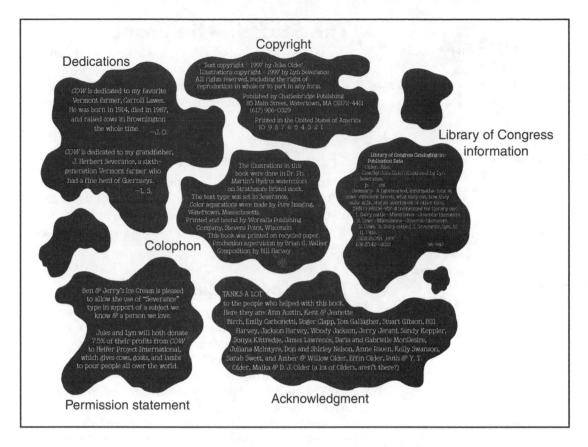

Copyright

Dedications

Text copyright © 1997 by Jules Older.
Illustrations copyright © 1997 by Lyn Severance.
All rights reserved, including the right of
reproduction in whole or in part in any form.

Published by Charlesbridge Publishing
85 Main Street, Watertown, MA 02172-4411
(617) 926-0329

Printed in the United States of America
10 9 8 7 6 5 4 3 2 1

COW is dedicated to my favorite
Vermont farmer, Carroll Lawes.
He was born in 1914, died in 1967,
and raised cows in Brownington
the whole time.   —J. O.

COW is dedicated to my grandfather,
J. Herbert Severance, a sixth-
generation Vermont farmer who
had a fine herd of Guernseys.
       —L. S.

**Library of Congress
information**

Library of Congress Cataloging-in-
Publication Data
Older, Jules.
Cow/by Jules Older; illustrated by Lyn
Severance.
p.   cm.
Summary: A lighthearted, informative look at
cows: different breeds, what they eat, how they
make milk, and an assortment of other facts.
ISBN 0-88106-957-4 (reinforced for library use)
1. Dairy cattle—Miscellanea—Juvenile literature.
2. Cows—Miscellanea—Juvenile literature.
[1. Cows. 2. Dairy cattle.] I. Severance, Lyn, ill.
II. Title.
SF208.O56   1997
636.2742—dc20   96-947

The illustrations in this
book were done in Dr. Ph.
Martin's Hydrus watercolors
on Strathmore Bristol stock.
The text type was set in Severance.
Color separations were made by Pure Imaging,
Watertown, Massachusetts.
Printed and bound by Worzalla Publishing
Company, Stevens Point, Wisconsin
This book was printed on recycled paper.
Production supervision by Brian G. Walker
Composition by Bill Harvey

Colophon

Ben & Jerry's Ice Cream is pleased
to allow the use of "Severance"
type in support of a subject we
know & a person we love.

Jules and Lyn will both donate
7.5% of their profits from *COW*
to Heifer Project International,
which gives cows, goats, and lambs
to poor people all over the world.

TANKS A LOT
to the people who helped with this book.
Here they are: Ann Austin, Kent & Jeanette
Birch, Emily Carbonetti, Roger Clapp, Tom Gallagher, Stuart Gibson, Bill
Harvey, Jackson Harvey, Woody Jackson, Jerry Jerard, Sandy Keppler,
Sonya Kittredge, James Lawrence, Daria and Gabrielle MonDesire,
Juliana McIntyre, Don and Shirley Nelson, Anne Rauen, Kelly Swanson,
Sarah Swett, and Amber & Willow Older, Effin Older, Ruth & Y. T.
Older, Malka & D. J. Older (a lot of Olders, aren't there?)

Permission statement

Acknowledgment

This copyright page, from Cow *by Jules Older, illustrated by Lyn Severance, includes many of the items often found in front matter.*

Other information besides the copyright appears here—see if you can find all of it in our illustration. You'll see the complete address of the publisher, how many printings the book has gone through, the *Library of Congress* Cataloging-in-Publication (CIP) data, the ISBN, and any acknowledgments of use of someone else's copyrighted material (though this can appear elsewhere). The CIP information helps get your book into the nation's libraries. The publisher submits the book to the Library of Congress, which assigns it its own number and creates basic cataloging information.

Picture books are reviving an old tradition in publishing—the *colophon.* The colophon provides information about the production of a book, such as the typefaces used, the names of the designer and typesetter, and the kinds of paint and paper the illustrator used. Often this appears on the copyright page, but if the information is lengthy the colophon may get its own page.

The Stuff in the Front

Now that we've gotten through the business of the book, let's move on to other stuff you might find in the front of the book. Logically enough, all of this material is called the "front matter" by folks in publishing.

"For Me!" Dedications

As an author or illustrator, you may want to dedicate your creative efforts to someone. The publisher will place the dedication page after the copyright page, or, especially in picture books, on the copyright page as the first item.

Tables of Contents

Just after the copyright page and dedication, you sometimes find a table of contents. The average board book or picture book won't have one, of course. But plenty of other children's books—like anthologies, chapter books, or informational works—do include a table of contents. Sometimes the table of contents is simply called "Contents." The amount of detail a publisher goes into varies, but you'll certainly find the chapter number, chapter title if there is one, and the beginning page number of each. If the book has sections, they'll appear too, and sometimes subdivisions of chapters will be listed (as they are in the front of this book). Glossaries, indexes, and other material will also get listed.

Vocabulary List

The **Library of Congress** is a federal agency charged with maintaining a collection of all books published in the United States, and with creating standardized cataloging information for libraries; most other countries have similar agencies. A **colophon** is an item in a book's front matter that gives information about how it was produced, from typefaces to the kind of paint an artist used.

Forewords and Introductions

After the table of contents, you may find either an introduction or a foreword—or perhaps both. Sometimes the foreword may be called a prologue. Generally speaking, a prominent expert or authority writes a foreword to a book. If you write a children's book based on astronomy, and John Glenn writes a few pages talking about your book and its merits, that's a foreword.

Typically an author writes an introduction to provide information integral to the understanding of the book or some background on the basis or making of the book. For a historical novel, for example, you may want to include an introduction to give your reader some background on the period of time in which your novel takes place.

Contents

This table of contents from The Forestwife *by Theresa Tomlinson shows chapter titles as well as chapter numbers.*

What's Between Your Head and Feet? Your Body!

It takes a while, but once you get past all the business and practical details, you get to the good stuff—the stories, the poems, the learning, the history—the content itself! Let's take a look at the *body* of the book. In a picture book, the body of the book is the story and the pictures that accompany it, in one straightforward narrative. For other kinds of books, the setup may be a little more complicated, and other elements appear.

Vocabulary List

In journalistic or creative writing of any kind, the "meat" of the story—or the story proper—is termed the **body.** Basically, the body of any work is the work itself without any extraneous information like the copyright page or the dedication or the index.

Chapter Books

The identifying factor of a chapter book—a novel for kids—is simply that the text is broken up into chapters. The chapters may or may not have illustrations. Seems easy enough, right? But you have choices. A chapter may just have a number, or it can have its own title. Look on your own shelves for examples. Get a sense of the length of chapters. Do they vary much? Are they longer in books for older children?

Alphabetical and Other Setups

Chapters aren't the only way the body of the book can be broken up. Authors can as be creative with the structure of their book just as they are with the content. Especially for picture books, the letters of the alphabet may break up and organize the body of the book. Jerry Pallotta, for example, introduces a variety of types of jets and explains how a jet engine works in his *Jet Alphabet Book.*

A chronological structure works well in books set up as diaries. Lisa Rowe Fraustino's *Ash,* for example, is written as the journal of a boy dealing with the breakdown of his older brother, while Patricia McKissack's *A Picture of Freedom* from the "Dear America" series follows the life of an enslaved girl on a Virginia plantation.

Other Elements

Chapters and other ways of putting the body of the book in order aren't all that can appear there.

You can also find …

➤ Pictures with captions and labels

➤ Tables

➤ Special elements like pop-ups

➤ Running heads (these go across the top of the page and help you know where you are in the book)

➤ Headers, subheaders (you'll see these throughout this book, as a way of breaking up the chapters)

Go to the Back of the Line—Back Matter

Children's books often include what we in the industry call "back matter." Basically, back matter includes anything of informational purposes other than the text—a glossary, recommended reading lists, an index, information about the book, games to play based on the book, and other material. Much of this is written by the author, but some may be added by the publisher.

More About Bugs for Lunch

More About Bugs for Lunch

There are more insects in the world than any other kind of animal. More than 800,000 insects have been studied and named, but scientists believe that there are probably millions that nobody knows about yet. It's a good thing that insects are food for so many creatures, or the world might be overrun with them.

The *NUTHATCH* is called the upside-down bird because it walks headfirst down tree trunks as it searches for food. With its strong beak, it pries out insects, caterpillars, and insect eggs that are hidden in cracks in the bark.

SPIDERS catch insects in webs and traps made of silk. Each species of spider has a distinctive design for its web or trap. When they catch more than they can eat at one time, most spiders wrap the leftovers in silk to save for a later meal.

BATS fly from their roosts to look for food as the sun goes down. But even in total darkness, they can catch insects. Bats send out a constant stream of sounds that are pitched so high that people cannot hear them. As these sounds hit objects, they echo back to the bat. When an insect flies across this beam of sound, the bat can tell exactly where the bug is and can swoop down to catch it in flight.

A *GECKO* is a small lizard that lives in warm climates. Many people like to have geckos in their gardens and backyards. They know that geckos will come out of hiding at night to eat moths and other insects that people find pesky.

Back matter in a picture book may include additional information, as in this page from Bugs for Lunch *by Marge Facklam, and can also include recommended books, sources, a glossary, or even an index.*

Are you a picture book author who's thinking, "I can see that in a book for an older child or in a nonfiction book, but not a picture book"? But we know of many cases when picture books have back matter, too, especially picture books based on folktales. Just what is in the back matter varies enormously. In the back of the paperback edition of the novel *A Wrinkle in Time,* there isn't much. Yearling Books includes descriptions of four other books by Madeleine L'Engle as well as a short biography with her picture. For an example of more extensive back matter, check out *The 20th Century Children's Book Treasury.* In this anthology of picture books, the reader will find "Biographical Notes" about each author, a "Guide to Reading Ages," and an "Index of Titles, Authors, and Illustrators."

Back matter in a chapter book can be lengthy. This is the first page of the back matter in James Giblin's When Plague Strikes.

SOURCE NOTES AND BIBLIOGRAPHY

So many books, magazine articles, and newspaper reports were part of the research for *When Plague Strikes* that it would be virtually impossible to list them all. Here I'll single out those that contributed significantly to the planning and writing of the book.

OVERALL

Four books stimulated my thinking when I was deciding how to treat the subject of plagues in history. They were:

Plagues and Peoples by William H. McNeill (New York: Doubleday, 1977). This fascinating book describes the decisive role that disease has played in the historical development of the human race. From it I gained a much clearer notion of how plagues like the Black Death could travel from one continent to another.

The Doctor in History by Howard W. Haggard (New York: Dorset Press, 1989). A history of medicine and its practitioners from prehistoric times to the early years of the twentieth

197

We urge you to browse books, specifically looking at the back matter. In fact, go out now. Pull several books from different age categories and just pore over the back pages. See what other authors and publishers have included. Think about whether or not you think it adds to the book. Do any of the books you examined seem to have something missing? Keep all of this in mind when working on your own book. A book can be put together from a large grab bag of components in many different ways, and you can be as creative with those components as you are with any other part of your writing.

Class Rules

Don't be afraid to mention your ideas for back matter in a proposal for a book. In fact, keep notes on all your ideas for any back matter and list those possibilities in the proposal with examples. You'll give the publisher a more complete vision of your work.

The Least You Need to Know

➤ A book contains many elements, each of which has a name and a purpose.

➤ Hardcover books have a jacket, which details specifics about the book, while softcover books must fit all the information on the cover.

➤ Business aspects of the book—copyrights, publisher information, and dedications—occur at the front of the book before the copy.

➤ The body of the book is your work—the book!

➤ Many books—even picture books—contain back matter. This back matter may include anything from a biography of the author, to suggested games to play, to an index or glossary.

Part 2

Finding Out What's Possible

Now that you know the basics, you still need to learn more if you are going to get to your destination. Here we clue you in on the different formats and age levels books get slotted into, and show you some of the genres within which you might be writing, from pure fantasy to the most straightforward nonfiction.

You'll also learn about the kinds of publishers, and the difference between books for series and books that work best as individual titles.

Think you're ready to launch your manuscript into the world? First, read up on how to get good feedback, and then proceed.

Chapter 8

Animal, Vegetable, or Mineral? Book Formats and Age Levels

In This Chapter

➤ A look at fiction and nonfiction

➤ What are board books?

➤ The lowdown on easy readers, story collections, and more

➤ The different kinds of books with chapters

➤ Who reads what, and we don't just mean children

You know you want to write for children, and you've even explored the classics and hot titles. By now you're probably on a first-name basis with the librarians and booksellers in town. But what about what you're going to write? Do you know the difference yet between chapter books and picture books? How about board books and easy readers?

In this chapter, we'll give you an overview of different children's book formats, and how they more or less align with different age levels. We'll also explain why you may be writing not only for children, but for adults, too.

Tell the Truth, the Whole Truth

When you tell the truth, the whole truth, and nothing but the truth in your books, you're writing *nonfiction*. Journalists write nonfiction; they retell the events of a story. But even though it is called a "story," the writer is trying to get at the facts. When you

read an article in *Time* magazine or *Redbook,* you are reading nonfiction. When you hear a reporter on the radio recount the details of a four-alarm fire, you're listening to nonfiction.

Nonfiction covers a wide range of subjects or approaches. Here are just a few examples:

➤ There are how-to books for children just as much as for adults. These are a specialty of Klutz Press; one example is *Coin Magic,* which tells how to perform 24 magic tricks.

➤ Books that present "just the facts" might introduce dinosaurs, such as *Dinosaurs! Strange and Wonderful,* by Laurence Pringle, or burial customs, as in Penny Colman's *Corpses, Coffins, and Crypts: A History of Burial.*

➤ Stories about real people, as long as they are based only on verifiable information, are biographies, a major type of nonfiction. Barbara Cooney's *Eleanor* is a picture book example.

Vocabulary List

Also known as an "informational book," **nonfiction** is writing in which the author re-tells the events of history with minimal embellishment, passes on knowledge, or presents activities or experiments. A biography, a guide to endangered species, a how-to, or a story about Mount St. Helens are all kinds of nonfiction writing.

If you like to do research and write about what you've learned, you can write nonfiction. We'll go into more detail about this area in this and the next chapter.

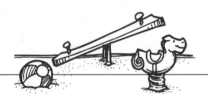

Stories from the Playground

Is nonfiction less creative than fiction? Not so, says nonfiction author Sneed Collard: "I actually began my writing as a self-indulgent and ignorant fiction writer. In fact, my first four children's sales were all fictional stories. The problem was, I was having so many interesting experiences as a biologist that I just couldn't help writing about them. Once I began writing nonfiction, I loved it. It provided me with a great excuse to learn more about biology AND could be just as creative as fiction. I'd go a step further and say that a nonfiction books offers MORE opportunity for creativity than fiction. It's extremely rare to find a fiction picture book that truly breaks new ground. Nonfiction, on the other hand, has not even begun to peak as far as creative possibilities."

Have Fun Lying

Obviously, the opposite of nonfiction is *fiction*. Fiction is what we make up, though it may have a basis in fact. As renowned writer Jane Yolen, author of novels, picture books, poetry, and much else, puts it, "Memory is just one more story. And sometimes not a very good one at that. It needs that sandpaper touchup, a bit of paint, a little lie here, and a bigger lie there—and so fiction is born." So although nonfiction can never be based on an entirely invented incident, fiction can find a basis in fact. Fiction is not truth, though it can hold truth within it. You'll find fiction at the other end of the spectrum from nonfiction, but as you will learn, there are interesting categories in between.

As with nonfiction, there are many types of fiction. We'll explore these in more detail in this and the following chapter.

Vocabulary List

Fiction is writing from the imagination, or writing containing elements of imagination, fable, or tale. Fiction is "made up."

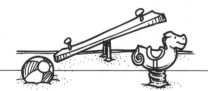

Stories from the Playground

Continuing her discussion of fiction writing, Jane Yolen offered a look at the evolution of her fictional works from a beginning in her life. She says, "*Owl Moon* is a compilation of lots of owling trips that my husband took with our children. *The Girl Who Loved the Wind* is a fairy tale allegory of my life. The *Commander Toad* books are pun-filled romps with a serious message at the core. Yet they each started with something real—a memory of something actual—and then went on to make something 'realer.' Bad grammar, but a true statement nonetheless."

For Baby Brother: Picture Books

After you've absorbed the fiction/nonfiction distinction, move on to formats. Very generally, children's books come either as heavily illustrated picture books, or as sparsely or not illustrated chapter books.

When people think of children's literature, picture books often come to mind. These are the books Mom and Dad read to you at bedtime, or the teacher read to you at story time. In a picture book, a line or two of text typically accompanies a page of illustration, though the amount of text can range from none at all to a paragraph or two.

Most picture books are also pretty short, not just because their audience—younger children—have pretty short attention spans. Most picture books are printed in full color, and that's expensive. Because books get printed on a sheet of paper that's printed on both sides, then folded and cut, picture books come in lengths of 16, 24, 32, 40 pages or sometimes more; 32 pages is the most typical length. A longer book with more text might be called an illustrated storybook or picture storybook.

If you did your homework and dug through the books a librarian and bookseller may have handed you, you probably read many, many picture books.

For Big Sister: Chapter Books

When kids move from picture books to reading books themselves—with chapters even!—they've entered the realm of chapter books. These range from easy-to-read novels for the elementary school crowd up to serious novels and nonfiction for teenagers, and from short books with illustrations to meaty 300-plus-page tomes with no illustrations to be seen. Think of the "Frog and Toad" books, *Island of the Blue Dolphins,* the "Nancy Drew" series, and *Bridge to Terabithia.* These are all chapter books of different types.

What's for Who? How to Tell

We hear you. It's all very well to make these big distinctions, but you need specifics. You want to know just what you are writing, to help you know if you are writing at the right level for your audience, and to help you describe your book to a publisher—and even to send it to the right publisher.

There are no hard-and-fast rules, but you'll begin to learn some rules of thumb. In general, to find out whom you are writing for—or to make sure you are writing for whom you want—you'll need to take a look at the following:

➤ Length. The shorter the book, the younger the child, usually. Because picture books are often read *to* children not *by* them, they may be the exception.

➤ Complexity of language and vocabulary. Your syntax and vocabulary can get more complex for older readers.

➤ The age of your main character. Generally, children read about children at least as old as themselves. You won't find too many 11-year-olds savoring a story about a third-grader.

➤ Subject matter. Are the concerns of your book the concerns of your audience?

You Can Throw 'em

Any parent of an infant or toddler knows *board books,* the simplest kind of picture book. You'll know one especially well when an angry 18-month-old child hurls one from across the room and hits you in the forehead with it! Be fore-warned: Flying board books can result in stitches. How can a baby book be so sturdy—and danger-ous? Well, these little titles are small but chunky and tough, made literally from paperboard or card-board, not paper, so they can stand up to the wear-and-tear of fat, dimpled hands. You'll even find plastic versions to play with in the bathtub.

Traditionally, board books consist of several thick, hard pages with one or two words of text and an illustration on each; there are usually no more than 16 pages. Repetition rules, too. For example, one page may say, "Peek-a-boo, cat!" Turn the page, and you'll find "Peek-a-boo, dog!" These books are simple, direct, and brief, just right for babies to experience in the lap of a parent. That's been your typical board book for generations.

Lately publishers have been converting lengthier children's picture books into the board book for-mat. Early and successful examples of such con-versions are the Margaret Wise Brown's titles of *Goodnight Moon* and *Runaway Bunny.* Now many other publishers of picture books are jumping on the baby book bandwagon and producing board book versions of popular picture books. This trend has gone so far that most of the books you'll find in the board book area of a bookstore didn't start out as board books.

In between the true board book and the picture book, you might find what are called "concept books," because they explore a concept rather than tell a story. In a way, they are nonfiction for the very young. See books such as Tana Hoban's *Colors Everywhere* or Suse McDonald's *Peck, Slither, and Slide* as examples.

Vocabulary List

Board books are short, thick, square-shaped (usually) simple books for infants and toddlers. They may tell a brief story or introduce basic concepts like colors or numbers.

Class Rules

We'll be saying a lot about word count and page length in this chapter. But use these numbers to help you figure out what a manuscript might be, not as rules for writing. As Jane Yolen says, "Should be, what an awful con-cept. A book should be as long as it needs to be, not some arbi-trary length. I must remind my-self that a story has a beginning and a middle and an end. Not a word count."

Read It Again!

You know the scene. Everyone bathed and tucked into bed. Suddenly you hear, "Mommy, can you read me a story?" So, you go in and read the story—beautiful picture books with glossy pages and crisp, short prose. These books aren't as short as board books, and fortunately, they're often considerably more interesting for adults. This, is after all, an age that loves familiarity. You'll get tired of reading a favorite book long before a child tires of hearing it.

Picture books probably account for more books on the shelves in the children's department than those in any other format or for any other age level. Children beg for them, parents love them as a vehicle for literacy, and people buy them as gifts for children *and* adults all the time. They can be fiction or nonfiction, and because they are read by adults to children, or perhaps used in school, they vary in length from a few hundred words to as many as 2,000. This is a very flexible format, allowing for all kinds of subject matter and approaches.

Can You Keep a Secret?

Author Larry Dane Brimner notes these basic distinctions among books for beginning readers:

➤ Easy-reading picture book: 32 pages

➤ Easy (or early) reader: 48 to 64 pages

➤ Early chapter book: 48 to 64 pages

Lengths vary from several hundred words to 1,500 words.

I Can Read This

Remember the thrill of reading your first book yourself? Children may start with those picture books that have fairly simple texts, but beginning readers soon crave more than books like those that relatives read to them. They want more. More words. More length. More to read. But be careful. You don't want to overwhelm this reading group. Because these books—given various names, as you can see in the sidebar—aren't read by parents to children, they must have simpler vocabulary than picture books do, vocabulary that beginning readers can handle.

The Arthur books by Marc Brown are a typical example of the first easy readers kids pick up. From there, *Frog and Toad* and *Amelia Bedelia* come to mind. You might also want to study an entire program, such as the Simon & Schuster "Ready-to-Read" books, and the careful gradations between the levels of its program. Easy-to-read books can be nonfiction too, as in the Harper "Let's-Read-and-Find-Out Science" program, actually originated by the now-defunct Thomas Y. Crowell publishing company in 1960, and still going strong 40 years and a change of publisher later. The best thing you can do to focus your energies in this area is immerse yourself in the books. Children don't spend that long on early readers, but that doesn't mean this is an area to ignore. Soon they'll be moving on to lengthier chapter books.

That's a Lot of Stories!

Parents, teachers, and librarians love collections, the cornucopia of books all bound as one for typically less cost than buying each individually. Some are put together from existing books by an editor. But others are original works, and a type of book about which you should know, if you like to write the kinds of stories that don't work too well in picture books but aren't long enough for longer books.

Folktales and Fairy Tales

Do you remember the stories of Hansel and Gretel? Sleeping Beauty? Both are fairy tales, a form of writing that developed from folktales. *Fairy tales* and *folktales* remain a great way of imparting culture and traditions to children. The only difference between the way we pass on folktales today and the way it was done ages ago is the medium. We have books, while in years past the stories were passed on orally.

You'll see plenty of well-known folktales and fairy tales made into picture books, but many don't work well for that audience. What to do, if you love these? Another approach is to put together a collection. Watch out for copyright infringement (for guidance, see Chapter 20, "They Might Take My Idea! Copyright Basics"). Virginia Hamilton's *The People Could Fly* and Howard Norman's *The Girl Who Dreamed Only Geese* are great examples of collections of retold folktales.

Can You Keep a Secret?

For more information on writing early and easy readers, surf over to "Targeting the Emergent Reader," an excellent article by Joan Broerman that examines this tricky area: www.underdown.org/early_rd.htm.

Vocabulary List

A **folktale** is a story that has been passed down orally and may appeal to both adults and children, whereas a **fairy tale,** though like a folktale in form, is told specifically for children and involves more literary elements or stylistic devices.

Short Stories and Poetry

You can also put together other kinds of collections. Short stories, which otherwise only find a home in magazines, can be collected for book publication, though extremely few short story collections for children are published. Poetry collections are a similarly tough sell, because the few publishers that do publish poetry look for an overall theme and a distinctive style. If there's any one type of children's book that can truly be said to be for "all ages," it's the collection.

Mom, Can I Get This?

Children can move from early reader books to true chapter books as early as second grade. Chapter books, especially those for middle-grade readers, are what we think of when we fondly remember classic novels for children—such books as E. B. White's *Charlotte's Web*, Laura Ingalls Wilder's *The Little House on the Prairie*, and Beverly Cleary's *Ramona the Pest*. For younger readers, these may have some illustrations, and be no more than 64 pages in length, but they range up to 200 pages or more.

Chapter books, which can be nonfiction as well, are just books with chapters. We include a number of kinds of chapter books in this category, but be warned: The term "chapter books" is used by some people only to mean books between early readers and true novels. Here is the range of all books with chapters:

➤ Easy readers with chapters or "early chapter books": 48 to 64 pages (approximately 6- to 8-year-olds).

➤ Young middle-grade: 48 to 80, longer if nonfiction (7- to 9-year-olds).

➤ True middle-grade: 80 to 160, occasionally more (8- to 12-year-olds).

➤ Older middle-grade or transitional: a bit longer (10- to 14-year-olds).

➤ Young adult or YA: up to 250 pages (12 plus).

It's difficult to make hard and fast distinctions between the different levels, so until you develop an intuitive sense of them, just write, and remember Jane Yolen's warning about word counts.

For the Backpack

Want to write something similar in form to books for middle-graders but more sophisticated in content? Don't forget the *young adult* audience. Loosely, that's teenagers.

Vocabulary List

Young adult (or **YA**) books are exactly as they sound. YA is the term used in the publishing arena to designate teens.

The publishing business started to target teens relatively recently. As noted in the October 18, 1999, feature "Making the Teen Scene" in *Publishers Weekly*, the trade magazine for publishing, "From *The Outsiders* in 1967 to *Smack* in 1998, publishers have consistently released books by talented authors who speak directly to a teen audience about sophisticated, though teen-appropriate concerns." That's not a long track record! It was authors such as S. E. Hinton, Walter Dean Myers, and Judy Blume who started to write more challenging novels for teenagers in the late 1960s, and the young adult category was invented in response.

Now here's the rub! Where to shelve teen books? Something like *The Catcher in the Rye* typically sits on the adult fiction shelves with the likes of *Memoirs of a Geisha*. And that's OK, because Salinger is, in fact, an adult author, too. He didn't set out to write a book exclusively for teenagers. But teens are likely to be insulted to find their books amid the board and picture books of younger children. For years, publishers, librarians, and booksellers have struggled over where to shelve teen titles. Sometimes there's a separate YA section. Sometimes there isn't. As a writer, don't concern yourself too much with this.

For Kid's Eyes Only—Not!

Of course, your audience of whatever genre you choose to write will be children. But not only children read children's books. Parents, grandparents, teachers, and librarians ultimately make the decision of what their children read, with the exception of books for teenagers, who have some control over their own spending. These people are the gatekeepers, and it's a fact of life that you must get your book past them to the child you want to reach.

Class Rules

Don't censor your writing for a teen audience. Adults sometimes underestimate the sensitivity and self-awareness that teens possess. Long before there was an official "young adult" genre, authors who respected teens were reaching them. J. D. Salinger's coming-of-age novel *The Catcher in the Rye* caused controversy among adults when it was published in the 1950s, but has been revered by generations of teens and is now considered a classic.

Sometimes, that can be a problem, especially if you want to write something that children will handle just fine but might not be approved by every adult. Still, the best children's books appeal to both children and adults. Always have, and always will. Some appeal more to adults than others do, as we noted in Chapter 6, "It's a BIG World." Should you, then, aim your writing at adults? No, because if you do, you may miss children altogether. Concentrate on your core audience, and if you do your job really well, maybe you'll reach adults, too.

The Least You Need to Know

➤ There are many different categories of writing to explore as a children's writer.

➤ Nonfiction writing is the truth and nothing but the truth.

➤ Fiction writing may involve some truth but ultimately requires imagination to tell about something that did not happen.

➤ Picture books are heavily illustrated with little text for the younger child. Someone other than the child reads the book to him.

➤ Chapter books have more text, and contain, of course, chapters. They get longer for older children.

➤ When you write, you will not only be writing for the child, but for adults, too. The "gatekeepers"—parents, librarians, and teachers—will often read or evaluate a book first, or actually read it to a child.

Digging Deeper Into the Book Pile

In the last chapter, we introduced the basic categories of writing for children. In this chapter, we'll delve deeper. Put on your oxygen mask because we're going under and immersing you in all the different "departments" of children's literature you may find in the bookstores and libraries. You now know the many formats of children's books, but you also need to know if what you want to write will be of interest to publishers. The possibilities are not endless.

In addition to giving you an understanding of all the different genres, we'll offer many titles for you to peruse at your leisure; you'll then obtain a more thoughtful understanding of each area.

Good Books (Literary Fiction)

Not all children's books are created equal. As in anything in this world, different qualities exist in the world of products. Look at champagne. Andre or Dom Perignom, anyone? How about chocolates? Not to sound snotty, but what would you prefer: Godiva or a Hershey bar? Let's face it. *Good* usually refers to the high end of any product out there. Well, it works the same in children's literature. There is a difference between good children's literature and lower-end works.

Vocabulary List

While the **format** of a book refers to its physical appearance—picture book or chapters, soft or hard cover—the **genre** of a book refers to the type of writing—fantasy, historical fiction, multicultural, or nonfiction.

To look at this from another angle, we'll use an example from adult literature. There exists a huge difference in the quality of F. Scott Fitzgerald's *The Great Gatsby* and popular women's writer Nicholas Sparks's *The Notebook*. One—*The Great Gatsby*—constitutes good, quality, high-end literature, while the other book—*The Notebook*—though popular, really isn't high-end literature.

Let's look at a few examples of quality and literary picture books:

➤ *Merette on the High Wire,* by Emily Arnold McCully
➤ *Zin! Zin! Zin! A Violin,* by Lloyd Moss
➤ *A Snowy Day,* by Ezra Jack Keats
➤ *Swimmy,* by Leo Lionni
➤ *A Bargain for Frances,* by Russell Hoban
➤ *This Land Is My,* Land by George Littlechild

If in your discovery of children's literature you haven't read one or more of the bulleted titles, we highly recommend you seek them out. Analyze them. Ask yourself, "What makes these books outstanding works of literature?"

Now we'll give you some examples of children's novels considered high-end, literary choices:

➤ *Tuck Everlasting,* by Natalie Babbitt
➤ *Catherine, Called Birdy,* by Karen Cushman
➤ *Charlotte's Web,* by E. B. White
➤ *A Wrinkle in Time,* by Madeleine L'Engle
➤ *The Lion, the Witch and the Wardrobe,* by C. S. Lewis
➤ *The Chocolate War,* by Robert Cormier (definitely for older young adult audiences, but great children's literature, nonetheless)

Again, if you haven't read the books on this list, go back and study them.

They're, Like, Soooo Popular: Popular Fiction

How many of you adults out there love a really great scare and pick up Stephen King night after night? Or how many romance novels sell directly off the racks in supermarkets, gobbled up by adoring fans of lovely heroines and muscle-ripped heroes? Now, now. Get your nose out of the air! Popular fiction appeals to the masses. And just as Mom and Dad may not always read Shakespeare, children don't always cuddle up to *The Secret Garden*. And why should they? You like Stephen King? They like "Goosebumps." You like romance novels? They like *Love Stories*.

Just a few examples of popular fiction for younger children:

➤ Any of the Arthur books by Marc Brown
➤ Any of the Maisy the Mouse books by Lucy Cousins
➤ The Berenstain Bears books

For the older reader, some popular fiction includes:

➤ "Dear America" novels
➤ "Goosebumps" series
➤ Matt Christopher's sport novels
➤ "Animorphs" series

Popular books and good books generally come from different publishers, or at least from different divisions within the same publisher. Depending on what approach you are taking, you'll need to seek out the right kind of publisher, and we'll explain the differences in the next chapter.

Pat Sat on the Mat (Control the Vocabulary)

In most cases, you can just sit down and write your story, using your judgment about vocabulary. But some series, easy readers in particular, are built around a carefully selected vocabulary list. When even *Make Way for Ducklings* proves too advanced, or when the audience delights in the simple rhymes and sounds, then books like *One Fish, Two Fish, Red Fish, Blue Fish* appear on the shelves. These books maintain simple vocabulary for simple vocabularies; they are controlled vocabulary books.

Most commonly found in textbooks, controlled vocabulary also inspired *The Cat in the Hat,* which Theodor Geisel (Dr. Seuss) crafted from a list of just more than 200 words for beginning readers,

Can You Keep a Secret?

Popular children's fiction characters are everywhere on your television set these days. According to the February 22, 1999, issue of *Publishers Weekly,* "nearly all of CBS's Saturday morning line-up is inspired by book titles," while the Maisy debut on Nickelodeon last year "boosted ratings for the time slot considerably."

Class Rules

Don't look upon books like *Pat the Bunny* or controlled vocabulary titles as the learning tools of children with low reading levels. Just because an elementary student may struggle with reading doesn't mean the kid wants to read "baby books." Thankfully, publishers are responding with "hi-lo" books. These books strive to provide interesting subject matter while still retaining simple vocabulary.

using every single one of those words and no others. If a publisher's guidelines call for a controlled vocabulary, then use their word list. You can assume that most children's publishers don't care about this, however.

Vocabulary List

Fantasy is a type of fiction in which the rules of the world are different—animals talk, magic works, strange creatures exist.

Swords and Sorcerers and Talking Bunnies

If we sound like we're hitting you over the head with the following concept, sorry. But it bears repeating: Whatever adults like, children like. Some areas, of course, are more popular with children than with adults. *Fantasy* books have proliferated within the children's literature arena for a long time. The *kind* of fantasy publishers want requires some study, however.

Let's take a look at some of the areas within fantasy and examples of some titles.

Traditional Fantasy

One of the best-known traditional fantasy titles ever remains J.R.R. Tolkien's *The Hobbit.* Coauthor Lynne still remembers fondly her fourth-grade teacher reading the book aloud to the class after lunch each day. "I was mesmerized by this world unlike anything I'd ever known or seen. It was captivating," she recalls. Besides *The Hobbit,* other books you might check into to further explore traditional fantasy include Ursula Le Guin's "Earthsea" books.

Even picture books cross over to the fantasy genre! For example, pick up any stories with witches and ghosts in the plot, or stories that involve imaginary friends and you just pulled a fantasy title for a child. Children know at an early age that these are fantasies, but they enjoy them. Moreover, oftentimes fantasies provide small children a way of dealing with their own feelings and developmental problems. What are monsters, for example, but manifestations of our own destructive impulses, or of our fear of some external threat?

Mon Dieu! *The Clock Is Alive! Personifications*

Bringing inanimate objects to life and giving them human qualities—personification—is not common in mainstream publishing (the "good" publishers), though you'll find it is popular. *Budgy the Helicopter,* by Sarah Ferguson, the Duchess of York, is a typical effort in this area, and was published by a mainstream publisher. Celebrities sell books, of course, regardless of the content. Your average author would not have been able to sell this same story to a publisher.

So personification is an area you want to avoid. Even if well done, an editor will assume it's the usual stuff—especially because many beginners gravitate toward turning an inanimate object, like a clock or a car, into something with human qualities.

Watership Down vs. Sammy Squirrel: Anthropomorphism

In the serious and wildly successful fantasy novel Richard Adam's *Watership Down,* the bunnies do talk. But any book with talking beasts better prove itself unique and original, or a publisher won't look twice. Again, the more substantial fantasies like *Watership Down* and *Redwall* are for a much older audience—at least young adult—and succeed because the authors create a rich and believable world.

Stories Dressed in Facts: Historical Fiction

Stories dressed in facts—this is an unusual way to describe *historical fiction,* but an accurate one. The most important thing to remember about this hybrid genre is this: They are stories, not fact. Though fact weaves itself in the tale—and oftentimes with incredible detail—the stories themselves are fiction, and get shelved in that section of the library or bookstore.

Classics in the category of historical fiction include, of course, Scott O'Dell's masterpiece, *Island of the Blue Dolphins* and the Colliers's *My Brother Sam Is Dead.* More recently, *Catherine, Called Birdy,* by Karen Cushman, set in the 1200s, and *Beetle Love,* by Karen Romano Young, set in the 1960s, suggest the range of time periods possible. For insight into an approach carefully crafted to appeal to a wider audience, see the "American Girls" books by the Pleasant Company, "Dear America" from Scholastic, and "American Diaries" books by Simon & Schuster—proof positive that kids love historical fiction.

Vocabulary List

Anthropomorphism and **personification** have much in common, but aren't the same thing. Anthropomophism involves attributing human characteristics to animals, from feelings to being able to talk. Personification is making characters out of ordinary nonliving objects.

Class Rules

Stay away from alliterative animal names—like Sammy Squirrel or Rocky Raccoon. "Ugh!" will immediately exit the mouth of an editor. Alliteration as a stylistic tool in prose is one thing, but when matched with an animal character, it's downright trite. You'll show yourself an amateur if you do it.

Neighbors Next Door and Far Away

One area of children's literature has developed only recently—multicultural literature. What is it? Most broadly defined, it's literature that simply takes into account the fact that we live in a multicultural and multiracial world. Many types of books fall under this definition, from picture book stories about a classroom of children from many different backgrounds, to stories based in a particular culture, such as Laurence Yep's *Dragon's Gate* or Christopher Paul Curtis's *The Watsons Go to Birmingham.*

Just what it is and who can write what about whom is the subject of considerable and sometimes bitter debate. On one side are writers who believe that they can imagine anything without the benefit of personal experience, while on the other side are cultural guardians so concerned with authenticity they'd limit writers to writing only about their birth culture.

Vocabulary List

If you yearn to tell a story of a child caught up in a historical event, or just living in different times, you are writing **historical fiction.** In this type of writing, the main character and often many others are invented, while the setting and other details are based on careful research.

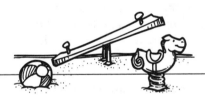

Stories from the Playground

You may be surprised at what you finally decide to write. Author of *Growing Up in Coal Country* and *A Coal Miner's Bride,* Susan Campbell Bartoletti confesses, "Given my interest in historical fiction and nonfiction, it's hard to believe that I was one of those kids that whined about history class. I didn't like class lectures. I didn't like taking notes, I hated the textbook. But I crave stories—all kinds of stories—and history just happens to be one of the places I look for stories."

Realistically, there is a middle ground. Visiting a country for three weeks is personal experience, but writing about it from anything other than a tourist's outsider perspective will be very difficult. Working in an immigrant community as a social worker may give one personal contact with it, but as a visitor and a caregiver, not someone part of it 24 hours a day, 7 days a week. But immersion works, as one can see in Paul

Goble's illustrated retellings of Lakota legends. Originally from England, he's made this his life's work and has received the approval of tribal elders. If you want to write about a culture other than your own, make it be one you've truly lived in, not one in which you are an outsider.

The Facts Dressed in Lies: Fiction in Nonfiction

Can You Keep a Secret?

For a more detailed overview of multicultural literature, read "Writing and Illustrating Multicultural Children's Books," available on-line at www. underdown.org/multicul.htm.

We've talked about taking facts and immersing them in fiction, but what about immersing story into truth to teach more vividly the concepts at hand? When you take a nonfiction concept—let's say the planets of the solar system—and, to teach about the planets, you weave a story line into the facts, then you're "dressing the facts in lies." You're also probably making the learning process much more accessible and interesting to a child. Let's take a look at the different ways authors use this vehicle to teach kids.

Telling a Story

The most tangible example of this area probably occurs with telling a story. The popular television program *The Magic School Bus* started life as a book series. It gives us a great example of fiction being use as a medium for fact. In the series, the teacher, Miss Frizzle, leads her students—Arnold, Phoebe, Ralphie, and Tim among others—on adventures in a school bus that transports them all over the world of science. The bus—and the kids—have traveled to the dawn of age, inside the human body, within the solar system, and beyond to learn. Essentially, the characters and the story remain ancillary to the lesson. But, no one can deny the powerful tool of the fiction incorporated into the lesson. "The Magic School Bus" books and videos fly off the shelf.

Some other titles you might want to read to obtain a better idea of this genre include: *Minn of the Mississippi,* by Holling Clancy Holling, *Cathedral* and similar books, by David Macaulay, or more recently *An Extraordinary Life,* by Laurence Pringle, and *Prairie Town,* by the Geiserts.

Drama

Where books like "The Magic School Bus" series maintain a light note while offering learning, books in this category use the techniques of fiction while sticking pretty closely to the facts.

We recommend checking out or buying the following books for good examples of factual books enlivened by the techniques of fiction:

➤ *The Great Fire,* by Jim Murphy

➤ Russell Freedman's books

➤ *The Tiger with Wings,* by Barbara Esbensen

Straight Nonfiction

As we noted briefly in the previous chapter, there are a number of kinds of straight nonfiction, books in which the author (and illustrator, if there is one) strive to present just the facts.

These include how-to books: Just as this book is a how-to for you to write and publish for children, many "how-to" books exist for kids. We mentioned Klutz Press as one publisher that specializes in these books, but you'll also find such titles as *Passport on a Plate,* presenting recipes from around the world, and *Handtalk: An ABC of Finger Spelling and Sign Language,* by Remy Charlip and Mary Beth Miller. From cooking to card games, from hula dancing to sign language, kids want to know how to do it all!

Some books present information: Take a look at the "Everything Kids" series in the cash wrap areas of bookstores. You'll find the *Everything Kids' Nature Book, Everything Kids' Money Book,* and *Everything Kids' Space Book.* In the book that covers money, there's everything a child might want to know about it—the history of money, all about banks, what goes into starting a business, information about investing, and a whole lot more. Informational books also belong in the library and in schools, such as Children's Press's "True Book" series, more than 150 books, all in the same 48-page format, all targeted at early elementary-age children, covering topics from geography and history to earth science and even to trucks and tractors.

Some tell the stories of the lives of real people: Otherwise known as biographies, these make up a big part of the nonfiction section, from the highly respected *Lincoln: A Photobiography,* by Russell Freedman to the popular *Britney Spears,* by Alix Strauss. Children enjoy real-life, nonfiction tales about other kids too. A popular example of this idea is Rebecca Hazel's book, *The Barefoot Book of Heroic Children,* which brings together the stories of some of the most exceptional children in the history of the world.

Or you might tell a story from history: In this category, the author tells the story of events of the past. Patricia Lauber, for example, wrote the photo-illustrated *Volcano: The Eruption and Healing of Mount St. Helens* about that recent eruption. James Cross Giblin wrote *When Plague Strikes* about three of the great plagues: the Black Death, smallpox, and AIDS.

In short, there are many ways to write both fiction and nonfiction. Publishers will be more interested in some kinds than in others, so your challenge now is to keep reading and figure out which ones are right for you.

The Least You Need to Know

➤ There are many ways writers can approach fiction for children.

➤ All fiction is not created equal. Just like any product there are good products and popular—but not necessarily good—other products.

➤ You should familiarize yourself with the different categories of fiction: literary, popular, anthropomorphic, fantasy, and historical.

➤ There are at least as many types of nonfiction as there are fiction, from fiction-alized stories about real events or people to nonfiction with fictional elements to "straight" nonfiction.

Chapter 10

Apples and Oranges: Kinds of Publishers and What They Do

In This Chapter

➤ Learn what a publisher actually does—from acquiring your idea to producing the final product

➤ Find out why a publisher is a necessity in children's literature

➤ Discover what happens to your book once it's produced and how it gets into the stores

➤ The difference between mass-market, trade, and institutional books

You know you want a publisher to pick your children's book and produce it, but don't have the foggiest idea what a publisher actually does. What really happens once someone calls and says, "Hey, we want to publish your book"? Many things. In this chapter, we'll give you an overview of the key responsibilities and abilities of a publishing house. We'll also discuss the book market, and particularly the difference between mass market and trade books.

Quiz—What Do You Know?

We're starting to get into information that is difficult to pick up unless you're an insider, either someone working for a publishing company or an author with a number of books published. What do you already know? Take this short quiz to find out. Decide if the statement is true or false or pick the one best answer for each question.

1. Publishers are best summed up as printing companies with staff that pick books to produce and others that sell them. True or false?

2. Printing a typical hardcover picture book costs …

    A. $2,000.

    B. $3,000 to $9,000.

    C. $10,000 to $20,000.

    D. $100,000 or more.

3. A "trade" book is …

    A. A book you can return, or trade in

    B. A book usually bought in a bookstore

    C. A book usually bought in a supermarket

    D. An inexpensive book

4. Paperbacks are always sold to what is known as the mass market. True or false?

5. Less expensive books sell in much higher numbers than more expensive ones. True or false?

Now score your test by checking to see if you picked the right answer. Count up your number of correct answers, and then check the following section to see what your score means.

1. False. Publishers usually contract their printing work with a separate printing company. As you'll learn in this chapter, they do, however, do many other things.

2. **C** is correct. Printing a picture book costs from $1.75 to $2.50 a copy for the paper, printing, and binding (called PPB for short) and publishers usually print at least 7,500 on the first printing.

3. **B** is correct. Read on for more about trade books.

4. False. There are mass market paperbacks, and there are more expensive trade paperbacks.

5. True. The logical answer is the right one this time.

If you got four or five answers right: You're a publishing insider, aren't you, or a book reviewer? You already know lots about the business, but keep reading. You might pick up a few tidbits.

If you got three items right: There are a few things you don't know, but you've picked up quite a lot, and we can help you fill in the blanks.

If you got one or two right answers: You've learned a few things, but you've got a ways to go. Keep reading, and you'll be an the road to being an expert.

If you didn't get any right: Keep this book by your bedside! We need to help you un-learn a few things on top of what you need to learn.

What Does a Publisher Do, Anyway?

When your first book idea appeared in the recesses of your mind, you may or may not have considered the role of a publisher in the process. By now, however, as you sit here reading this, you've discovered that the vast majority of children's literature is published, produced by, and distributed by or through a publishing house. From the biggies—like Random House and Simon & Schuster—to smaller presses—like Dragonfly and Northland—publishers fill a need for an author, and authors fill a need for a publisher.

Obviously, a publisher needs new stories to publish. But why couldn't you go it alone? What need do you have for a publisher? As you travel deeper into this book, you'll find some answers to that question. For now, we'll briefly say that a publisher has skills, equipment, experience, access, a reputation, and money that you probably do not. Even with the money, the other ingredients may be difficult to purchase.

Yes, publishers need you. You may be surprised to learn just how much you need a publisher.

The Professionals

Question: Do you think a publisher does little more than print books? That the wheels on the printing press rumble through the building? If you think that's the role of a publisher, you're thinking too small. Publishers do a lot of things, many of which you can't do on your own.

Getting the Ball Rolling

When you send a manuscript off to a publisher, the envelope enters an office much like any other office. If the publisher agrees to publish it, that's just the beginning of a long and complex process that ends with a book appearing on the shelves of a bookstore.

Let's say your manuscript is accepted. In publishing terms, it has been acquired. In the adult book world, the person acquiring that book is often called an *acquisitions editor.* (We'll go into the process more in Chapter 19, "Oh Boy! A Contract!") She may then hand the book on to someone else to develop it, someone called the *development editor.* Now that we've mentioned these terms, you need to forget about them. In children's books, those two roles are still mostly fulfilled by one person. The person who signs you up also edits your book. What does the publisher do besides send you a check?

Vocabulary List

An **acquisitions editor** signs up manuscripts for a publishing company, while a **development editor** actually edits them. At most children's book publishing companies, one person, the editor, does both. Children's publishers believe that it makes sense to have the person who cared enough about a book to acquire it also be the person who works on it.

Professional Manuscript Preparation

So you've signed a contract and written your book. After your creativity takes form on paper, now the publisher takes over. Your editor works with you on making what you've done even better. She may urge you to reshape the book in major ways, changing its structure, or adding material. Or she may just go through the book line by line, making suggestions or asking questions where needed (not surprisingly, this is called line editing). When the editor is done, the book may be copyedited, a careful process of checking grammar, punctuation, spelling, and house style. Many people think an editor does this; actually, it's the last step in the process and is usually done by a specialist.

If your book needs an illustrator, the publisher then chooses one, signs a contract, and pays him or her. The book has to be designed, which may be done by someone on staff, or by hiring a freelancer. The designer chooses typefaces, stylistic elements, gets the look of the pages right, and perhaps even works with the illustrator to get the art just right. Or a separate art director may do that.

Overseeing Production

Eventually the book will be ready to be printed, and someone else gets involved, if he hasn't been already. If the designer wants to do something fancy with gold ink, or the book needs to be longer than usual, you can bet the editor has already been talking to the production manager/coordinator/editor (depends on the publisher). The production manager works with printers and with costs. What kind of paper can we print this book on? How fancy can we make this jacket? Can I get this printed for 5¢ less a copy at Printer A or at Printer B? Depending on the book and the creativity of the production manager, his or her contribution can make a big difference.

With a standard paperback novel for adults, for example, the cover design is often highly important to the editor, but the actual paper the book will be printed on isn't. There will be a narrow range of acceptable papers available, taking into account cost, quality, and what the competition is doing.

Things are different with children's books. The great range of age, education, and life experience of the children's book customer (from toddlers to teen and their parents!) mean that the design and marketing of these books often require a much more specialized approach to production. At the publisher for which Harold works as an editor, for example, they produce several books with transparent acetate covers. Such special elements—everything from elaborate artwork on each page to groovy fonts to unusual paper—require the expertise and contacts of someone who can dig up the raw materials and then implement the processes necessary to accomplish the final product. Moreover, this person keeps the cost within budget.

Meanwhile, another person has been involved. A managing editor keeps track of where the book is in the process from start (manuscript) to finish (on the shelves at the store). This editor deals with strict timelines to ensure the book arrives out on its intended publication date, or *pub date.*

We're compressing the process a lot here, and we'll go into it in more detail in Chapter 23, "What If I Don't Like the Pictures?" and Chapter 24, "The Rest of the Process," but the point is that several specialists work on the book before it gets out into the world. Much of what they do may not be apparent to the consumer, but without their involvement, the standards a book is produced to will not be as high.

Sales Force One—or More!

The publisher also takes care of distribution, which begins with a sales force. A publisher's main goal, after all, is selling your book. Sales representatives from the publisher approach their accounts—everyone from Barnes & Noble to Amazon.com to independent bookstores and back—with information about your book. A sales representative takes orders before the book actually goes to print, thereby gaining a good idea of the number needed immediately in stores.

The big guys like Simon & Schuster and Random House hire an entire force to cover major accounts and geographic areas, while smaller publishers often work with "commissioned reps," who handle sales for many publishers at once and receive commissions of the sales they create. These representatives meet with book buyers for each store and show them the hot titles on their lists.

Team Effort: Marketing

Along with the sales force, the marketing department will devote time to the proper positioning of your book in the marketplace. Think catalog here. The sales representatives carry catalogs of all upcoming titles. Let's say your picture book tells the tale of an egotistical, sparkly fish that learns to share. The marketing department will write the copy for the catalog describing your book and gather all materials for the sales force to aid them in selling the book. Moreover, the marketing department may design in-store displays (like sparkly,

Vocabulary List

When a publishing house acquires a book, the house determines when the book can reasonably expect to hit the shelves in finished form. This date, which may change several times, but will eventually be printed in catalogs and advertised to buyers, is called a **pub date,** short for publication date.

Class Rules

Let's say you decide to self-publish your book; you will then assume all responsibility for selling and distributing the title, too. Most major chains loathe accepting materials not "in the system." Most stores are just not set up to accept product outside of their established accounts and established distributors. You stand a better chance of getting into a store if you pursue a contract with a publisher.

life-size fish that a bookstore may hang from the ceiling or use in a window display with your book). Additionally, the marketing department designs—especially with children's books—activity packets to accompany the book that stores may use in events focusing on the title.

Not to beat a dead fish, er, horse, but let's look at our pretend title. The marketing department charged with designing an activity packet around the shiny fishy might have sent stores materials like photocopies of line drawings of the main character with sequins and beads so children attending a story time where the picture book is read can then create their own shiny little swimmer.

From activity packets to in-store sales displays, the marketing department works with the sales department to get your book out there!

A Pocket Full of Marbles and Money

When you work with a publishing company in the production and distribution of your book, you're working with experienced professionals who know how to get your book in the hands of the reader. Again, the publisher fronts all production costs and pays you an advance. The professional quality of a publisher's product usually exceeds that of a self-published tome. And booksellers and other buyers know the publishers and are willing to take the time to check out their book.

Pineapples and Oranges—and Bananas? Different Kinds of Books

Understanding what children's publishers do also means you need to understand that they aren't all selling their books to the same customers. You know the saying "That's comparing apples and oranges"? Well, comparing trade and mass market books is like that.

Pineapples—Trade Books

Trade books are our pineapples. When publishers come together and talk of "trade" books, what are they talking about? Well, they're talking about books of all kinds for general readership, usually of higher quality, usually of higher price, and usually to be sold in bookstores—the book trade. Okay, as opposed to what other readership? As opposed to a school and library readership, or mass market publishers, who produce the popular books we talked about in the previous chapter. Trade publishers, therefore, produce trade titles. Publishers sell their trade titles—distribute their trade titles—through the book trade—meaning bookstores. Trade books can be either hardcover or paperback.

Don't confuse trade paperbacks with mass market paperbacks. Generally, trade paperback books still adhere to the higher quality of a trade hardcover. Also, trade books virtually always remain larger in format than a mass market book. And while you may find mass market books on racks at newsstands and in supermarkets, you won't find trade paperbacks there. To reiterate, trade books appear in bookstores and usually high-end retailers.

What should you send to a trade publisher? Well, you'll need to study the books they publish to see just what genres and formats they publish, as we explain how to do in Chapter 16, "The Publishing Maze." But in general, the "good" books we mentioned earlier are the kinds of books trade publishers seek.

Oranges—for the Masses

Now let's take a look at the other end of the book publishing spectrum—mass market. We've already mentioned that mass market refers to paperback books that you can find in supermarket or newsstand racks. Other places you may find mass market books include budget retail establishments like Kmart and Target. The big difference between mass market and trade is cost. Imagine you're in the supermarket checkout line. Suddenly you notice the latest Danielle Steel novel that you've been dying to read as a guilty pleasure hidden from friends and relatives. Wow! Instead of the $24.95 price tag on the hardcover at Barnes & Noble, this pocket-sized paperback in the rack only costs $5.99! Welcome to the world of mass market. These books are low-end, high-volume titles. No frills. No fancy book jackets. Just text on inexpensive paper. Oranges, in short, and very different from those trade pineapples.

The Childish Masses

The premise of high-volume, lower-end quality of mass market books runs pretty much the same in children's publishing—but not quite. According to a late 1990s article in *Publishers Weekly*, "The Children's Mass Market Business," by Sally Lodge, "children's mass market publishing business" is a "license-driven game," featuring some recognizable big "mass market" publishers—such as Western Publishing—but recently showcasing several competitors—such as Landoll's.

Mass Appeal: What Publishers Want

The big deal in mass market books for kids is licensing. The mass market publishers seek licensing of favorite kids' characters and then churn out as many book titles as possible—from coloring books

Can You Keep a Secret?

Whereas a mass market publisher of children's books may release more than 500 titles or more a year, trade publishers of quality children's books won't even publish 50 titles in a year! Moreover, the quantities printed and sold of those 500 or more titles will probably exceed the print runs of most—if not all—of the trade released titles several times over. That's mass market!

to workbooks to storybooks based on beloved characters. This isn't all that different from what the adult mass market publishers are doing. Name recognition is everything, but for adults it's Danielle Steel, John Grisham, and Stephen King, while for children it's Disney characters, Teletubbies, and Barney. Opportunities for authors are limited, as a result. They don't want your original stories, though they may hire you to turn out a dozen stories featuring their characters.

Bananas? The Institutional Market

As if the pineapples and oranges of trade and mass market publishing weren't complicated enough, you also need to take note of publishers that concentrate on schools and libraries, also called the institutional market. These publishers may overlap in their approach with trade publishers, producing quality books that sell to bookstores *and* to schools, or they may aim squarely at those institutions. You'll find clues to a publisher's identity in their catalog, so be sure to study how to read one in Chapter 16.

Double Vision! The Blurring of the Boundaries

You also need to know that things are changing in publishing: We call it a blurring of the boundaries. Lately, publishers are producing "high-end" mass market books, which can as easily sit in a Borders as in a Wal-Mart. These books, though still softcover, are made from high-quality materials. At the same times, trade publishers are creating inexpensive versions of their books, and reaching into the mass market. Perhaps not as inexpensive as a generic coloring book, but certainly less than the $15 price of a hardcover, these books run the gamut from classics like *Goodnight Moon*, priced reasonably at about $6, to *Blue's Costume Party*, a $4 stapled softcover based on the popular Nickelodeon character.

As a result, it's not as easy as it used to be to get a sense of what a publisher is doing. They may be doing a lot of things at once. You need to work harder to find out where the right home for your manuscript is.

The Least You Need to Know

➤ You really do need a publisher in order to achieve proper manufacturing, distribution, and sales of your book in the children's literature world.

➤ Self-publishing is when you, the author, produce, sell, and distribute your work. You do not work with a publisher on any of the process.

➤ Working with a publisher offers you the luxury of a professional and experienced team of players.

➤ Books may take form as either a trade title or a mass market book. Lately, the lines are blurring between the two types of publishing.

Keep 'em Rolling: Series

Perhaps you have a manuscript and wonder if it might be the beginning of a series. Or perhaps you've already planned out a whole series of books. Move over, "Baby-Sitters Club." Step aside, "Hardy Boys." In this chapter, we'll take you step by step into the world of writing books for a series, and get you thinking about what works for a series and what doesn't. We'll also give you an overview of the different genres of "hot" series books.

Editors are used to getting letters and manuscripts from authors who have written one story, or maybe just have an idea for one story, and are proposing a 24-book series complete with accompanying dolls and coloring books. And those editors are used to rejecting those proposals, because the author doesn't actually have a good idea for a series. Or, worse, the author's sent her idea to a publisher that doesn't publish series. So if you've got an idea for a series, what should you do with it?

Vocabulary List

Books linked in theme, purpose, characters, style, or content can be part of a **series.** Each subsequent book in the series continues one or more of these elements. Often the series will also have a title, just as a book does.

Class Rules

Don't assume a book with one or more sequels *is* part of a series. Although sequels may feature many of the same characters as the first book, a series goes on much longer. The five books in Lloyd Alexander's *Prydain Chronicles* are more a set than a series. Think "Baby-Sitters Club," "Animorphs," and "American Girls" as examples of series.

What's the Big Difference?

First, we need to ask, "What's the difference between writing a single book and developing a *series?*" Actually, that's like asking, "What's the difference between one baby and quintuplets?" With one baby, you possess a single unique person who remains distinctly his or her own person, unattached in birth to any other human being. Quintuplets, however different or unique from each other, are also alike in genetic coding and shared space! Books in a series are no different. Each book contains new content, yet continues with the same "genetic code"—content, theme, format, characters, or purpose. The books are linked much like multiples are linked.

And what exactly is the appeal? According to Ginee Seo, executive editor of Harper-Trophy in an interview for *Children's Writer* (December 1997), the appeal of a series—much like the appeal of any single book—is "compelling writing, great characterization and a really good hook." Writing for a series, or originating your own series, is no less challenging than writing individual books.

Series or Single Title?

Every series begins with one book, right? But not every book is part of a series. In fact, the vast majority of titles on the shelves for kids sit there as a "one-shot wonder" of sorts, and so they should remain. Many authors write only this kind of book. In fact, numerous fine children's books started as one book and remained one book. Consider such Caldecott medal-winning titles as *Mirette on a High Wire,* by Emily Arnold McCully, Peggy Rathmann's *Officer Buckle and Gloria,* or Allen Say's *Grandfather's Journey.* Compelling characters in all of them, but they were published as single titles, and, in spite of their success, have not spawned a series.

It's tempting to take a character or idea one loves and build a series out of it. But it may not be a good idea, if only because the publisher who might be interested in a story that stands nicely on its own would not be interested in it as part of a series. For the most part, trade publishers publish single. Other kinds of publishers—mass market and institutional—produce series. So proposing a series to a publisher that doesn't want them is as fruitless as submitting a manuscript for a single book to a publisher that only publishes series.

Let's Get Series Now

What elements set a series apart from a single title? As an example, take one of the most popular children's book series ever, the "Nancy Drew" mysteries. Like many series, it's fiction. In the series, our sleuthing teen unravels tales of the unknown and uncovers mysteries. Each story involves a different plot and scenario, but two common elements—Nancy and a mystery—remain throughout the series. Style, format, and length also do not vary. For lengthy series such as Nancy Drew, developed by independent companies called *"packagers"* or *"development houses,"* there might even be a "bible"—a notebook detailing all the character quirks, dress guidelines, history, and other information—to ensure consistency from book to book.

You'll find other, similar elements in common if you analyze other well-known fiction series such as "Goosebumps" or "Sweet Valley High" (these are a staple of mass-market publishers). Children reading on their own, in the middle grades or as young adults, buy these books for themselves.

The kind of writing you do for a series is different than the kind of writing you do for single titles. Single-title books can stand on their own. Books written for a series, especially for a planned series, often cannot, or are intended to be consumed one after the other like potato chips. Are fiction series like the ones we've mentioned the only ones? No, there are others, and we'll go into them now.

I Didn't Mean to Do That: The Unintended Series

What if you write a book and never even consider it will evolve into a series? What if the one book you write becomes so "tickling" to kids that they yearn for more? What if the concept is so engaging

Vocabulary List

A **packager** or **development house** is a company much like a publisher, except its work stops with the completion of a manuscript, or in some cases with the printing of the books. A publisher puts its name on the books and handles the rest of the process.

Class Rules

Editors at publishers like Charlesbridge, where coauthor Harold used to work, don't like to see manuscripts proudly presented as the "first book in a series." They mostly publish single titles. If a book is a phenomenal success, they might want to do another, but at the beginning such publishers prefer for authors to put their energy into one book instead of planning the first 12.

that the public wants more? That's exactly what happened with Laura Numeroff's delightful picture book, *If You Give a Mouse a Cookie*. Kids loved the idea of "if, then" that Numeroff explored. Finally, after myriad antics the mouse comes full circle back to the beginning and the cookie. Children immediately embraced the simple concept and funny actions of the little mouse and girl in the story and wanted more. Numeroff responded with *If You Give a Moose a Muffin, If You Give a Pig a Pancake,* and *If You Give a Cat a Cupcake.* The author's single title resulted in a series of four. Voilà! The unintended series. Of course, this doesn't happen all that often.

School and Library Publishers

Not all series books fit into the fun category like the "Animorphs" or "The Boxcar Children" books. Some series books are downright bookish! Or, rather textbookish! We're talking about publisher-developed nonfiction series titles developed by publishers specifically for schools and libraries. These are the bread-and-butter of institutional publishers, sometimes confusingly called "educational" publishers—but they are not textbook publishers. As noted by Dorothy Hinshaw Patent in her May/June 1998 *Horn Book Magazine* article, "as trade book publishers have cut down on the number of science books they publish, institutional publishers have rushed to fill the gaps, producing more books than ever. They have come out with every conceivable kind of series, especially in biology—life cycles of animals, habitats of the world, and so forth."

These series come in different forms. Some are short, and focused on a specific subject area, such as 12 books on 12 different habitats. Others are identified by a specific design, length, and vocabulary level, such as the "True Books" of Children's Book Press. There are hundreds of titles within this series, grouped into series within the series, on subjects such as national parks, continents, and transportation. Or one subject area, such as biographies, will be the focus of an ongoing series that just keeps adding titles.

Series nonfiction generally doesn't pay well, but it can be a kind of training ground. Noted writers like Seymour Simon started out writing series books for Franklin Watts. Now he publishes with top-level trade publishers.

The writing experience itself may also be different than writing for trade publishers. When asked whether he found writing for library publishers like Children's Press to be different from or similar to writing for trade publishers, Larry Brimner, the author of *Brave Mary, Dinosaurs Dance, E-Mail, A Migrant Family,* and many others first pointed out a difference that is not as great as it used to be: "There was a time when one could look at books published by educational publishers and identify them by their appearance. They looked 'text-bookish,' as if they belonged in schools. Today, thankfully, this is largely no longer the case." However, he says that any manuscript that does not fit into an existing series or serve to launch a new one will be a very hard sell. Also, as noted in our story, the publisher's focus on the school market may restrict what an author can do.

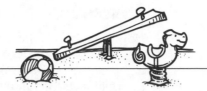

Stories from the Playground

Larry Dane Brimner notes one significant and perhaps surprising difference between institutional and trade publishers: "I've also found that because of their reliance on educational consultants, school and library publishers sometimes restrict a writer's artistic expression. A phrase that is artfully crafted and expressed may be rewritten because the consultant may not understand why an author has begun a sentence with a conjunction or used a fragmented sentence and doesn't understand how these departures from 'school English' can be used as teaching points by teachers. This typically is not the case with trade publishers, where an author is much freer to express himself with language that is artistically crafted."

Writing for institutional publishers, then, can be different from working with trade publishers. Know this from the beginning and you're less likely to be disappointed.

Easy Readers

You may have heard the potato chip commercial with the slogan, "Betcha can't eat just one." Adults like to devour things they like, such as potato chips, cookies, or even books. Kids are no exception. When they enjoy something, they want more. Especially new readers excited about reading.

And that's why series are also a staple of the easy-reader market. Easy readers can be just single titles, but series are a more common approach, such as the "Frog and Toad" or "Henry and Mudge" books. These series books have frequent illustrations, but have more of an emphasis on the text than a picture book does. Typically, you'll find a breakdown of reading grade-level or age-level on these books.

Easy-reader books share several characteristics:

1. They include many illustrations.
2. The illustrations, however, remain secondary to the text.
3. New readers can easily whip through them and grab another in the series.

These books ignite imagination, as well as a love for reading.

Can You Keep a Secret?

The best-sellers of 1999 reveal the success of historical fiction series. On *Publishers Weekly's* list of books that sold 100,000-plus copies sits *Dear America: My Heart Is on the Ground; The Diary of Nannie Little Rose, A Sioux Girl*, by Ann Rinaldi, and *The Royal Diaries: Elizabeth I; Red Rose of the House of Tudor*, by Kathryn Lasky.

Historical Fiction

How many of you have plodded through a boring history textbook, one devoid of any illuminating dialogue between historical figures or fascinating, more personal facts? Wouldn't you love to read conversations between Ben Franklin and Thomas Jefferson as they made history? Infusing history with modern relevance and the story beyond the mere facts remains a challenge for all historical writers. Historical fiction is a staple of children's publishing, but the success of the Pleasant Company's "American Girls Collection" has made this a much more active area.

This isn't to say that straight biography, autobiography, and history books are a bust in children's departments, and that you should dedicate yourself to historical fiction in series form. Jim Murphy, James Cross Giblin, and Russell Freedman and others are still writing quality nonfiction, which sells very well to libraries and to the larger bookstores. But children, teachers, and parents all over have embraced the influx of the "American Girls" series, the "Dear America" series, and others. It's not for everyone, but it's a part of what's out there.

We urge you to stop by a local bookstore, tackle the children's department manager, and ask to see all the latest historical fiction for kids. You'll be amazed by the number of titles, and if you pick one up, probably find yourself immersed within the pages.

Getting Down on Your Knees

If you've concluded that you do indeed have a viable idea for a series, you next need to take care in getting it to a publisher. Choose the kind of publisher carefully, of course, researching their program to make sure that they do publish the kind of books you envision. For the more mass market fiction series, such as "Goosebumps," look to packagers rather than publishers. You'll find information about them in reference books we cite in Appendix B, "Resources."

Then you will probably need to send in a proposal. We'll have a lot more to say about how to write to publishers and send them manuscripts in the following chapters, and this isn't all that different, but a proposal is more than just a letter and a manuscript. You'll want to check the guidelines for the publisher, but you'll probably need to include a plan for a number of additional books in the series, a statement about the overall focus of the series, and some evidence that this particular idea will succeed.

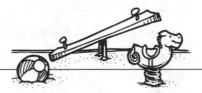

Stories from the Playground

Bruce Balan, author of the *Cyber.kdz* series, notes that there are always exceptions to the "rules": "A fiction series requires a proposal that will sell your idea to an editor. As editors see thousands of these proposals, yours must stand out. So not only do you need a new or fresh idea for your series, but it is very helpful to find an interesting way to present it. I sold 'Cyber.kdz' with a proposal that was written as a series of e-mail communications between myself and the fictional kids of the books .... 'Cyber.kdz' taught me that you don't always have to follow the 'rules.' I was told repeatedly that it was impossible to sell a series without prior series writing experience as well as middle grade fiction experience (for a middle grade series). I had neither. Remember, there is always the exception!"

If you're an unpublished author, you may not get anywhere, no matter how good your idea. You need credentials, so our final suggestion on series is that if you want to write one, your best bet may be to develop your "chops" as a writer with other books, perhaps single titles, perhaps by contributing to existing series. Many packagers hire writers to actually write the books in a series, after they are outlined by the author of the series. Many institutional publishers extend some of their series with new books from other authors. Look around and learn about the world of series before jumping into it, and you're more likely to succeed.

The Least You Need to Know

➤ Not every book develops into a series, but sometimes a single title may delight audiences and spawn a series.

➤ Series books contain a common thread that links the books, such as a theme, character, or story line.

➤ Fiction for middle-grade and young adult readers is often published in series form, particularly by mass market publishers.

➤ Institutional publishers often publish nonfiction series for use in schools and libraries.

➤ Recently, fictionalized history series such as "Dear America" have proven successful with the younger set, but many different genres, from mystery to romance, also proliferate on the bookshelves.

➤ Craft a proposal if you want to write a series and be sure to send it to the right publisher.

Chapter 12

Is It Ready to Hand In?

In This Chapter

➤ Find ways to ensure your manuscript is ready to send to a publisher

➤ Find out why the opinions of your friends may not prove the best in determining how "good" your work is

➤ Learn about critique groups

➤ Discover the best ways to receive a good critique of your work

➤ Learn about children's writing programs and classes

Perhaps you've heard fabulous things about your writing abilities. Everybody exclaims, "That's such a great story!" But, in reality, you need more than the opinion of your neighbor's sister. You need to seek out ways to garner the right type of criticism—things that will help you improve your manuscript and make it publisher-ready. We'll give you several options now for improving your writing and discovering just when the time is right to hand in your manuscript.

Rabbit's Friends and Relations

You may remember that Rabbit, in the Winnie-the-Pooh stories, had a horde of friends of relations, none of whom were much help in getting Pooh unstuck from his hole. Like Rabbit, you will tell your closest and dearest friends and relations about your aspirations to write a children's book. And, of course, they will support you and your creative side. After you get your first story down on paper, these will be the people you automatically turn to for a review of your efforts. Invariably, they'll all exclaim, "Fabulous!" "We loved it!" "It'll sell a million copies!" This sounds encouraging, doesn't it?

In reality, your relatives and friends—though well meaning—aren't the best choice if you seek an honest and educated response to your work. Nothing against Mom or your hubby but, in most cases, they don't possess the skills necessary to adequately provide you the feedback you need to improve your manuscript. Now, we're not saying that you shouldn't rely upon your loved ones to support and guide you. Absolutely, you should. What we are saying is that you must depend upon others—experts—to provide you with criticism. Ugh! Criticism. It seems like such an ugly word. In truth, criticism helps you become a better writer. Let's begin the process with you.

Reading Aloud

Writers everywhere know the merits of reading their work aloud. We believe that virtually all writers practice this powerful editing tool. Coauthor Lynne, who teaches high school when she's not writing, requires her students to read their papers aloud before turning them in. "Sometimes you can read something over and over again silently and not see an awkward sentence or hear a dead 'beat,'" says Lynne. "Only through reading aloud can you pick up on and actually hear the problems." If you find yourself elaborating or wanting to leave something out, that's a clue that there's a problem.

One Is the Loneliest Number

The first person you should read your book aloud to is none other than you! Stand up. Pick up your clean, typed (or printed) sheets of creative genius, and begin to read out loud. Though you may feel funny at first, you'll soon become comfortable with the sound of your own voice and begin to perceive and hear where changes need to be made. If you hate being alone, pull the dog in the room and read to your pet.

Guided Responses

After you've listened to your own words and made any changes from your review, pull in an audience to hear your words. Now is the time to gather sisters, brothers, uncles, neighbors, and coworkers together. But don't ask them to listen and tell you what they think. Instead, give them specific tasks. Ask them to tell you how the story sounds and if they can catch any problems, such as an awkward word or a confusing phrase. You may even want to give your audience a *response sheet*.

Here is an example of a response sheet you might offer to those people listening to your story. You may even choose to let the parties read your story silently first and then respond after your reading.

1. What is your gut reaction to the story? Did you feel any emotions while reading it/ listening to it? If so, what did you feel?

2. Please read the story aloud. Are there any awkward breaks in the text? If so, where are they?

3. Please note any word choices that you think are wrong or not precise. Is there a word I could have used? What?

4. What age do you think this book targets?

5. Why do you think this book will be purchased?

6. Who is my audience?

7. Please mark egregious grammatical errors and correct, including:

   ➤ Comma splices

   ➤ Misplaced modifiers

   ➤ Misspelled words

   ➤ Change in verb tense

   ➤ Punctuation errors

   ➤ Run on sentences

   ➤ Fragment sentences

8. Finally, what do you like best about this story? What don't you like about this story? How might I improve upon this story?

Vocabulary List

In the writing process, often a writer relies upon a peer editor to better the manuscript. For writers or peers with little experience editing, sometimes a **response sheet** is used. On the sheet, the writer lists certain ideas, devices, or grammatical points for listeners to consider. Then the person listening or reading the manuscript need only go through the response sheet to help clarify the writer's problems or strengths.

The Director's Chair

This may sound strange, but another way to get a different perspective on your writing is to have someone else read it to you. You'll hear it afresh, and because they won't be familiar with it, you'll notice problems more easily than if you were reading it yourself. When you read the story, you can juice it up with drama and fix the rhythm of it, but someone coming to it cold won't be able to do that. Sit with a copy of the text and make notes as your mouthpiece reads.

Class Rules

Be careful during your reading to a room of kids. You'll want to read expressively—but not read with over-the-top dramatics. Kids naturally gravitate toward drama. You may con them into loving your book when, in actuality, they loved your performance of the book. Choose short selections from your work and from two published books. Watch their re-actions. To which were they most attentive? Where did they react spontaneously to the action?

Can You Keep a Secret?

Another great way to gauge whether kids love your tale or not is by reading your story at the local bookstore. Offer to read your piece, mixed in with similar selections from published books, and lead a story-time session in the store. The manager will love you! If you lead story time, the manager won't need to pull an employee from the sales floor or cash register to read to the kids.

Apples of Your Writing Eye: Children

You've read solo; you've coerced your friends and family into listening to your work. Now comes the true test of your skills: Read to children. After all, you want to write for them. They may not provide you with knowledge of whether you've dangled a modifier or misused a word, but what they do provide remains more valuable. Children will offer you a direct emotional response to your story. Because children love being read to, though, don't take their enthusiasm as a sign that what you've written is ready to go (and above all, don't offer it as a sign of the quality of your work when you write to a publisher. Just about any writer sending a manuscript to a publisher can claim that kids love it). No, if you want to use children as critics you have to learn to interpret their responses and even to guide them.

Start with children who don't know you. Your own children or neighbor's children are hopelessly biased, and you wouldn't want it otherwise, would you? Instead, gather a junior focus group. How do you go about wrangling together a group of kids to listen to your work and provide unbiased feedback?

You go to where the kids are. Depending upon the age your book targets, seek an audience either through a day-care center/preschool, elementary school, or middle/high school. You'll benefit from finding a group of kids that you don't know instead of seeking out your friends' children.

When you're in the classroom, be as thoughtful as you can in setting up your reading. It should be fun for the children, but also useful to you, a market re-searcher. Find at least two published books with sto-ries of the same type as yours, and of similar lengths. Type them out like yours. Practice reading all of them so that you can spend as much time as possible with your eyes on the children. Watch their reaction. How is their body language? Listen for spontaneous "aahs" and "oohs." Listen for whispering and other signs that you've lost their interest. How they react may tell you more than what they say afterward, but do ask them questions too. Ask them if they had a favorite and why, or other questions that will bring out comparisons. This will help you avoid giving them a hint that they should like a particular one.

But you can't just step into your local school and start reading. You need to follow a process. If you know an educator who happens to teach the same grade or level of kids to which you're targeting your book, ask him or her to host you for a reading in the class. Then you need not gain permission through the office, which may involve filling out forms and having a background check done on you. If you don't know an educator (which is more likely the case), you can approach your local schools and explain that you're a children's writer hoping to gain some feedback on your work from kids. You may have to let the principal, teacher, and parents read your manuscript first to gain access to a classroom. Unfortunately, due to the dangers of our world, schools act as the protector of kids as well as the educator. If you don't have any business on a campus, they'll be wary of you until you prove yourself and your objectives. Because literacy and literature-focused programs remain integral to the classroom, you'll probably succeed in finding a school where you can read your work to kids.

Know-It-Alls: A Critique Group

Every writer—from the novice to the expert—knows the merits of joining a writer's group and receiving critiques on his or her work. We highly recommend you seek out a local writer's organization or club and join. If you can't find one, then create one.

You'll find the experience and keen eyes of other writers a tremendous asset to your own writing. You, in turn, will also provide an invaluable service to your fellow club mates: your keen observations about their work. Generally, club members will all bring their work "to the table" where a read-around occurs. Each member reads another members work and responds to it. Sometimes, copies of your work are required for all members who then take them, read them, and report back at the next meeting on your story.

Beyond the great instructional feedback you'll receive, the camaraderie between members extends beyond the meetings and the critiques. It's comforting to know that there are others with aspirations like yours, learning the ropes, writing, hoping one day to publish their book. The group can serve to keep you focused toward your goal and intent on retaining your dream.

Critique groups can be tremendously helpful, but they can also err in two very different ways. If the group is too supportive, with most comments being along the lines of "What a wonderful story," everyone will feel great about his writing, but won't be pushed to improve it. On the other hand, if the group nitpicks every line, or is never satisfied with anything, its members won't know where they stand. Strive for balance in your group.

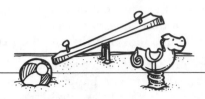

Tales from the Playground

Lisa Rowe Fraustino says: "A successful and lasting critique group is like a family, with all its commensurate joys and foibles. Commitment and caring are its lifeblood. We are very vulnerable to each other as we lay our writing open for criticism. Through it we strengthen our manuscripts and our own characters. But the very best aspect of being in a strong critique group isn't, to me, the critiques, but the camaraderie and support involved. Once a month we are not alone with the page." She knows what she says—her group has produced several published writers.

Can You Keep a Secret?

Several major universities offer specialized programs in writing for children. One of the best programs, a MFA in Writing for Children, comes through Vermont College of Norwich University. For more information, go on-line to www.norwich.edu/grad/writing/program.html. Others offer summer institutes—there's probably one near you.

Another valuable aspect of critique groups is that information of the right kind seems to naturally gravitate toward them. One person in the club may have heard of a conference where editors and published writers will review manuscripts. Another member may tell of a writer coming to town and orchestrate a meeting. A third may have news of changes to the editorial staff of a publisher. The "brain trust" within these groups is wonderful. It's like having several personal trainers for your creative spirit. So, what are you waiting for? Grab your manuscript and join a writer's group.

Writing Classes

Ah-ha! The personal favorite of your coauthors. You should never, never stop learning the writing process. Writing classes, seminars, conferences—hey, all improve your writing and help hone your craft. Each year, all over the United States, writers meet for workshops and classes, usually taught by experienced authors. In some cases, participants learn from each other and each other's writings. These are great settings in which to get objective and often skilled feedback on your writing.

Beyond the workshops and classes, specialized programs in writing and even writing children's literature do exist. And if a college degree in writing isn't what you envisioned or what you want, local colleges, universities, and extension campuses typically showcase a host of composition, writing, and English classes for those who just want to improve their writing skills. See what's available in your area—and when considering teachers, apply the criteria we suggest for writing consultants later in this chapter.

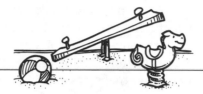

Stories from the Playground

Not all authors favor the group approach. Says Charles Ghigna: "Stop attending workshops. Read other writers if you must, but for heaven sakes save your soul and stay away from how-to workshops and conferences. At worst, they'll drain you of your creativity. At best, they'll have you writing like everyone else. Keep what little originality you have left from childhood. Protect it. Nurture it. Let it run wild. That's all you have. That's all you need. The only way to learn to write is to write. There is no other way. Workshops and conferences can only take you away from the real work—the real world of writing." The perspective works for Ghigna, who has authored more than 25 books including *Tickle Day: Poems from Father Goose*.

Critiques by Professionals

What about critiques from professionals, such as freelance editors or published writers? Well, your writing group may include a few professionals who already are offering you advice without charging you. So why pay a fee? Or if you've got money to spend, why not use it on a class? Certainly, if you take a class, you should receive some good input. But good writing consultants can provide you with the insight and detailed criticism that will most improve your writing, while also bettering your chances of publishing your work. The trick is finding the good ones out there.

Good Guys and Bad Guys

The burden is on you to find the good professional over some fraud posing as a professional and charging a fee to make money. Believe us, they're frauds out there. They prey on writers wanting to succeed—even at great expense. Most real writers—professionals—consider their work an art form. Though they do charge for the classes and critiques they give, if they have time for them at all), writers actually like to offer sage wisdom to fledglings and nurture their success. After all, we were all in the same place at one time. Also, don't be misled by those who call themselves "agents" and want to charge you a "reading fee" to evaluate your work. You are not likely to get useful feedback for that fee—or any help finding a publisher. So how do you go about finding an honest and learned writing consultant? You act like a detective and do your research. As you come across possible candidates, ask yourself—or them—these questions:

➤ Who recommended this person? How did I come across him or her? If someone you respect—such as another writer in your writing group—highly recommends the consultant and offers concrete examples of who the person has helped, then you possess a bit of information lending itself to the credibility of the individual. If, however, someone who no one has ever heard of approached you, be wary.

➤ Has the person actually published any writing? Ask for the title, the publisher, and where the book can be found today. Look for a writer with a track record of publishing with a publisher—not self-publishing. Ask to see the books and make a gut judgment on the talent of the author yourself. If the books are poorly made and lacking creativity, you'll hold a clue as to whether this is the writer to review your work.

➤ Ask for references. Who else has the consultant helped? If the list includes a few established and respected writers and *you can verify* the consultant actually helped the writer or the agent actually garnered a publisher for the writer, you're in good shape. But if the consultant can't provide references, run.

➤ Ask for a resumé. Where did the consultant or agent previously work? Other publishers? As an editor? At a fast-food chain? You get the idea. The more established the consultant or agent is within the publishing community, the better your chances of receiving a strong critique that will prove helpful in your aspirations.

➤ Finally, don't automatically run from a substantial fee. Many good professional writers must charge a fee to weed out many silly requests of their time and talent and to allow themselves time for their own work.

The key to finding a professional is asking questions. Just as all law-enforcement agencies run background checks on future cops, you need to run your own background check on anyone charging to look at your work. If you want good feedback on a manuscript, you're best off working with people you know—the people in your local children's writer's group, the staff at the local college, and even your own friends and relations. With some guidance provided by you, of course.

The Least You Need to Know

➤ Although well meaning, relatives and friends may not prove the best choices for critiquing your work. For one, they are biased. You need to seek out unbiased parties to look at your work.

➤ Start with yourself. Read your work aloud and listen to the language, words, and beats to begin the editing process. Have someone read it to you.

➤ Join a writer's club, take a class or two, and seek out professional perspectives of your work.

➤ Don't forget kids want the straight scoop about your story. Observe their reactions to your work carefully.

➤ When seeking the help of a professional, thoroughly check out the individual's credentials.

Part 3
Out into the World

Once you've got a manuscript that is ready to go, you need to know just how to send it, what to say in a letter with it, and whether or not you need to include illustrations. Feeling unsure, and thinking some name-dropping might help? We'll let you know just how it might, and how it might not.

We'll help you get that manuscript to the right spot in the maze by looking at some publishers and their catalogs, and then looking beyond them to some parts of the children's market that aren't so fully explored. Finally, we'll explain just how important you are to publishers, and how you can best contact them and start to work with them, once that first precious personal letter comes.

Know the Rules, If You're Playing

So you've finished your manuscript and you're ready to stick a copy of it in an envelope and send it off to dozens of publishers to see how many of them are interested. If that's your plan, or something like it, hold on a minute—you're already breaking two of the basic rules. Following the rules won't guarantee that you get published, but it may save you some time, spare you some grief, and help you come across as a professional.

In this chapter, we'll show you how to prepare your manuscript and a letter to go with it, untangle the mysteries of unsolicited manuscripts and multiple submissions, give you tips on writing cover and query letters, and suggest some alternate ways to get in the door at companies that have closed theirs.

The Basics

It's hard not to obsess over the treasured story or nonfiction work you're about to send off into the world. You want it to be just right. Should you type it double- or single-spaced? Should you write a letter to go with it? What else do you need to send? Fortunately, what you need to do is pretty simple.

Sew a Label on It

Getting your manuscript ready to go is straightforward. First of all, type it, using double-spaced lines. Editors do get the occasional handwritten story, and usually don't bother to read it. On the first page, either upper right or upper left, put your name and full address. That's important, in case the manuscript gets separated from your letter and envelope. Skip a few lines, and put the title. Skip a few more and start the story. If you prefer, you can skip straight to a second page and start the story there, but that's not necessary.

Make sure the manuscript is easy to read. Type it using both capitals and lowercase letters; ALL CAPITAL LETTERS MAKE A STORY HARDER TO READ. Though the fancy typefaces that come ready-to-use with word processing programs are tempting, don't use one of them either; good old Times Roman or Courier is just fine. A book might use a fancier typeface, but right now, your goal is to make your manuscript as easy on the eyes as possible. And that means that white—not pink, not neon yellow, and not textured—paper is your choice.

Break the manuscript up into paragraphs, with breaks between them. Start a new page when you come to the end of another one. Don't try to type if out as if in book form. That's particularly important if you've written a picture book; 32 pages, each with one line on them, are a bit irritating to read. Editors are used to imagining how a book would be laid out, so we prefer a standard format, whether that means the manuscript is one page or 200 pages long. If you want to, you can put a line break wherever you imagine a new page, but that's optional and if the book is published might well be ignored by the editor or illustrator.

Vocabulary List

The envelope a rejected manuscript gets returned in is a **SASE,** standing for **stamped, self-addressed envelope.** It carries your complete address in the space where the address belongs, and is large enough and has enough postage for your manuscript.

After the manuscript is ready, make a copy of it. Never send out your original and only copy.

Send a SASE, Don't Be Lazy!

If a publisher doesn't like your manuscript, you'd rather not know about it. But to keep track of who has seen it and who hasn't, you need to enclose a *SASE* (pronounced *say*-zee). Always, always include a stamped, self-addressed envelope for the publisher's response and the return of the manuscript. That can be expensive, especially if a novel is involved, but don't take a shortcut and include an envelope "for response only," as some writers have started to do. That sends a message that you don't care enough about your work to get it back. Sure, you kept a copy, but can you bear to imagine your work being thrown out or recycled? Maybe you can, but don't let a publisher think so.

Dear Editor

You may not know the individual to whom you are sending your manuscript, or even know his name, but do include a brief cover letter. Again, it's the professional thing to do; we'll go into what you need to write in it later in this chapter. How do you figure out what publisher to send it to? Flip to Chapter 18, "So, How Does It All Work?" Right now we're getting the format down.

The Envelope, Please!

Put your manuscript, SASE, and cover letter in an envelope. If the manuscript is only a few pages, you can use a standard business-size envelope. Don't use something smaller, such as an envelope you might use to send a personal note. Publishing is a business, after all. If the manuscript is longer, use a plain manila envelope. You can type up an address label, but a neatly handwritten address is fine too. Send it all by the good old U.S. Mail.

And Then You Wait

You'll also need patience, but don't send that with your manuscript. Hold onto it. Most publishers these days need a minimum of three months to get through their submissions, and some take much longer than that. If you want some assurance that the publisher received your manuscript, use the inexpensive "Delivery Confirmation" option from the U.S. Postal Service, or include a stamped, self-addressed postcard and the request that it be returned to you when your package is opened.

That's it. Letter, manuscript, SASE, envelope, and patience are all you need to make an unsolicited submission to a publisher.

What's an Unsolicited Submission, Anyway?

Children's publishing is a strange business. Thousands of manuscripts arrive annually through the doors of most publishers, all so that they can publish perhaps 20 books. Truly, many are called but few are chosen. These many manuscripts are *unsolicited,* meaning they were not requested by the publisher, but many publishers do read them, in the hopes of finding the next Margaret Wise Brown or J. K. Rowling. Maybe that's you.

Vocabulary List

An **unsolicited manuscript** or **unsolicited submission** is the same thing—a manuscript that a publisher did not solicit, or ask for, from an author. You send **solicited** or **requested** manuscripts in response to a letter or phone call from a publisher, and you should always write that on the envelope.

Though the odds are long, the unsolicited manuscript is your foot in the door. You'll have to find out which publishers read them (we'll tell you how to do that in Chapter 18), because not all do. Thanks to this policy, children's books are one area of publishing in which you don't need an agent or a friend in the business, because if you follow the rules and have chosen the right kind of publisher, you've got a chance of finding a home for your work.

When your manuscript gets to a publisher, the envelope is opened, probably by an intern or an editorial assistant. He may then read it himself or leave it for a junior editor to read. What a cruel fate! You had hoped it would be read by Mr. Olympian Bigshot or Ms. Children's Publishing Wonder. Don't be discouraged. Mr. Bigshot and Ms. Wonder are so busy with the authors and illustrators they have in their stable that even if they read your manuscript and loved it, it's unlikely they'd publish it anytime soon. Editors at their level see many more "publishable" manuscripts over the course of a year than they can actually publish.

Vocabulary List

The **slush pile** consists of all the manuscripts that a publisher has received from writers the publisher doesn't know. They will be read, eventually.

Fortunately, the junior editors and assistants reading the unsolicited manuscripts are exactly the people you want to reach. They don't already have well-known writers to publish. They can rise up in their company by discovering writers with promise. So they spend as little time as they can filing and typing letters, and as much time as they can mining the *slush pile,* as publishers call the high stacks or file drawers full of unsolicited manuscripts.

Some publishers, of course, don't accept unsolicited submissions. If you aren't a published author or don't have an agent, they won't read your manuscript. This seems terribly unfair, and your natural response might be to try to find a way in through a back door. There *are* ways to do that, and you'll hear about some of them later in this chapter and in Chapter 17, "Deeper into the Maze: Other Kinds of Publishers," but it may not be worth the effort. The companies that have closed their doors most likely have ongoing relationships with a number of authors and illustrators already. You can spend a lot of energy and time making contact with an editor at one of those companies only to discover that they just don't have room for your manuscript. Consider spending that time instead on finding out about companies that really want your work.

I've Been Waiting Forever

You're almost ready. You've typed up your manuscript, readied your SASE, and fixed a few publishers in your sights. But your acquaintance, Savvy Writer, tells you that it can take six months or longer to hear back from a publisher. Even the "fast" ones don't promise a response in less than three. You know that the first editor to read your work may not fall in love with it: It might not be to her taste; he might be having a bad day; or she might be distracted by a phone call. It could be years before you get it to the right person. But Savvy suggests a solution. Why not send your manuscript to a bunch of publishers at the same time, say 20 or 30?

It's tempting to resort to *multiple submissions* and send copies of your manuscript to several publishers at once. You'll keep track of who you sent it to, and if one of them offers to publish it, you'll let the others know. Think twice before you do this. You may be helping to kill the goose that lays the golden egg by overloading the publishers that still read the slush pile, causing more of them to close their doors. You may be wasting paper and postage on your mailing of 37 copies of your manuscript when further research would have helped you target three or four. And some publishers are keeping their doors open by only reading manuscripts that are clearly identified as *exclusive* to that publisher.

What to do? National organizations such as the Society of Children's Book Writers and Illustrators suggest allowing a publisher three months to respond to a submission. If you haven't heard by the end of that time, you write to the company and withdraw your submission. You may still hear from that company, because it may not be able to match up your letter with your submission, but you are free to submit it elsewhere.

Whether you choose to submit your manuscript exclusively or to a short, targeted list, is up to your own sense of ethics, but do not resort to scatter-shot multiple submissions. No week goes by at Charlesbridge, the publishing company where coauthor Harold used to work, without the need to open and return a novel, sometimes even a novel for adults. This is a waste of time for both staff and authors, because Charlesbridge doesn't publish novels, and never has. A minor inconvenience? Not necessarily. Not too long ago Franklin Watts, a major publisher of nonfiction for the library market, closed its doors to unsolicited submissions because it was spending too much time returning fiction submissions. It has no fiction program.

Vocabulary List

An **exclusive submission** is a manuscript sent to only one publisher. A **multiple submission** is a manuscript sent to two or more publishers at the same time. A **simultaneous submission** is the same as a multiple submission.

Can You Keep a Secret?

You've sent your manuscript to a publisher that receives 6,000 manuscripts every year, and publishes only 60 books, most by its current authors. The odds against someone even reading your manuscript look very long. But many of those submissions will disqualify themselves; they're badly written or have been sent to the wrong publisher. Yours might be one of only a few hundred truly worthwhile manuscripts.

Dear Somebody

After you've got your sense of ethics settled, you are ready to launch your manuscript into a sea of many other manuscripts. With your name and address on your manuscript, no publishing credits to cite, and no specific person to write to, why write a letter to go with the manuscript? Why not just put the manuscript in the envelope and send it off? Because a letter is the polite and professional thing to do, even though the envelope says "Submissions Editor" and your letter has to have "Dear Editor" as its salutation.

Vocabulary List

A **cover letter** is the letter that accompanies your manuscript. A **query letter,** on the other hand, is a letter you send to a publisher to ask, or query, if it is interested in seeing the manuscript.

Covering a Cover Letter

The absolutely necessary elements of a *cover letter* are few:

➤ Your name and address.

➤ The publisher's name and address.

➤ The date.

➤ The salutation: "Dear Editor."

➤ The title of your manuscript.

➤ The type of manuscript it is.

➤ A brief and tempting description of your manuscript.

➤ Your signature.

Class Rules

We've heard published authors saying that a Post-it note with a brief greeting is all that you need to send with a submission. We don't agree. If you know the editor, fine, but otherwise you're assuming a degree of acquaintance by being so informal. Write that letter, and let your professionalism and personality shine.

What Not to Include

The list of what NOT to put in a cover letter (or include with it) is much longer, but the most important items not to include are …

➤ Your resumé.

➤ A marketing plan.

➤ Endorsements.

➤ The statement that your children loved it (of course, they did).

➤ Apologies for your lack of experience.

➤ A lengthy plot summary.

A good cover letter is simple and business-like. It has the information that is needed, and no more, and does not distract the editor from the business at hand, which is reading your manuscript.

"Query First": Letters About Manuscripts

Sometimes you'll find another hurdle in your way to just sending off your manuscript to a publisher. Some publishers, particularly for novels or longer works of nonfiction, require a *query letter,* in which you ask them if they want to see your manuscript or not. This procedure has advantages and disadvantages for you. On the one hand, it may save you postage and copying costs. On the other hand, it gives the publisher the opportunity to say no before even seeing your manuscript.

If a publisher does not require a query first, and your manuscript is short, it's usually better to just send the manuscript. That saves you the time you would have spent waiting for a response to your query, and it lets you put your best foot forward—your manuscript.

Can You Keep a Secret?

Editor and writer Jackie Ogburn has written a thoughtful and funny guide to cover letters and query letters, complete with sample letters showing what to do and not do. You can read it on-line at www.underdown.org/covlettr.htm.

If you must query, or choose to do so to avoid sending out your 500-page fantasy epic, remember that your letter is meant to intrigue the reader, so that he will want to read your manuscript. If your manuscript is fiction, including a paragraph or two from it can be effective. Choose a passage that displays your style to good advantage. If you have a nonfiction piece, think about what it is that makes your subject interesting. And be sure to include sample chapters, or an outline, if the publisher's guidelines request them.

That's a No-No!

The quality of your writing will get noticed, in the end, but be sure to avoid the common mistakes that might mean that no one actually bothers to read your manuscript, or dismisses it quickly when he does.

Neatness and Spelling Count

You thought you could stop worrying about spelling and punctuation when you left school, right? No, presentation counts in publishing, and you will lose points for spelling mistakes, bad grammar, and even bad style. An editor is learning about *you* as he reads your cover letter and manuscript. If you come across as a sloppy typist or a careless speller, he may expect that to continue if he were to work with you.

Harold has seen it all in the slush pile:

➤ Authors who trumpet their "exclusive submissions."

➤ Authors who get the name of the publisher wrong.

➤ Even authors who get his name wrong (and it's so unusual, he can't understand why they didn't take the time to check it).

And he has seen plenty of bad grammar, poor style, and even almost illegible photocopies. We don't want to make it sound like publishers discriminate against the spelling-challenged or against someone who missed the semester on grammar in elementary school. But we do assume that the appearance of your submission says something about how much you care about your manuscript. If you care enough to get your friend who knows grammar and spelling (and we all know someone like that, if we ask around) to check over your cover letter and manuscript, then you're the kind of author with whom many children's book editors want to work.

Pink Envelopes and Other Horrors

Feverish visions of the tottering heaps of manuscripts that make up the slush pile understandably drive many to desperate measures in an attempt to get them to stand out from the rest. "If they read mine first, maybe they'll appreciate it better." Actually, you're more likely to come across as naive, so avoid these ploys and variations on them:

➤ Express delivery of any kind—your wait will be just as long after the manuscript arrives.

➤ Pink, neon yellow, or decorated envelopes—editors evaluate your writing, not your taste.

➤ Enclosures of food, stuffed animals, or toys—they won't fit in the files.

➤ Faxing your manuscript—you can't send a SASE and it's harder to read.

A plain envelope, white paper, the right postage, and a SASE are all you need.

More Than I Need to Know

What would you think of a building contractor who put more time and energy into an unnecessary (but attractive) screening wall than he did into the simple ground-level patio he was constructing for you? You'd wonder about his sense of priorities and worry that the effort he put into the wall took time away from his work on the patio.

That's how editors react when someone sends a five-page marketing plan to go with a three-page picture book manuscript. The marketing department can take care of that, if they publish the book. They feel the same when they see a plan for a lengthy series, when they work for a publisher that prefers to sign up single titles. And they react the same way when someone tells us about his life at great length, or encloses a detailed resumé, when nothing in his experience relates to the piece he has written.

When Harold was an editorial assistant at a large company, a group of assistants developed an irreverent rule of thumb: "The quality of a manuscript goes down as the amount of other material enclosed goes up." Put your effort into your manuscript. An editor cares about that, and nothing else.

The Wrong Kind of Bedtime Book

The time-honored tradition of parents putting their children to sleep by reading them a book should not extend to your reader's reaction to your manuscript. Any editor or other reader of manuscripts sees hundreds of manuscripts a year, and will be quickly put to sleep by certain too-familiar kinds of submissions. Though you'll find exceptions, most editors at hardcover publishers, the ones you'll be targeting, will get very sleepy when they encounter …

➤ Cute, fluffy animals.

➤ Writers imitating a popular author and claiming they are the next (fill in the blank).

➤ Stories that contain thinly disguised moral lessons.

➤ Memories of someone's childhood.

We could give other examples but you will need to find from your own experience what will get a reaction (even if it's just a personal rejection letter) and what doesn't. Imagine that poor assistant, slumped in front of a stack of 100 manuscripts to read by 5 P.M. Then imagine her jumping up and running into her boss's office, and saying, "Hey, this one's got something different about it." That's the reaction that you want to get. In fact, we'd go so far as to say that an unusual, unconventional, difficult-to-publish, but wildly creative manuscript is more likely to get a response than one that plays it safe, follows the rules, and just isn't that different from anything else.

So, go for it! Write your best, not what you think someone wants to see, and send it in the right way.

The Least You Need to Know

➤ Manuscripts need to be typed, double-spaced, on plain paper, with your name and address on the first page.

➤ A submission to a publisher needs a short cover letter, the manuscript, a SASE, and a stamp.

➤ Multiple submissions are multiple copies of the same manuscript sent out to more than one publisher; avoid them if you can.

➤ A good cover letter is short and doesn't get in the way of a manuscript, while a good query letter makes an editor want to ask to see a manuscript.

➤ Avoid certain kinds of submissions, unless you want to put a manuscript reader to sleep.

Chapter 14

Who Draws the Pictures?

In This Chapter

➤ Why you don't need to include illustrations even if your book will need them

➤ What to do if you really want to illustrate

➤ What you can do and not do if you want to give instructions to an illustrator

➤ How to approach photo research, the only area in which authors have to work on illustrations

➤ Let yourself relax and enjoy the magic of illustration

Children's books have better illustrations than ever before, printed to exacting standards, in a wide variety of styles. Visual riches can be found in any decent children's bookstore or library. This treasure trove can be daunting to an aspiring author. Maybe you think it's your responsibility to provide illustrations in addition to your manuscript. Maybe you want to illustrate. Maybe you want to give careful instructions to an illustrator on just how your carefully nurtured manuscript should be illustrated.

We're here to tell you to relax. Whether you like it or not—and some people don't like it at all—publishers almost always put themselves in charge of choosing and overseeing illustrators. You're best off sitting back and letting it happen. Often enough, the results are magic.

But I Can't Draw

Looking at the end of the publishing process and seeing a gorgeous picture book, it's easy to assume that the beginning of the process must be more than just a manuscript. You obviously also need the illustrations that go with it. As a result, it can seem to an editor reading letters from aspiring authors that every other one includes an apology for the lack of illustrations, or sketches or computer art offered as a substitute, or even a complete set of illustrations done by someone the author knows.

In fact, in just about every case, a publisher does not want or expect an author to include illustrations when sending a manuscript. Why should you be responsible for illustrating your story, after all? Your skills are in working with words, not paint or pastels.

Can You Keep a Secret?

Just because you're written a picture book doesn't mean you need to make the pictures. Check a publisher's guidelines just to be sure, but you'll find that in most cases all an author has to do is write.

My Brother-in-Law Can

Not quite as often as finding that apologetic letter, editors will open a package and find a manuscript and a carefully rendered set of illustrations, all done by the author's brother-in-law, or daughter, or neighbor, or best friend from college, or—you get the picture. As we said before, these aren't needed, but sometimes authors want to include illustrations for good and personal reasons. They like the person and enjoy working with him, for example.

This can get sticky. Here's the scenario: You know an artist whose work you like, and you think that this person is just the right match for your story. You make careful color photocopies of some paintings they have done, and send them along with your manuscript, confident that you're doing the right thing. Unfortunately, you aren't.

Publishers almost always choose the illustrators for their illustrated books—picture books, chapter books with illustrations, or other types of titles. They hire and pay the illustrator. And they might not like the illustrator you have chosen. As a result, you might reduce the chances of their responding to your manuscript the way you want them to. Those illustrations might not show your work to its best advantage. Or the publisher might not like being told what to do.

There's a simple rule of thumb to follow: Don't include the illustrations done by someone you know, unless that person is Maurice Sendak or you're genuinely comfortable with the idea that doing so might reduce the chance that an editor will be interested in your manuscript. To rephrase a popular bumper sticker: Friends don't ask friends to illustrate their stories.

I Hired Someone

It doesn't happen too often, but there's another scenario we need to mention, so we can head you off in case you are considering it. Sometimes writers go out and hire an illustrator in the hope that this will increase the chance that they will get a story published, or perhaps so that they can have more control over how it is illustrated. (As we explain later in this chapter, publishers normally don't let an author have too much to say about how a story is illustrated.)

If you're independently wealthy and can also afford to hire a designer, and maybe pay to have a book printed and distributed, this could be an effective strategy. For most of us, though, this strategy is no more likely to succeed than is hiring your brother-in-law. A good illustrator will most likely charge you thousands of dollars to do the work. He or she will want this money up front, because there's no guarantee your book will ever end up published. And even if you do find a good illustrator, there's also no guarantee that a publisher will share your aesthetic tastes. Traveling to a national writer's conference or taking a writing class from an experienced author would be a better use of your money.

Why Don't You Get Dave Caldecott?

So you've accepted that you can't hire your brother-in-law, but you'd still like some say in how your book looks. Maybe you've heard that a beginning writer is better off if his story is matched with a famous illustrator. So you've got some ideas as to just who you'd like to see illustrating your story. Well, there's no harm in mentioning your ideas to your editor, if you are offered a contract, or even including them in the letter you write to accompany your manuscript.

Just don't get too attached to your preferences. Illustrators you're likely to know—unless you're a children's librarian or reading teacher and spend your days immersed in the latest children's books (lucky you)—are the top-of-the-heap people, the Caldecott winners, the professionals who've been around for a long time. Even if a publisher agrees that a particular illustrator would be a wonderful choice, these well-known artists are just the ones who are least likely to be available.

The Publisher's Job

Simply put, the publisher chooses and hires the illustrator. For you, this is a blessing and a curse. You aren't responsible for finding an illustrator, but you also can't insist on having the illustrator you want. This can be hard to take. You see the story as yours, and so you want the book to follow your vision. Try to step back a little. Yes, the story is yours, but turning it into a book is a true team effort, and one that's coordinated by the publisher, who happens to be paying the bills. In addition to the illustrator, perhaps a dozen or more people will be involved in taking what could start out as a two-page typed manuscript and turning it into a sturdily bound 32-page full-color book. You'll learn more about some of those people in Chapter 21, "Make It Better," and Chapter 22, "My Editor Doesn't Understand Me." For now, understand that with so much of the time and expense that works that magic being the responsibility of the publisher, it's no wonder that the publisher wants to be the one deciding who illustrates a book. And after all, they've probably got more experience than you do in making that kind of decision.

But I Want to Illustrate

We know some of you still have an objection. Forget about brothers-in-law and famous illustrators—you want to illustrate your book yourself. You've always had some talent, and you don't see why you should split the money you'll be paid with someone else.

Be Real: Can You?

Your dreams of being an illustrator could be realistic, if you went to art school and studied illustration. If you didn't, and you are self-taught or have just taken a few classes, how can you assess your abilities? Just as you can get a manuscript critiqued at a local children's writer's conference, sometimes you can show your art to a professional at such a conference and get his feedback.

Class Rules

If your abilities as an illustrator aren't up to professional standards, do yourself a favor and don't include them in a submission to a publisher. Harold says that in reading the submissions that come to him in his job as an acquiring editor, nothing has him reaching for a form rejection letter faster than amateurish illustrations, be they watercolor, crayon, or computer clip art.

If you can't get a professional's feedback, try self-assessment. Choose a publisher that you feel could be a good match for your book. Research the company's most recently published books, following the procedures we outline in Chapter 18, "So, How Does It All Work?" Choose three that have illustrations that are similar in style and medium (such as paint or pastels) to yours, and get your hands on them through your local library system or bookstore. Look through all of them carefully. Check how the artists show characters in different situations, how they choose to use or not use different perspectives. See if you can get a sense of their pacing and how they create excitement. Look closely at how the illustrators depict movement and facial expressions. Whether or not they are showing animals or people, and regardless of whether the style is realistic or cartoon-like, evaluate how lively and real the characters seem.

Then turn to your own work. Are your characters as lively as those you see in the published books, or do they seem stiff or clumsy? Are your illustrations as varied and interesting? Does your book have pacing like theirs? Does it build to a climax? In short, can you confidently say that your work is at least as accomplished as that which you see in these published books? If you can't, then don't include your art with your manuscript. Don't even include a sample. You could come off as less professional, and you could make an editor worried that you might be difficult and object to someone other than yourself being chosen as illustrator, even if you say that you wouldn't mind. You can always show your art to your editor, but don't do that until *after* you have a signed contract. When you do, send it with a note asking what he or she thinks. If you get a positive reception, then you can ask if the editor would mind considering it for your book.

For Professionals Only

If you are a professionally trained illustrator, or an especially adept self-taught one, then you can follow a slightly different path when preparing a manuscript. To be considered as the illustrator of your own manuscript, you can take one of a few different approaches.

The simplest one is to include samples of your work with the manuscript, and mention in your cover letter that you would like to illustrate the manuscript. These samples could be related to the story or not, but in any case should be color photocopies or printed samples, sometimes called *tear sheets*. Don't send slides, which are a hassle to deal with, and *never* send original art.

To push even harder for consideration as an illustrator, the best way to show your abilities is to send a *dummy*. Like a dummy of a person, this is a stand-in for an actual book. To prepare a dummy, break up the text as you would in a book, remembering to leave a title page, a copyright page, and any other necessary pages outside of the main text. Reread Chapter 7, "What's in a Book? A Guided Tour," if you aren't sure what to include in a book. Tape or glue the pieces of text onto separate pages, ideally of the same size and shape as you intend the finished book to be. Add sketches where you intend to have illustrations—you don't have to complete all the illustrations at this stage. Do two or three finished pieces. Then make color copies of everything so it won't be the end of the world if anything gets lost, and send the copies.

> **Vocabulary List**
>
> **Tear sheets** originally were work an illustrator (or writer) had done that had been torn out of a magazine or other source. Now a tear sheet can also be a photocopy of such a sample. A **dummy** is a manuscript laid out in book form, with sketches of all the illustrations and at least two or three finished pieces.

Doing all the art for the book won't do more to convince an editor that you are the right person for it. After all, editors usually choose an illustrator before any art for a particular book is done. Doing all the art will just take you extra time, time that could be wasted if another illustrator does the book. Even if you are

129

chosen, you may find that after you start working with the professionals at your publishing company, you have to take a new approach and jettison some or all of the work that you already did. In this and all these other scenarios, be prepared to be flexible.

Best Foot Forward

If you're an illustrator and a writer, as far as a publisher is concerned you're really two different people. One of you might be the author of a book, and the other might be the illustrator. You might end up working on the same book, but you might not. In this situation, you've got to put your best foot forward, or it might end up firmly in your mouth.

Often the best way to do that is to have the publisher consider your ability as an illustrator separately from your ability as a writer. In this book we've given you plenty of guidance if you want to put your best foot forward as a writer. Much of what you should do as an illustrator is similar. You should send away for guidelines—the illustrator version. When you send in samples, you should include a cover letter and a SASE if you want them returned, and you should take some care to get them to the right companies.

Illustrators do some things differently:

Can You Keep a Secret?

Theresa Brandon has created a fantastic on-line resource for aspiring illustrators at www.theresabrandon.com. From her home page, click through to "The Drawing Board for Illustrators," where you will find a FAQ file, articles, pricing information, and more.

➤ Send samples to the art director, not the editor. If you don't have a name, that title, or the words "Art Department," should get you to the right place.

➤ Contact as many companies as you want to at the same time, because you are hoping to be put on file for future projects, not to get a job right away.

➤ Consider sending color postcards, if you don't want the expense of a full-scale mailing. Include your address and phone number (and e-mail) so that a publisher can request more samples if interested.

➤ Some companies still have portfolio review days. With careful planning, you can have your portfolio seen by several companies on a trip to New York.

One thing is the same for illustrators as for writers; it can take years to break in, so be prepared to keep at it.

Instructions to the Illustrator?

OK, you know that you're not an illustrator, and that your job is to write. But you have some instructions you'd like to pass along to the illustrator, or you'd really like to see what he's doing and make sure that it fits in with your vision for the book. Be prepared for a shock. Though policies vary from company to company, many publishers do not allow the author to have contact with the illustrator while he or she is at work. Some may show you the sketches, but some won't even do that. How can you have an influence? There are a few different paths.

Not in the Manuscript

Many authors, particularly those who have written a book with very little text and proportionally more reliance on illustrations, want to include guidance for the illustrator for the manuscript. This can range from general instructions as to how the characters "should" look to page-by-page advice on what to illustrate, where to have page breaks, and so on. Including this attempted guidance in a manuscript is a bad idea, however.

Editors and illustrators alike are experienced at reading unadorned manuscripts and envisioning how they would turn into picture books. Experienced authors know this, and happily cede control of this area to them. So if an editor sees notes to the illustrator in a manuscript, he or she may assume the author is inexperienced, or would struggle with letting the illustrator do his or her job. Either way, those notes would be a strike against you, so resist the temptation to provide such guidance in the manuscript.

What's OK—and What's Not

Don't worry, your voice will be heard. Your advice may not be followed, of course, but it will be heard. Just be sure to provide your guidance in an appropriate manner.

If your story relies on surprise elements in the illustrations, or a page turn at a specific point, you have justification for saying so in a cover letter when you submit it. But if you just have ideas about the color of someone's hair, or how a house should look, keep these to yourself until your book is underway, and even then, be prepared to accept that your editor or illustrator may have different ideas. Offer your ideas in a letter or phone call, but don't expect them to be followed.

Be Flexible

So, be flexible. If your story is based on childhood memories, offer snapshots as reference materials, but don't expect every detail to be kept the same. The illustrator needs to find an independent vision. If your story calls for characters with different hair colors, and you see one as blond, one as brunette, and one black, don't be surprised if the illustrator makes different choices.

Laying Out the Book

Sometimes it can be useful for the author to lay out the book as it would appear in print. You can get a sense of whether you've provided what's needed—sort of the reverse of the exercise of typing up a published picture book text into manuscript form. In this case, you're looking to see if you've created enough different scenes, some of which can be set in the same place, as long as something new happens.

Cut up a copy of the manuscript and see what happens when you spread it out across 28 pages, which are the usable pages in a picture book. In some places, you might put text on every page, while in other places you might put text only on one page of a two-page spread. Is there enough? Too much? What happens when a page turns? Does the story just continue, or is there a new direction or a surprise? Compare it in your mind to books you've read.

You'll find that you get a better sense of how your manuscript might work in book form. Do not, however, send this to an editor as part of a submission. She won't want to see it. Use it, learn from it, but keep it to yourself.

Photo Research: The Exception

In one notable area, publishers not only allow the author to contribute to the illustration process—they sometimes insist upon it. This is when the book being created is photo-illustrated. This type of book spans the age ranges, from the photo essay, a nonfiction picture book with minimal to a considerable amount of text, to the photo-illustrated book for a middle school or high school age child.

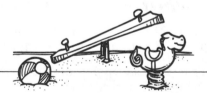

Stories from the Playground

Nonfiction writer Ginger Wadsworth advises that researching photographs can be just as important as researching information. Find out who controls the right to reproduce a photograph you'd like to use in your book; it could be a private photo agency, a government agency, a historical museum, or an individual. Have a tentative budget ready for the photographs you suggest using, and in many cases publishers will pay the fees, or help you pay them. If you're clever, even high fees can be OK, she notes: "Do you want to spend $300 on a picture (the price for the black and white cover photo of my book, *Rachel Carson, Voice for the Earth*)? My publisher said yes after I had obtained the right to use several family photos for free."

When making a submission of a book that is to be photo-illustrated, either because that's the only kind of book the publisher does, or because that's the way you want to see it published, and you know that this publisher is open to it, it's OK to include samples, and lists of possible sources. You may be required to do the photo research, so the publisher wants to see that you are ready to do the job.

Allow for Magic: It Happens!

Can you imagine *Goodnight Moon* without its familiar and charming bunny family? Of course not. And yet it didn't have to turn out that way—in the early stages of the book, the characters were to be humans. The idea of them being bunnies developed later. Almost all books go through changes, of course. But it's the illustrations that can really transform a story and make it much more than it was when it was just a manuscript.

Noted picture book author Tony Johnston was pleasantly surprised when G. Brian Karas showed the characters in Three Little Bikers as sheep. She hadn't imagined them that way, but they were fun. So relax. Work on your writing and let that magic happen when it's the illustrator's turn to work. We'll fill you in on what will actually happen after the book gets underway in Chapter 23, "What If I Don't Like the Pictures?"

The Least You Need to Know

➤ Heave a sigh of relief—you don't have to provide illustrations to go with the picture book manuscript you've written.

➤ If you want to illustrate, make sure you measure up to professional standards before sending your work to a publisher.

➤ You don't need to send all kinds of suggestions and information to an illustrator.

➤ The only kind of book for which an author has to work on the illustrations is a photo-illustrated book.

➤ Illustrators add unexpected and magical things to your words, so sit back and let it happen.

Chapter 15

I Know Somebody Who Knows Somebody ...

In This Chapter

➤ Find out why calling editors or otherwise trying to make personal contact can be a bad idea

➤ How agents can help, and how they can take up your time

➤ How to use names you know, and how not to use them

➤ The value of conferences for making contacts, and how not to blow it

➤ Contests as a way to a contract

You've probably already learned that a number of children's publishing companies, particularly the larger and better-known ones, have closed their doors to unsolicited submissions, or deal with so many thousands of manuscripts each year, and take so long to respond, that their doors might as well be closed. After spending years honing your skills, reading the latest books, and learning about publishing companies, you are frustrated.

Maybe you think you've got a solution to this problem. Knowing someone is *the* only reliable way to get someone to even look at a manuscript, and that's all you need, right? After he does, he'll recognize its brilliance. Or maybe you've come to believe that your work doesn't even have to be brilliant to be published, as long as you have a friend in the business. After all, there are plenty of children's books published every year that are less than brilliant. Someone must know someone for that to happen.

As is usually the case when dealing with a nugget floating in the pool of common knowledge, there is some truth to this, but the truth is a little more complicated than you might think. In this chapter, we'll sort through the various strategies people have used to vault over the slush pile straight into the inner sanctum, and show you what might work for you, and what won't.

Closed Doors: How to Pick the Lock

If a publishing company won't read an unsolicited manuscript, then it's reasonable to think that the way to get someone to read it is to get someone else to ask for it. If you don't know anyone with connections, what better way to do that than by making a phone call and asking for an editor?

Sounds good, but most editors just don't like getting calls from authors eager to "pitch" an idea and get the OK to send it in. These calls are time-consuming, and the better-known editors have so many people calling them that they usually instruct receptionists, company operators, and assistants to do everything they can to avoid putting through calls from writers they don't know.

Such calls are no better liked at companies that do read all submissions. Harold says that he always advises writers at conferences not to call him to get his OK to send something. "If someone calls, it's just another opportunity to say no, and since it's impossible to evaluate a manuscript on the phone, and good manuscripts may not sound good in a phone call, I'd rather just get a letter and a manuscript. That's what I need to see anyway," coauthor Harold says. And keep in mind that even if you do "get to yes" and have an editor's request for a manuscript, that probably won't affect how the editor views it when he finally does read it, days or weeks later. The editor might not even remember your conversation.

You may be wondering if a personal visit to a publishing company might be more effective than a phone call. We urge you to put that out of your mind right away.

Can You Keep a Secret?

Read a funny and footnoted version of an imagined phone call to an editor in Wendy McClure's "Let The Mail Prevail! A Guide to Etiquette, Status Calls, and More." Find it on-line at www.underdown.org/etiquet.htm.

While there are instances of writers with dynamic, persuasive, charismatic phone personalities and deep pockets for their phone expenses occasionally getting to talk to an editor, paying a personal visit just won't work. If you show up at a publishing company without an appointment, you won't get past the receptionist, and at best will get to leave your manuscripts, which will most likely join the slush pile. Want to visit *with* an appointment? You'll have to call to make one, and even if you get through to an editor, he won't want to meet with you until he's already working with you.

No, cold calling and knocking on doors, which are tough as a technique in just about any sales job, are not at all effective in children's publishing. Some other ways of making personal contact can be, however, so read on.

Secret Agents

On hearing about all the closed doors in children's publishing, many authors set about trying to get a *literary agent*. Indeed, publishers with rules against unsolicited manuscripts do not apply them to agents. Provided that the agent is someone an editor knows, which isn't always the case since anyone can call himself an agent, submissions from an agent will be treated with almost as much attention as mail from an author the editor knows well.

Of course, an agent doesn't just help you get your foot in the door. What does an agent do? Agent Jennie Dunham of Dunham Literary notes three main functions:

➤ "Submit material to publishers." Agents can submit manuscripts to any publisher and know who to submit to from their full-time, first-hand experience.

➤ "Negotiate contracts." Agents understand the terms and may have the clout to get a better deal than an individual author can do.

➤ "Collect monies and distribute them." Agents handle payments from multiple publishers and check royalty statements.

All this sounds great, doesn't it? The question is, should you take time out from sending manuscripts to publishers to send them to agents, so that you will have someone who will be sending manuscripts to publishers for you?

Vocabulary List

A **literary agent** acts on your behalf, selecting and writing to publishers with your manuscript, negotiating with the publisher, and generally going to bat for you. Some also work with you to help you develop your career.

To Agent or Not to Agent?

Indeed, agents open doors. But first you must open theirs, and that's a challenge too. Finding an agent to represent you can be as difficult as finding a publisher, because the established, reputable agents are as selective about new clients as publishers are with new authors, if not more so. The time you spend trying to find an agent, a search that may not succeed, could be time spent on trying to find a publisher. In the end, as agent Sandy Fuller notes in the sidebar, some authors feel they must have an agent, while others may be able to manage on their own.

Not Now

We can't say if you need an agent or not. Everyone's circumstances are different. To help you decide, you might want to know about a small survey Harold once did. He asked 10 published authors if they had had agents when their first books were accepted by a publisher. Seven of them did not. Of the three that did, two made the contact that led to an offer, only then turning to the agent to handle the negotiations. A few years on, 8 of the 10 had agents, who were much easier to find after they were published.

The bottom line, then, is that you may be able to get a foot in the door without an agent, and save the time and energy you would have to put into finding one. For information on selecting agents, see Chapter 31, "Building a Career." For now, know that agents are good to know, but no guarantee of success.

Stories from the Playground

Agent Sandy Ferguson Fuller of the Alps Arts Co. says: "I think the decision whether or not to contract with an agent is a very personal one. In today's market, it is probably advantageous to have an agent to 'get in the door' *if* you're able to convince a reputable, experienced agent to take on your work. So many writers are trying to get published that it's better to go in 'solicited' or 'agented'—and of course many publishers won't review unsolicited or nonagented work. An agent knows the ropes and shortcuts, has the contacts, understands contracts, etc. It is worth a standard 15 percent commission to secure a solid relationship with an editor and a publisher.

"That is *not* to say that a writer can't tackle the market without an agent. If an individual has the time, desire, and savvy to research potential publishers, make the contracts, and submit in accordance with guidelines, many publishers still can be approached without an agent."

A Friend in the Business

Maybe you are one of the lucky folks who knows someone in the business—an author, illustrator, or, best of all, someone who works at a publishing company. Understandably, you want his help, and if you believe in your manuscript as much as we hope you do, you probably believe that he will be happy to give it. As your friend, he may feel obliged to pass on your manuscript to an editor he knows, or perhaps to let you mention his name in a cover letter. That may not mean that he likes your manuscript. More to the point, he probably really cannot help you get published. An editor will be more likely to write you a personal letter if you send in a manuscript with the "endorsement" of someone the editor knows, but will still evaluate it as stringently as if she'd plucked it from the slush pile. Editors won't be predisposed to like your manuscript because your friend does; editors trust no one's evaluation but their own.

Go ahead and use a contact like this if you have one. But don't be a pest to your friend, and realize that he is more likely to be useful to you if you ask him about his experiences. He'll enjoy talking about himself (who doesn't?) and you'll get to increase your knowledge.

A Name on the Envelope

If you don't have an agent, maybe it will help to send your manuscript to a specific person, have someone like your lawyer send it out on your behalf, or proclaim your affiliation with a professional organization.

To a Particular Person

Does it help to have an editor's name on an envelope? Some writers believe so, and will go to the effort of calling publishers to get the names of editors if they haven't been able to find them out in other ways (*Literary Market Place,* among other books, lists staff by name, but gets out of date and doesn't include everyone). But if the editor doesn't know you, the manuscript is likely to be shunted to the slush pile anyway. If you do put a name on an envelope, make sure that you've spelled it correctly. Make sure that editor still works there—don't rely on three-year-old writer's guides. And don't mix up one letter with another envelope (we've seen it happen).

We've seen some authors take what looks like a creative approach and send their manuscript to the head of a division or company, or to someone in the marketing department. In the first case, the hope is that the big boss will pass it on, and because it comes from him or her, the manuscript

Class Rules

When you mention someone in a letter who suggested that you contact an editor, make sure it's someone that editor actually knows, or at least that she will recognize the name. Harold has often been amused to receive letters proclaiming "So-and-so suggested that I send you the enclosed manuscript. He thinks it would be just right for your list." But Harold had no idea who that so-and-so was.

Can You Keep a Secret?

Who reads their own mail? Who needs to find exciting new authors so that they can move up? Assistant and associate editors, that's who. If you have the name of someone at this level, because it was mentioned in a newsletter or at a conference or someone you know knows the person, use it. The less established editors want to hear from you.

will then be treated with more care. Sorry, but those manuscripts just go into the slush pile, sometimes after sitting around for weeks in the head honcho's office. In the second case, an author might hope that he has an idea that will excite someone in the marketing department, who will then send it along to editorial with an endorsement. Sorry again, but people in marketing have their own jobs to do, and these too just get passed along—if they aren't simply thrown out. And that's the greatest risk in sending a manuscript to someone whose job description does not include reading manuscripts. If it's so badly misdirected, the person who receives it might think you are clueless and not pass it on.

From Your Lawyer

Writers without agents sometimes ask their personal lawyer to send in manuscripts on their behalf. The letterhead is usually impressive, and you may feel confident that with your lawyer involved from the beginning, a company won't mess around with you. Unfortunately, most lawyers know nothing about publishing or how to write to a publisher. One lawyer, for example, contacted Harold after a trade show. Harold had not attended the show, but the lawyer must have picked up his business card at the company booth. So the lawyer opened his letter by mentioning having met at the show, a meeting that could not have happened, and then proceeded to briefly introduce three different clients, one of whom didn't even write children's books. Needless to say, Harold was not impressed. If you don't have an agent, keep it simple and write on your own behalf, because it's with you the publisher will be working.

I'm a Member of ...

Some writers mention their membership in professional organizations, and may even note them on their envelopes. This tactic can work, particularly if you belong to the Society of Children's Book Writers and Illustrators (SCBWI) in the United States or the Canadian Society of Children's Authors, Illustrators, and Performers (CANSCAIP) in Canada, the two national children's writers and illustrators organizations. A few publishers with closed doors actually open them to members of these organizations, on the reasonable assumption that someone who belongs to one of them has been working on his writing and learning about the market for a little while, and so is more likely to be sending something interesting and well targeted. See Appendix B, "Resources," for information on how to join. If you belong to another, less relevant organization, such as the National Writer's Union, it may not hurt to mention it, but it won't earn you any credibility.

Conferences and Schmoozing

Perhaps the best way to make contact with an editor is to go to a writer's conference, like those sponsored by the SCBWI and other organizations, and actually meet someone.

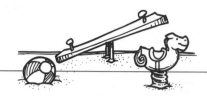

Stories from the Playground

Marilyn Singer's first three books were signed up and published in quick succession. Her fourth, *It Can't Hurt Forever,* was not. She picks up the story: "If there's one thing a writer must have, it's perseverance. And luck. And *contacts.* I went to my first SCBWI conference and met Liz Gordon, then an editor at Harper & Row (later to become HarperCollins). I introduced myself and asked if I could send her some stuff. She said yes, and off went the novels. Back came a note. Was I was willing to do extensive revisions on *It Can't Hurt Forever?* Was I willing? You bet I was. I revised my novel and Harper published it."

As Marilyn Singer's story illustrates, meeting editors at conference really can work for you. But there are ways to do this, and ways not to do this. Understand from the beginning that editors are normal human beings who do not enjoy being besieged by eager authors. They do expect to meet people at conferences, but they don't respond well to pitches or to manuscripts thrust in their hands (or slid under the door of their bathroom stall, as has happened). They particularly do not like it when someone relentlessly promotes herself, badgers them for advice about her 300-page story about her puppy, or plunks down next to them at lunch and attempts to lock everyone else out of the conversation.

There are always one or two people like that at conferences, and they may succeed in getting the editor's attention, but not his respect. Like Marilyn, be polite, and don't expect someone to take your manuscript away with him. A conference is not an opportunity for a smash-and-grab raid. In the long run, you'll do even better to get involved with the organization sponsoring the conference. You'll get to know more editors if you help plan a conference than if you only attend one, and you're more likely to impress them with your professionalism too. Most editors have published writers they met at conferences, but they are usually the folks who've been in it for the long haul, not the ones who show up at one conference, alienate (or amuse) everyone by being so pushy, and then disappear, never to be seen again.

Editors also attend trade shows at which publishers show off their books to booksellers, librarians, or other organizations of people interested in children's books. These shows are a great place to go to find all the latest children's books under one roof, all organized by publisher. They are not a great place to go to meet editors. Editors at these shows may be looking after their published authors or attending meetings, and though they may be polite and listen to a pitch, they'll have forgotten it by the time they leave for the day. Take catalogs and guidelines, if they have them, and use the show to find out about publishers you didn't know, but a show is not a place to sell a manuscript.

Faking a Contact

We mention the option of faking a contact—claiming you met an editor when you didn't, pretending to have been referred by a famous writer, or some other ruse—in a cover letter only to urge you *not* to do this. If you're found out, you can forget about working with that editor, or, if you are found out later, you'll destroy the trust that had built up. Even if you're not found out, you'll be worried that you will be, and you'll never be entirely comfortable. And, of course, making up things like this is just wrong.

Win a Prize!

Some companies with closed doors crack them open for contests. The Margaret K. McElderry Picture Book Prize offers a contract for a picture book to an unpublished author/illustrator: Text and art must be by the same person. You also can't already be under contract with another publisher or have an agent. This is a prize for someone just getting started, but please check for the latest information, as it may not be an annual event. Delacorte offers a similar prize at the other end of the age spectrum: the Delacorte Press Prize for a First Young Adult Novel. This award allowed Christopher Paul Curtis, winner of the 2000 Newbery Medal, to get his foot in the door. Smaller companies have prizes too, such as Milkweed Editions, which sponsors a contest for a middle-grade novel. Even if you don't win in a contest like this, your manuscript will be read, and you may hear from someone.

In addition to publishers' contests, organizations like the SCBWI offer awards and grants, some of which unpublished authors can win, and use as a credential in a submission.

Useful But Not Essential

In the end, all of these ways to find or create or make use of a contact can be useful, but you can get yourself discovered without a contact too. To some extent, the way you choose to submit manuscripts should suit your personality.

Do you think that there's a right way to do things, that there's one right publisher for your manuscript? Can you be stubborn in going after that? After you find that one right publisher and start to correspond, keep at it. That's what Bruce Balan did with a submission to Green Tiger Press (a small company now gone in a merger). It took him a year and a half, but Green Tiger Press eventually accepted a manuscript that he was convinced was right for them.

Are you a people person? Do you enjoy meeting and getting to know people? Then spend some time going to writer's conferences and other events. Don't try to hand a manuscript to every publishing insider you meet. Talk to them and find out what they do. Keep in touch with them. Later, when you have the right kind of manuscript for them, you can send it to them. Or if it's not right for them, maybe they can tell you who is. We know several authors who got published this way.

Are you systematic? Then do your research. Set up lists of publishers to contact and go down the list. Keep at it until you make a contact or decide you need a new system.

There are as many ways of getting published as there are people. Just stick with it, and don't be discouraged by initial rejections.

The Least You Need to Know

➤ Phone calls and office visits don't help you make contact with an editor.

➤ Agents can submit manuscripts to publishers you can't, but it can be just as time-consuming to find an agent as to find a publisher.

➤ Putting a name on the envelope or in your cover letter is only useful in certain circumstances.

➤ Conferences and contests are good ways to make contacts.

➤ Faking a contact or going out of your way to create a contact aren't worth your while. It's possible to be published without knowing someone.

Chapter 16

The Publishing Maze

> **In This Chapter**
>
> ➤ The difference between a publishing house and its imprints
>
> ➤ Why you must submit one at a time, not simultaneously, to imprints
>
> ➤ How to choose an imprint that's right for your manuscript
>
> ➤ Learning about imprints at a large publisher and a smaller publisher by analyzing their catalogs

Learning about publishing companies is like going into a maze of names. Publishing houses come in many sizes, shapes, and structures. Some have one simple name. Others have different divisions. Still others not only have divisions but also may have several "imprints" within them. "What's an imprint?" you may ask. Follow us and find out.

In this chapter, we'll explain how the larger publishing companies spread out the books they publish among different mini-publishing houses under the umbrella of the overall company. We'll also put this knowledge to practical use by learning about the books a major publisher and a smaller independent publisher publish from an examination of their catalogs.

Companies, Divisions, and Imprints

It's overwhelming enough that there are hundreds of companies to learn about, but you'll quickly notice that many of them seem to have separate entities within them with their own names. To which do you send a manuscript? To the company as a whole? To its children's book division? Or to even smaller parts of the company, which, strangely enough, all have their own names?

Dad, What's an Imprint?

Those small subdivisions are usually called *imprints*. What *is* an imprint? An imprint is literally the name that appears on the title page and spine of a book, such as "Dell Yearling," or "Viking Books." Both of those are parts of larger companies, in these cases Random House and Penguin Putnam, respectively. Each imprint usually has its own editorial staff, and sometimes its own marketing staff, but shares all the other resources of the company. Still, the company hopes that each imprint has a separate, recognizable identity, kind of like a brand name. When you think of Pepperidge Farm Goldfish, you think of a tasty crunchy snack. When you think of Penguin Books, what do you think of? Well, maybe imprint names aren't quite as well known as snack foods!

An imprint is not a division. Several imprints might make up the children's division of a larger company. Nor is it a "line." A line might be a part of an imprint; the easy-to-read line of Bobo Books, for example, which also has a picture book line and a nonfiction line. Sometimes an imprint is started up from scratch. Other times it carries a name that used to exist as an independent company that has been absorbed into a larger one. The company keeps the name because it means something to its customers.

Still confused? Don't worry. It will start to make sense as you get to know the companies, and the in-depth look we're doing later in this chapter into two catalogs will help.

One at a Time, Please

You need to understand what an imprint is because in most cases, you send manuscripts to individual imprints, not to the overall publishing company. Blue Sky Press and Cartwheel Books, for example, are two imprints at Scholastic—and very different, as you will see if you look at their catalog. You would send one of them a manuscript, not Scholastic. If that imprint is not interested, they will return it to you, and usually won't share it with other imprints at the same company.

Vocabulary List

An **imprint** is a part of a publisher with a distinct identity, name, and staff, usually concentrating on a distinct type or mix of books.

Class Rules

The different imprints at a publishing company act independently of each other, except when they don't. They don't share manuscripts, and they have their own staff. But never send the same manuscript to two imprints at the same company. They can't both acquire it, and management at the company will prevent them from competing for it.

There are limits to the independence of imprints, however. Most companies do not want their imprints to compete with each other. People at most companies will accept your decision to send a manuscript to several different companies at once, but will feel you are being gauche if you send it to two imprints at the same company. For example, Dial Books and Viking Books are two different imprints at Penguin Putnam. Both publish picture books. You know that they won't be sharing manuscripts, but does that give you an opportunity to send the manuscript to both? No.

In the admittedly unlikely event that both are interested in it, and both want to acquire it, the company will realize there is a conflict when both imprints bring it to the meeting at which they get approval to sign it up. At this point, one will be told to bow out, and all you will have gained is a group of people—the ones at the losing imprint—who are annoyed with you. Since publishing people move around, and since you may end up not publishing at the winning imprint for the rest of your career, this is not good.

There are also exceptions to the general rule that imprints have separate staffs, and that's another reason not to send manuscripts to multiple imprints at the same publisher. Charlesbridge, where Harold used to work, is the imprint for nonfiction picture books, and Whispering Coyote and Talewinds are both fiction picture book imprints, but each with a different emphasis. The same staff works on all three. If you sent a manuscript to Talewinds after it was turned down by Whispering Coyote, you'd just to be sending it to the same people again.

Door Number One, Door Number Two

Now that you know what an imprint is, you may be inclined to sit down and send your manuscript to any imprint that publishes children's books, but slow down. One reason a publisher branches off into imprints is to specialize and narrow the focus of each. Imprints typically have tight guidelines about the "type" of books each produces, though in some case that type may be a specific mix—there is such a thing as a Swiss Army knife of an imprint, which publishes everything from board books to young adult novels, with other "blades" of the knife perhaps being reference books, an easy reader program, and photo-illustrated nonfiction.

Let's use a fictitious example to understand why you need to choose the imprints you are sending manuscripts to. Say two imprints at one company both produce books with historical themes for children. You just wrote a young adult novel based on a boy serving in the Civil War. Your book contains facts galore about history, all woven into an edgy, realistic tale. At first glance, you think, "Hey, I'll send my manuscript to both imprints—one at a time, of course!"

Unfortunately for you, while both imprints produce books with historical content, as you've learned by glancing through their catalog, the focus of those titles may differ greatly. One may only produce textbooks, with an emphasis on historical fact. The

Class Rules

To find out what kinds of books a publisher produces, write to ask for guidelines. The guidelines will tell you a little about the imprint and how to submit manuscripts to it. And they may tell you how to get a copy of a catalog. Or try searching for the publisher on-line. Many companies now make their guidelines and complete catalogs available on the World Wide Web.

other may only produce picture books based on history. Your young adult title, though extremely good, doesn't fit either imprint, and sending it to either of them is just a waste of your time and theirs.

To make sure that you choose the right imprint you have to do research. Get the imprint's guidelines, which will usually start with a short statement about the kinds of books it publishes. Go to a bookstore and browse for books with that imprint name on them.

Even better, take a look at the catalog of that imprint, which might be part of a larger catalog for the company to which the imprint belongs. You'll find more useful and specific information in there than if you call and quiz an assistant in the department about the kinds of books they publish. The poor assistant will want to get you off the phone and will be brief and general in describing the program. But the catalog will be full of information from which you can put together a detailed profile, as we're about to demonstrate.

The Big Guys

As you learned in Chapter 6, "It's a BIG World," publishing mergers and consolidations have created several large publishers in New York. In one way, they have narrowed the market for you, but fortunately, since imprints are independent, and all of these publishers have several children's book imprints, you can still submit your manuscripts to each of them.

Or you can if their doors are open. Writers often complain that they can't send manuscripts to these companies unless they have an agent or are published. Fortunately, not all the doors are closed. A look at the companies listed in the Children's Book Council's member's list reveals about 30 imprint members that are part of larger companies. Sixteen, just over half, won't look at unsolicited submissions. The others will, though three require you to query first, and you may have to wait several months for a response.

What Are They Like?

You'll find a surprising variety of imprints at the big guys. Some are personal imprints run by one well-known editor. Others are general-purpose imprints covering the gamut from board books to young adult novels. Some are known for solid nonfiction for the library market. Others are known for innovative picture books that get snapped up in bookstores. They all tend to be slow to respond to submissions, however. So it helps to get to know them a little better. We've talked elsewhere about the importance of targeting your submissions. This is one reason why: It will save you time in the long run if you can cut your list of possible publishers from 30 to 10. You'll spend less time waiting. How? Study their catalogs. We'll show you how.

I'd Like You to Meet ...

We happened to have on hand a copy of the Simon & Schuster Children's Publishing catalog for fall 2000. It's a good example of a large, corporate publisher with several imprints.

Their catalog is pretty sizable, and lists six different imprints on the front. Flipping through the pages, we notice that they have been grouped into two sections, with Atheneum, Simon & Schuster, and Margaret K. McElderry in one, and Aladdin, Little Simon, and Simon Spotlight in the other. Rabbit Ears and Meadowbrook also get a mention: Rabbit Ears seems to be the book-and-cassette line for Little Simon, while Meadowbrook seems to be a separate company whose books Simon & Schuster distributes. We'll concentrate on the main six.

Atheneum's section starts with a big splash about a picture book, and goes on to cover a mixed list of about 25 books, including picture books, novels, and both picture book and chapter book nonfiction. Some are designated "An Anne Schwartz Book," and there's a small section for "Richard Jackson Books." We make a note to find out if these two personal imprints within Atheneum have separate submissions policies. We can't tell from the catalog. We get a general impression of a high-quality list that includes such well-known authors as Eve Bunting and E. L. Konigsburg. Two books get two-page spreads with information about marketing and promotion being done, so the company is definitely aiming for the bookstore market with those, but mostly the books seem to be aimed at the review-driven library market.

Then comes Simon & Schuster, and not surprisingly, since this carries the name of the company, this is a large list of nearly 40 books. It's a more wide-ranging list, more middle of the market, including not only picture books and novels like those on the Atheneum list, but a couple of celebrity picture books, gift and anniversary editions of famous books, and even investing tips from a teenager. There's overlap with Atheneum, but more of a focus on consumers, judging by the subjects of the books and by the emphasis in several cases on marketing campaigns that will help booksellers sell copies. Still, many manuscripts could fit at either one.

Margaret K. McElderry Books is a freestanding personal imprint (about which you'll learn more in Chapter 22, "My Editor Doesn't Understand Me"). Of 10 books listed, some are picture books, a few are middle-grade novels, and there are also two books beginning an early reader series and a young adult novel by Margaret Mahy, the famous New Zealand author. Browsing the pages, one sees none of the flash and promotional push we've seen earlier. All the books give the impression of being aimed quietly but firmly at children, and seem likely to sell mainly in the library market.

The other imprints in the catalog are quite different in focus from these first three, which had their differences, but all of which publish jacketed hardcover books. First up is Aladdin Paperbacks. This imprint publishes a mix of paperback series and reprints of previously published hardcovers, ranging from picture books to young adult novels. How do we know that some of these are reprints? In some cases, it says so in the blurb. In others, we recognize the book as one that came out a year or two ago. We'll check their guidelines, but this doesn't look like an imprint open to direct submissions.

Then comes Little Simon. This looks like a mass-market imprint, judging by the lower prices ($3.99) and presence of board books, pop-up books, and books with tie-ins to well-known cookie and cereal brands. At first, Simon Spotlight seems similar to Little Simon, but then we notice that all the books are tied to TV series and movies (in fact, to shows like *Rugrats* and *Blue's Clues,* which air on Nickelodeon, a cable channel owned by the same company that owns Simon & Schuster). Will either of these imprints be interested in your own original story, using their characters? No, but they might hire freelance writers, and it might be worth investigating what procedures you would have to follow in order to be considered.

We've found three imprints that seem likely to take submissions, though we'll have to find out if their doors are open, and three others who might be sources of freelance writing. Not bad. We could dig even deeper into the exact kinds of books each publishes, and we'll show how to do that in the following section, where we're looking at just one imprint.

Can You Keep a Secret?

Look in the section under the price and ISBN for each book in many catalogs, and you'll see who owns and can license the subsidiary rights. If it says the publisher's name and "all rights," that book either came in as an author's submission direct to the publisher, or was commissioned. Some rights may be held by an agent, a foreign publisher, or a book producer. Checking this information helps you get a feel for how many books have come as author submissions or are brought in from other companies.

The Little Guys

Looking again at the Children's Book Council (CBC) members, we find about 40 imprints that aren't part of larger corporations, though some are still pretty large companies. And there are many more who don't belong to the CBC, but can be found in market guides like those we list in Appendix B.

For the most part, these companies are more open to unsolicited submissions—about two-thirds of the CBC members will look at them, sometimes after a query. The percentage is better than it looks, too, because some of the ones that don't are highly specialized companies producing only a few books a year. They have their doors closed in self-defense, but most writers wouldn't have meshed with them anyway.

Those that are open are usually quicker to respond to submissions (by which they mean one to three months), and more likely to make personal comments.

What Are They Like?

Smaller, independent publishers are more diverse than the larger ones. This is where you'll find companies publishing for specific religious, cultural, and racial groups. You'll find companies with a regional focus, publishers for children with special needs, and publishers specializing in folktales, in arts and crafts books, and in the history of Williamsburg (you can look it up—they're a CBC member). You'll also find companies publishing for the general market, going head to head with the big guys, sometimes with considerable success.

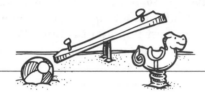

Stories from the Playground

Alexandra Siy, who has published with both kinds of publishers, has this to say: "Working with Charlesbridge [an independent] has been wonderful .... My experience with [an imprint at a corporate publisher] was much different. Once the books were published, it seemed that no one cared about them anymore. Even while working on them, there was far less dialog between myself and the editor, and I had no part in the layout of the book. My advice to beginner writers is to seriously consider small publishers (despite the lower advance) because they will probably be happier with their relationship with their editors and publisher and with the final product."

Why should you bother with these companies? They don't pay as well and they may not have as much marketing muscle as the bigger companies. But you are more likely to get personal attention at a smaller company. You may also find that unless you're lucky or have a potential best-seller on your hand, a smaller publisher is more likely to take the risk of publishing an unknown, or the risk of publishing something a little different.

I'd Like You to Meet ...

For our case study of a smaller and independent publisher, let's take a look at Boyds Mills Press. Based in Honesdale, Pennsylvania, this respected publisher is part of the company that publishes *Highlights for Children*. And as you'll see in the catalog, that magazine is the source of some of their books. For our study, we've sought out both the fall and spring 2000 catalogs, since they don't publish that many books in one season. This gives us a larger sample and lets us see if there are differences from one season to another.

Both catalogs feature about 15 new books, published under just one imprint, Boyds Mill Press. There are also a number of new paperbacks, reprints of hardcovers that they'd published previously. That might tell us something, but we'd better leave them out, because they are too far down the road from the time they were signed up; they are becoming paperbacks two, three, or more years after they were first published. They don't really tell us much about current interests.

Looking just at the table of contents of the spring 2000 catalog, we learn something right away. There's a backlist section, organized by grade level. And that tells us that Boyds Mills sees teachers and school libraries as a good chunk of the market they are trying to reach, if not the most important chunk. We don't see the emphasis on promotional support we saw for the Simon & Schuster imprint. Since they are interested in the school and library market, we aren't surprised to find a good amount of nonfiction (four titles), two historical fiction picture books, and some picture books with learning components (one explores math concepts, and there's also a counting book).

We also spot two collections of poetry, one made up entirely of originals, the other a compilation. Though there isn't a separate section of the catalog, we notice that the text about these books mentions an imprint called Wordsong. All of these are for children 12 years old or younger.

The fall catalog confirms some of what we were starting to conclude from the spring catalog. There's more poetry, collections again, and we decide that we should get one or two of these from the library before sending in our own poetry. There are activity and craft books, but they seem to be connected to *Highlights,* so before shipping off our dog-eared manuscript of "101 Popsicle Stick Activities," we are going to query to see if they accept these materials, or just reuse them from the magazine. As in the spring, there is a novel for middle grade readers. We are also interested to see three books with a religious connection: There's a picture book biography of Saint Nicholas, a history of Jerusalem, and a story of King Solomon. And there's a middle grade collection of 15 biographies of athletes who "battled back" from something. Good thing we looked at this—it's not just a repeat of the spring.

Can You Keep a Secret?

Use catalogs to find out about the *kinds* of books an imprint publishes, such as historical fiction or easy readers, not to study specific subjects. If a catalog includes a book about the death of a pet or an unusual summer vacation, that does not indicate a strong interest in that particular subject. Stories with such subjects could be published by any general purpose imprint, because they address common childhood experiences.

What have we seen? We've seen a diverse list aimed at the school and library market, probably not with much orientation to bookstores (no books by celebrities or brand-name connections, and they don't mention any big marketing campaigns). If you're writing historical fiction picture books, or collections of poetry, or middle grade novels, this company is worth some more investigation. There seems to be a separate imprint for poetry books, so an author of poetry would want to inquire and find out if poetry is considered separately, perhaps by different staff. We didn't see any young adult novels or nonfiction, we didn't see any easy readers, and we didn't see any fantasy. We could have looked this closely at the first three imprints in the Simon & Schuster catalog, by the way.

Could you divine all that we did from a catalog? Possibly not. We knew what to look for, and knew what it meant. But as you learn more about today's children's book market, and as you spend time reading catalogs, you'll become better able to get useful information from them. Once you've learned from a catalog, you can continue your investigation of publishers in ways we'll go into in Chapter 17, "Deeper into the Maze: Other Kinds of Publishers."

The Least You Need to Know

➤ Publishing companies may have many different parts, but imprints are the ones a writer wants to get to know.

➤ Imprints are independent units within companies, each with its own focus.

➤ Choose your imprint carefully, especially at large companies where different imprints will have very different programs.

➤ Catalogs are useful tools in figuring out the kinds of books each imprint publishes, and you should take some time analyzing them.

Chapter 17

Deeper into the Maze: Other Kinds of Publishers

In This Chapter

➤ The importance of picking the right publisher

➤ The magazine market

➤ Educational publishers

➤ Niche and regional publishers

➤ Checking out new publishers, on-line and off

➤ Watch out for the subsidy publishers

So you've been knocking on doors at the big guys and the smaller guys and you're still not getting anywhere? There's more out there than you might think. After a quick reality check to ask whether you've been knocking on the right doors, this chapter will open even more doors—the doors to the magazine world, to educational publishers (they don't just publish textbooks!), the doors to regional and niche publishers, and the doors to new publishers.

Sorry, I'll Try Next Door

You learned in the last chapter how to figure out what a publisher does—and what books they might want to see—by analyzing their catalog. But did you do the right thing with that knowledge? If you learned that Publisher Q publishes picture books, but you didn't notice that all of them feature contemporary children, you might send them your poetically retold Middle English folktale, to no avail.

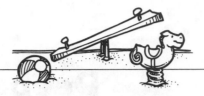

Stories from the Playground

Experience taught Larry Dane Brimner that, "Authors today must know the books that individual publishers publish. I learned this with my first book sale. I'd sent the book to the late Ann Troy, of Clarion Books, and she kindly responded with a letter telling me that I'd written 'a terrific book that is going to be perfect for somebody's list. Unfortunately, sports books do not do well on the Clarion list.' She encouraged me to 'find the right publisher.' Had I done a careful study of the Clarion list to begin with, I would have known that it rarely publishes sports-related nonfiction. My subsequent study led me to Franklin Watts because the book I envisioned, the book I'd written, was similar to books it published. My book would fit with the list."

Like Larry Dane Brimner, you might send your manuscript to the wrong place if your knowledge of a publisher is superficial. Nine times out of 10, you won't hear from an editor that you simply chose the wrong house. You'll just get a standard rejection letter and be none the wiser.

So dig a little deeper before you throw up your hands—but not too deep! Sometimes at conferences, Harold has heard authors complaining that they wish they knew exactly which editor published which book, so that they could send that person their book, which happens to be just like it. You don't need to dig that deep. An editor who happened to publish a farcical story about a dog who learned the importance of good manners might not want to see another farcical story about a dog. If that editor went to another publisher, that company might not want to publish such a story. But either publisher could be open to a story with an animal as the main character. So it's more important to get the focus and approach of the publishers correct. Editors come and go, but unless they are sufficiently influential to change a publishing program, few change the focus of the company.

Should you be concerned about the focus of a publisher just because you don't want to waste the time of the editors there? In these times of overwhelmed editorial staffs, maybe you should be, but let's not forget the purely selfish and practical point that you waste your own time if you send a manuscript to a publisher who just isn't going to be interested in it. Yes, the publishing maze is confusing, but you'll save yourself time in the long run if you do enough research that you can target your submissions carefully and follow the latest guidelines of the publisher.

Class Rules

Every editor has stories about wildly inappropriate submissions—novels for adults sent to publishers of picture books, picture book stories sent to publishers of library nonfiction for teenagers—and their mantra is "Find out more about us!" Emma Dryden of Margaret K. McElderry Books dramatized this point by heading a list of things she wishes beginning writers knew with these two items:

1. I wish more beginning writers were familiar with our backlist and current titles before submitting their projects to us.

2. I wish more beginning writers submitted their materials according to our specific submission guidelines.

Magazines

So you've followed our advice and tried every single one of the publishers that might be interested in your piece on bee behavior or your story about two children learning to take care of a puppy. Your critique group loves it, you think it's fun, but you struck out? Either it's time to put it aside or it's time to try elsewhere. To start with, try magazines.

There are quite literally hundreds of magazines for children in North America, some—like *Highlights for Children* or *Cricket*—publishing for a general audience, others focusing on a very specific interest or audience. Some are for preschoolers, while others are for teenagers. You'll find magazines tied to many religious denominations, magazines focused on math or social studies or nature, magazines for girls, and magazines for boys. Magazines can be pretty specialized, such as *Gball,* a girls basketball magazine, or *Pack-O-Fun,* a craft magazine. Whatever your interest, you are likely to find at least one magazine that matches up. In fact, given that magazines can more effectively target a small market then book publishers can, you'll find a wider and more varied range of opportunities among magazines than among book publishers.

Writing for magazines *is* different than writing for book publication. If you mostly write for younger children, understand that a magazine piece needs (or demands!) fewer illustrations than a story for a picture book. If you write for older children, here's your market for true short stories, or if it's nonfiction that grabs you, for journalism, for pieces that wouldn't fly as chapters in middle grade nonfiction but that come to life on their own.

To understand the difference, immerse yourself in it. Get your hands on some children's magazines in an area that you think interests you. If you write picture books for five-year-olds, for example, check out *Ladybug*. Type up a story from the magazine and compare it to yours. Is the length all that's different, or can you see how a picture book story needs more illustration? Does the story develop differently? How about the vocabulary? Try reading several issues of a magazine and then several books intended for children of the same age, and reflect on the differences you notice.

Magazines work differently from books too. Many pay per word, or pay a flat fee per article. You can expect to receive anywhere from $25 for a very short piece to hundreds of dollars for a longer article. That doesn't sound like much, but it's a credit you can cite, and experience, and usually magazines only buy one use of your work, so you can sell it elsewhere. Check their guidelines carefully—some accept submissions generally, others want material for specific theme issues, while others commission work from you on the basis of your writing samples and stated interests. Magazines also specify how many words they want for certain kinds of pieces, where book publishers will ask for "long enough to tell the story." Follow those guidelines carefully.

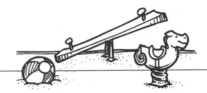

Stories from the Playground

Sneed Collard writes for both books and magazines: "For a long time, I viewed magazine writing as a way to break into books, but magazine writing has its own rewards. First, you can write about a topic without spending as much time on it as a book requires. Second, I enjoy the more journalistic, 'snappy' approach that magazine articles allow. Third, magazine articles provide great 'spin-offs' from books—and earn you additional income. Last, especially with the 'testing fever' these days, several companies are gobbling up magazine reprint rights like crazy. I've now made more money from some of my magazine articles than I have from my books!"

Magazines are a big market, and a great place to get experience. And who knows? You may decide this is the place for you, or at the least a great complement to what you want to do in books.

Educational Publishers

Educational publishers are another market worthy of investigation. They don't just publish textbooks. Schools today want all kinds of supplementary materials, from activities to poems to stories, in all curriculum areas. To meet this demand, educational publishers may buy the right to republish a book already sold in bookstores for their school audience. Or they may seek out original work.

When you are just getting started, it will be difficult to make headway at the really big companies, such as Harcourt, Macmillan/McGraw-Hill, and Houghton Mifflin. Look instead for companies producing supplementary materials. Companies such as Continental Press, Frank Schaefer, Mondo, the Wright Group, and Carson-Dellosa are producing series of "emergent reader" books, grade-by-grade anthologies of stories to read, and poems, activities, and even games to go with math, social studies, and science curricula. Language arts is no longer the only time of the day when children read; with the rise of the "whole language" movement, or increased interest in what is known as "reading across the curriculum," educators have come to understand that children need to read in many contexts. These companies are meeting the demand for such materials.

How can you find out about companies like this? If you're a teacher, you already know about them. You will find them listed in some market guides, but to really learn about these companies, there's no better way than to go to a national or regional convention of such teacher's organizations as the International Reading Association, the National Science Teacher's Association, or the National Council for Social Studies. You'll get a catalog listing all the publishers attending, with their addresses, and you'll be able to go from booth to booth learning what they publish, and taking notes.

Educational publishers won't all want original material, and some only work on commission (they hire you to write something specific), but this is a relatively unknown market, and one that might be just right for you. A few examples:

➤ Silver Moon Press publishes historical fiction in American settings for older readers.

➤ The Education Center, a teacher-resource material publisher, puts out calls for such things as "short-short" stories (525 words) for anthologies.

➤ Caeden Books produces little, stand-alone reading books.

Going back to school just might be the right move for you.

Can You Keep a Secret?

How do you find out about the smaller educational publishers? If you can't go to a teacher's convention, Rozanne Lanczak Williams, who has built up a career working with such companies, suggests your local teacher supply store. Browse through the aisles and make notes on books similar to what you write. Contact those publishers and request guidelines.

Regional and Niche Publishers

The publishers you are most likely to know are the ones that publish for the national market. You'll find their books from Florida to Alaska and probably in British Colombia and Newfoundland, too. They publish general interest books for a wide audience. But what if you want to tell a story about a local hero or explain how the tide affects the bay? You might do well to find a local or *regional publisher*. What if you want to reach a child with a specific problem or background? Then you want a *niche publisher*. Both of these kinds of publishers do not try to reach every child in every part of North America, but rather to reach specific children.

How do you find a regional publisher? You'll find them in the market guides (including a "Guide to the Small Press Market" available to members of the SCBWI—see Appendix B, "Resources"), or on-line, but that may take some sifting and sorting. Perhaps the most direct way is to go to where the customers are. In your community, where would you go to buy a book like the one you have written? Go there, and look through the books on display. Note who published them. Call them up, or write to them, and find out if they accept submissions. If you live in Oregon and want to write a book about the art of the Indians of the Northwest coast, you'll come across Sasquatch Books. If you live in Maine and want to do a story about life as a Maine fisherman, you would find that Down East Books is the place for you. Every region of the country has one or more regional publishers. You just need to find them.

To find a niche publisher, again, go to where the customers are. In this case, that's not necessarily a bookstore. Harold receives frequent questions at his Web site from the authors of stories about children overcoming emotional problems or dealing with a physical disability. In the larger children's bookstores, you may find a special section for these books. But it might also be worth your while to ask a child psychologist or school counselor to let you look through his shelves. If they do any "bibliotherapy," handing children books to read that are tailored to particular problems, you may find a sizable collection.

Christian and Jewish and other religious publishers also publish for a niche market, in this case parents seeking books that speak to their particular faith or that more generally support values with which they feel comfortable. You'll find Christian bookstores in just about every community, and the Christian Booksellers Association has conventions at which you can investigate this market.

What other niches are there? There's one for just about every interest or lifestyle, though not always for children. Some publishers specialize in environmental themes, some specialize in craft books, some in New Age values. Whatever your interest, there's likely to be a niche you can call home.

New! New! New!

It's easy enough to get the idea that publishers are closing down and merging, and that the number of outlets for your writing is decreasing every year. The big publishers certainly are bigger then they used to be, but new publishers and imprints appear every year. "New Hats in the Ring," in the July 31, 2000, issue of *Publishers Weekly,* lists nine new imprints—you'll find similar articles from time to time. Some are completely new companies, notably Handprint Books, Christopher Franceschelli's new company, founded after he left Dutton in 1997.

Other new companies already existed in some form before, and won't be much of an opportunity for writers. In that article, three new imprints are packagers or British publishers going direct to the market, and so will not have much interest or room for new material. Three are editors moving to new houses or starting new imprints— Megan Tingley Books at Little Brown, Richard Jackson's "return" to his personal backlist at Simon & Schuster, and David Reuther's SeaStar imprint at North-South. All three will be looking at new writers, but all three are stocking their new imprints mostly with authors and illustrators with whom they have been working for some time. And the remaining two are tightly focused, drawing on existing material or authors: the Family Heritage Series of the Vermont Folklife Center, based on stories from their archives; and the Everything Kids series, a mass-market line spun off from a similar adult line.

There are opportunities at companies like these. But they are not necessarily an opportunity to clear out your drawer-full of already-rejected manuscripts. New companies may be just as selective as old ones, so send them what they want. Keep your eyes open, read *Publishers Weekly,* read your favorite newsletter, and update your market guide every year.

E-Books and the Internet

We've mentioned electronic publishing in Chapter 6, "It's a BIG World," but it bears repeating that this area is getting a lot of attention from traditional publishers. So far, there don't seem to be many new opportunities for writers to get books published

Can You Keep a Secret?

For guidance to this brave new world, see *The Writer's Online Marketplace,* by Debbie Ridpath Ohi (Writer's Digest Books, 2000). She founded the now defunct and much lamented www.inkspot.com. This is a good guide to the online market and to electronic rights.

Class Rules

You aren't really publishing your work if you have to pay the publisher. It's that simple! Whether you are subsidizing print costs for a real book, or paying the costs of converting to electronic format, or paying a one-time or monthly fee to be listed on a WWW site, you are entering a world in which companies make money from authors, not from people buying books.

(though there is lots of freelance writing), because much of the electronic publishing being done consists of new editions of books already available in print form. And so far, those books are mostly novels and technical books, because these translate more effectively to on-screen versions. Technically, it's more difficult to display color picture books on computers or hand-held readers.

However, new companies such as ipicturebooks.com are publishing picture books, including original works, and others are likely to come along. If you do work with an electronic publisher, expect to be paid royalties, and do not expect to pay "listing" or "production" costs. If your work is good enough to be published, then the publisher can make money from selling it, not by charging you.

For similar reasons, avoid the many "manuscript display sites." As noted in the article "Display or Misplay" in the October 2000 *Writer's Digest,* these WWW sites charge to display your manuscript, promising that editors and agents will come and look at them. Unfortunately, because the sites aren't selective, editors don't find them useful—looking at them is just like looking at the slush pile—so few if any editors find manuscripts this way.

All Is Vanity? Vanity and Self-Publishing

Because the Internet is no help, and considering how difficult it is to find the right home for your manuscript, you might be tempted to publish your manuscript yourself. To do that, you could turn to what's politely called a subsidy publisher but is more accurately known as a vanity press, or you could actually go it alone and arrange for editing and illustrating and printing and marketing and distribution yourself. Think twice before you do either of these.

A Lot of Work in Vain

What is a subsidy publisher? Simply a publisher whom the author pays to publish a book, rather than the other way around. These companies are also called vanity presses for a very good reason—they rely on the vanity of those who want to see their work in print, even at considerable cost.

If you really believe in what you've written, why shouldn't you do this? The problem is that the money you pay will only buy you a stock of books, printed to uncertain standards, which you will likely have to market yourself. No vanity press in existence can get your book true national distribution or do the marketing needed to get the books sold.

Vanity presses come in many guises, some of them seeming to be endorsed by respectable people. There are poetry anthologies going under the name of "National Library of Poetry," and "International Library of Poetry," which are nothing more than vanity collections. Some of the electronic publishers charge you a fee to prepare your manuscript and another one to keep it listed. This is just another form of vanity publishing.

Going Solo

Instead of working with a vanity press, why not do what a publisher does and work directly with a printer, and hire all the other services needed to put a book out on the market? As you will discover in more detail later in the book, a publisher does a lot. If you are to replicate that, it will cost you a lot. Let's say you want to *self-publish* your photo-illustrated book about the animals of the Smoky Mountains. You'll need to hire an editor, a designer, a copy editor, and someone to do the marketing. You'll need to find a way to sell it. Perhaps you'll have to do that yourself. And you'll need to make arrangements for the book to be distributed—difficult to do, because the independent distributors aren't likely to work with someone with one book and no track record.

Vocabulary List

Self-publishing is the term used to describe when an author pays for the costs of manufacturing and selling his own book and does not depend upon a publishing house for any of the process of getting the book on the shelves of stores and libraries.

If you only need to reach a local or specialized market, and you can take the time to do that yourself, this could work. Otherwise, self-publishing might be a better option for you after you've actually been published, as we explain in Chapter 31, "Building a Career." The publishing maze is large and complicated. Carry a ball of string, and don't lose track of the different ways out of it.

> **The Least You Need to Know**

➤ There are magazines for every age level and interest, and they can be great markets for writers.

➤ Educational publishers can be an opportunity—and teacher's conventions are a good place to find out about them.

➤ Smaller publishers focusing on regional and specialized subjects may be the home you need.

➤ New publishers come along every day. Read the fine print to determine how new they truly are, and what their needs are.

➤ There is a lot of heat and noise over electronic publishing, but so far few new opportunities.

➤ Don't be driven by the difficulty of finding a publisher to consider a vanity press, and think carefully about self-publishing.

Chapter 18

So, How Does It All Work?

In This Chapter

➤ Why publishers need you

➤ How to go beyond the basics and play the game the most effective way

➤ How to respond to an editor's interest

➤ The importance of persistence

➤ What goes on behind a publisher's doors, and why it sometimes seems like nothing is happening

By now you know the basics of getting your children's book published, but you need to know how to put it all together. You need to know how the system works—to the extent that it does. In this chapter, we'll show you why, even after the mergers of 1990s, children's book publishers still need you, and how you can best approach them. We'll also explain what's happening behind the doors of a publisher when you don't get a response.

Publishers Need YOU

At this point you may not believe it, but publishers need you. Without authors, most publishers would not exist. Your creative energy produces works too distinctive to be created by in-house writers, and it's those creations that the trade market, at least, demands. Some publishers do seem to have little need for fresh talent, but every one of the authors they publish was a beginner at some point.

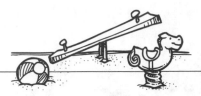

Stories from the Playground

Why are a publisher's books called a "list"? The answer probably goes back to the time when there were no catalogs and a publisher informed the public about available books by printing a list of them. Today publishing insiders use several "list" words. At the "top of the list" sit the book or books for which the publisher has the highest hopes. The "front list" refers to this year's books and the "backlist" to previous years' books; backlist income is predictable and often vital to a publisher. And the "midlist" author is the author whose sales may not hit peaks but are reliable book after book. Publishers who aim to publish "only best-sellers" may hope to reduce their midlist ranks, but the midlist is still a good place to be.

Publishing works on a never-ending cycle. Every publisher must create a minimum number of new books every year, or run short of income. A publisher releases two or three "lists" each year, grouping its books into fall and spring bunches, possibly adding a winter or summer group. Why? That's just the way it's always been done, though mass market publishers tend to release books throughout the year. The publisher's business is built around a certain number of books, be it 5, 10, or 50, that it must have on each list.

And that need for a full list is where you come in. Authors leave even the most stable of lists. They get restless and move on, their editor leaves and they follow, or they cut back their output or even stop writing. So every publisher needs some fresh blood from time to time. If they get it by luring an author over from another publisher, then *that* publisher needs to fill a space on their list. There is always some flux in publishing, and that change brings opportunity.

Play the Game by the Rules

To get anywhere in this business, you need some talent, persistence, luck, and an understanding of the way things work. The first three, you provide, and the last one, we hope you're finding in this book. So far, we've given a lot of detailed advice. Here, we're pulling it all together and highlighting important strategies.

The Union Makes You Strong

No union of children's writers exists, of course, but there are national organizations of children's writers and illustrators and you should not only belong to them but also get involved with them. We've said it elsewhere, but it bears repeating! The occasional genius can go it alone, but the resources of the Society of Children's Book Authors and Illustrators (SCBWI) and the Canadian Society of Children's Book Authors, Illustrators, and Performers (CANSCAIP) (see Appendix B, "Resources," for more information) are worth getting access to, and local conferences are well worth attending.

But do more than that. Get involved, for the local critique groups, for the support of other writers, for the opportunity to have regular contact with editors. Go to one conference and you might get a chance to talk to an editor for a few minutes. Become an active member of your local chapter and you will get to know editors over phone calls and letters and at the conference.

That contact is valuable. Coauthor Harold will testify that although he's met many authors and illustrators at conferences, the people he remembers are usually the folks who organized them, or who helped out during them, and not the person who asked him in the hall if he would mind looking at her manuscript. Has he published many books by these folks? No, but more than average, and they've certainly got more of his attention. So, get involved.

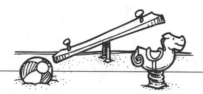

Stories from the Playground

Lisa Rowe Fraustino, author of *Ash* and *The Hickory Chair*, among other books, has this to say: "Five out of the six books I have contracted to date have been with editors I met at conferences and developed a rapport with. And the sixth book is in a series published by the same house but a different imprint than one of my regular editors, and without my prior contact with the house I doubt my proposal would have been taken as seriously."

What she's not saying is that for years she was one of the organizers of a conference in eastern Pennsylvania, and that it was through that work that she met these editors, including Harold.

Catalogs, Conventions, and Guidelines

It's good to get to know editors. It's vital to get to know publishers. We've shown you how to analyze a catalog. Do that for all the publishers who might be a home for your manuscript *before* you send it to them. You might end up dropping half of them from your list, saving yourself time and postage.

To get all those catalogs, you can write publishers and send the right size SASEs and wait for them to come back. Or you can go to a conference. National and regional teacher, librarian, and bookseller organizations have them every year, and in their exhibit halls dozens and dozens of publishers set up booths showcasing their latest books and giving away their latest catalogs. For booksellers, there's BookExpo America (BEA), and regional shows like the Southeast Booksellers Association show. For teachers, there's NCTE and IRA and NCSS and NCTM and their regional variants. And for librarians there's the American Library Association and regional conferences like the Texas Library Association convention. Often, the public can get in for the day to wander the exhibit hall, or if not, you can get a day ticket through a teacher or librarian you know.

Can You Keep a Secret?

The very best place to learn about trade publishers may be the convention of the American Library Association. Publishers display their latest books and give out catalogs. Held in January and June, ALA conventions will be in Washington, San Francisco, New Orleans, Atlanta, Philadelphia, and Toronto from 2001 through 2003—sooner or later it's coming to a city near you, or one where you know someone. Find out more at www.ala.org.

Spend a day at one of these conventions, going booth to booth. Take catalogs and make notes. Look at the books. You may get a chance to chat with some editors, but don't try to push manuscripts into their hands; that's not why they are there. Learn about their interests. At the end of they day, you'll be exhausted but you will leave much better informed about the latest in children's books than you were when you started.

Scope Out the Competition

Don't assume that your idea is so original that no one else has ever thought of it. Find out what other books are out there that are similar, just so you can say in a cover letter how yours is different. It's not enough to say "I wrote this because I wanted to find a book on (fill in the blank) and there wasn't one at my local bookstore." Most editors won't believe this and may well be able to think of several books you didn't find. Anticipate them, and tell them about the similar books and the ways in which yours is different. This is particularly important for nonfiction, but you can do it for fiction, too.

Waiting Patiently—or Not

After you get your manuscript out there, be prepared to wait. Of course, don't just wait. Use that time to write another manuscript, to start research for a new book, or to read the five latest Newbery winners. When you do hear from a publisher, you most likely will get a form rejection letter, photocopied, without even an individual's name. Don't be disappointed. Every author starts out getting these. But check the rejections carefully. Don't leave your returned SASEs lying around unopened. There may be a golden opportunity inside, so open that envelope, and be ready to spring into action.

Follow Up Everything

If you keep at it, and do everything right, and have a little luck, there will come a day when you hear from an editor. Nine times out of 10, if not 99 times out of 100, your first actual contact will be a short rejection letter or maybe even a note scribbled on a form letter rejection. Do not be discouraged that this is "another rejection." Be encouraged that someone has taken the time to write to you. Respond, but be sure to respond appropriately.

When You Get a Nibble

The least encouraging positive response you can get is a short note scribbled at the bottom of a *form rejection letter*. It may say "We hope to hear from you again" or "Thanks for your submission" or "We don't publish this kind of story but we would like to see [something] from you." Notes like this may not seem like much but at most publishers, very few manuscripts will get even this much of a response. The message? You are in the ballpark, and someone wants you to know it, even if you aren't ready to take the field as a starter. Submit to this publisher again.

More encouraging is a short rejection letter. Even if it's written in generic language—"Thank you for submitting *XYZ*. We enjoyed reading it, but are sorry to tell you that it is not right for our list"— you can be encouraged that an editor has put his or her name at the end of the letter. This is an invitation to write to that editor again, with a different manuscript. Accept this invitation!

Vocabulary List

A **form rejection letter** is a short, anonymous letter, usually photocopied, saying something like this: "Dear Author. Thank you for your submission. We appreciate your sharing your work with us. Unfortunately, your manuscript does not meet our current publishing needs, and we are returning it to you herewith." Anything more personal than this is encouraging!

A letter that rejects your manuscript but provides detailed reasons why should set off a celebration in your writer's heart. To write such a letter, an editor has taken a half-hour or more out of her busy day (or has asked an assistant to draft a letter and then reviewed it). This editor is interested in you. If she doesn't ask to see the manuscript again, do not send a revision unless you can see ways to deal with every single one of the concerns expressed in the letter. If she asks to see a revision, do your very best to think through what she says and make changes that not only do what she asks, but that create a satisfying new whole. Don't be in too much of a hurry to get it back. That editor is not expecting to hear from you right away. She hopes you will take your time and reread what you've done, mull it over, read it to your critique group, and only send it back when you are sure it's ready.

Not Too Much!

After you have made contact in this way, this is not the time to clear out your drawer and send in every story you have ever written to this editor. She's not expecting it. Remember that it was one story that drew that response. Are you confident that a new story you've written is as good? Then send it. Can you say the same of that story you put aside a year ago, not sure of what to do with the ending? Probably not. Read it over. Do you really want her to read it? After all, you want this editor to think highly of you, and, realistically, she just isn't going to want to publish several of your stories right away.

So unless the editor specifically asks you to send her everything you've ever written, pick and choose and send her only your best work.

Class Rules

Want to know a surefire way to ruin a budding relationship with an editor? Deluge her with manuscripts, call her often when you don't hear from her, e-mail her all your latest ideas. Coming across as overeager or desperate won't get you better results, and might cool her interest in you. Strive at all times to be professional.

Not Too Aggressive!

At the same time, remember that you aren't the only author the editor's working with. She's juggling dozens of active titles and probably corresponding with dozens of other authors, on top of meetings and planning sessions and conferences. You are not going to suddenly start to get your manuscripts back from her within a few weeks. You should not call her a day after you calculate she would have received the manuscript to ask her what she thinks. Even if she read it when it first came in, she needs a week or two to mull it over. Let her get in touch with you. Even if she takes a couple of months, don't worry. There might be lots of other things going on. If you don't hear from her within the industry-standard three months, then a note or preferably a phone call is a good way to get in touch.

Publishing is a people business, and acting like a professional from the time you first write to someone right through the time you see your book appear on the bookstore shelves is as important in helping you go on to another book as is the quality of your writing.

You Can Get It—But You Must Try

Persistence leads to success. We make no guarantees—except to say that without it you won't get anywhere. Most published writers will tell you that they spent years learning, and going from form rejections to nibbles to regular correspondence and finally to publication. And even after that first book, they kept learning and growing and recovering from setbacks. Breaking through to a first book is no guarantee of a second or third. You have to write new manuscripts, they have to interest an editor, and your books have to do well enough that editors (and readers) want more down the road.

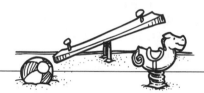

Stories from the Playground

Sometimes persistence goes right back to childhood. Writer Elaine Landau told us:

"When my mother was pregnant with me, a palm reader said that she would have a girl who was destined to become a writer. And my mother did give birth to a baby girl who showed a keen interest in writing. But she felt certain that I'd never make a decent living writing and tried her best to discourage me. I continued to fill notebooks with poetry and essays. When I went to college, she insisted that I take a practical major like business. I tried but after just one term I switched to an English and journalism major.

"Today I'm the author of over 150 children's books. If you have that dream, don't let anyone discourage you. Just keep writing."

What's Going On in There?

Sometimes, though, you don't hear back, or all you get is a form letter. Even a form letter tells you something, if you think about it. Whoever it was that read your manuscript decided that your submission did not warrant a personal response of any kind. You don't know if that's because the manuscript didn't measure up, or because you sent it to the wrong publisher. After trying several publishers and getting only form letters, though, you may want to go back to your word processor, or try another manuscript.

Why does this happen? Why can't publishers respond personally to all submissions, so authors won't be left guessing? Let's look behind the office doors of a publisher to find out, and understand why persistence is so important.

Behind Closed Doors

It is not true that editors have a peaceful job, reading manuscripts, deciding which ones they like, setting them into motion as books, and then watching them bob away on the stream. Any editor is likely working on dozens of books at various stages of completion, all of which need his personal attention, and on top of that spending time in meetings. We'll give you a peek into the lives of a few editors in Chapter 22, "My Editor Doesn't Understand Me," but for now, please take it as a given that no editor has much time to spend on reading the submissions.

At most publishing companies, assistants, junior editors, or retired editors come in one day a week read the "slush." They then pass on the 10 percent or so that they feel might interest an editor. Don't worry—even if the reader is a new assistant fresh out of college, it doesn't take much training to weed out the poorly written or badly targeted or just plain unoriginal writing, and pull out only what might be good enough. The editor will still reject most of what he sees, but at least he's not spending as much time sorting through it.

Class Rules

If you don't like competing with thousands of other people, children's publishing is not for you. There are well over 10,000 members in the Society of Children's Book Writers and Illustrators, and plenty more who aren't members. Keep striving to write your best and most creative work, so you can stand out in this crowd.

Help, I'm Sinking!

Unfortunately, the system doesn't always work this smoothly. Publishers also get completely overloaded, and then you may not hear at all, or not for a long time. The sad fact is that when people at publishing houses get busy, it's the slush pile that suffers. Editors can always read it tomorrow, or next week, but if a book is due at a printer, or a writer is waiting for comments on a manuscript, or an illustrator needs guidance, that must come first.

So manuscripts pile up, on desks, in file cabinets, and in bookcases (and that's why it's called a slush *pile*). Typically a publisher will have a backlog of a month or two, and will deal with it in batches, between busy times. But it can get worse. If a company gets publicity in a writer's magazine, or a staff person leaves, hundreds of manuscripts can pile up, and the publisher may resort to closing its doors to more submissions until it can get caught up.

It's also true that more people are writing, and writing better, than used to be the case. Ten years ago, a publisher might have received 2,000 manuscripts and queries in a year. That's a lot, but manageable. If three people each read 10 or 20 manuscripts a week, they can keep up with it. Today, that same company, with perhaps the same number of staff to deal with the manuscripts, is getting 6,000 manuscripts. That's scary.

Do I Know You?

Faced with this situation, and perhaps not needing to find many new authors, many publishers have thrown in the towel and stopped reading submissions unless manuscripts come in from someone they know, or from someone with an agent, or someone with a previously published book. A few ask you to "query first" (send a query letter) so they have the opportunity to judge if the book you've written even sounds like something they would publish. To many writers, it can seem that most publishers have closed their doors. That isn't true, as we noted in Chapter 16, "The Publishing Maze," but certainly more are closed than used to be. And as more publishers close their doors, the ones left must deal with more mail. It's little wonder that it can be three, four, five, six months, or more before some publishers respond.

Lost in the Shuffle

A final reason that it can take so long to hear from publishers is that they are seeing more manuscripts that do not deserve an immediate rejection. Thanks to the work of organizations like the SCBWI, more manuscripts than ever are coming in that have possibilities. There are still plenty of manuscripts that can be rejected quickly, perhaps after reading only a few lines. But manuscripts that can be read all the way through, and need to be thought about, are the ones that take up a reader's time. And there are more of these.

As we have suggested before, the competition is tough. Keep at it and at the end of the process, after making that contact with an editor, perhaps revising a manuscript several times, may just be a contract. And then you are on your way to publication.

Can You Keep a Secret?

Harold recently judged a contest for unpublished authors, mostly reading the first chapter of a novel. Of more than 70 submissions, very few were easy to reject. Many, though perhaps after revision, could be published. In competition this strong, sometimes it can be hard to get noticed.

The Least You Need to Know

➤ All publishers need fresh talent. You need to put your best foot forward when approaching them.

➤ Get to know publishers and editors at conventions and conferences.

➤ Be restrained when you first hear from an editor, at least in your response. Later you can celebrate all you want!

➤ Persistence is a key to success, but no guarantee.

➤ Publishers get swamped by manuscripts and often take months to respond.

Part 4

Working with a Publisher

You've made it over the transom, and now you're working with a publisher. Or at least you're about to be, because they've sent you a contract. So to start with, we'll help you figure it out, and explain how copyright law affects what you do.

Once you start working with an editor, you'll have to revise. So we tell you what to expect and how best to deal with the process, and then go on to tell you just what editors themselves are like. Of course, you won't just be working with your editor, so we show you what happens once an illustrator gets involved, and give you an idea of how you will and will not be a part of this. Other folks join the team, too, and we'll introduce you to them.

Chapter 19

Oh Boy! A Contract!

In This Chapter

➤ What contracts are all about

➤ How you will be paid and what you'll have to do

➤ The mysteries of subsidiary rights

➤ Legal terms and other arcane knowledge

➤ Negotiating tactics

At some point, if you stick it out and build your talent and have some luck, you will hear from an editor that he would like to publish your manuscript. The excitement generated by this phone call or e-mail or letter might lead you to unquestioningly hand over your first-born child, if requested—put on a green eyeshade and negotiate the terms of a contract? You can't be bothered. You're going to have a book! But we urge you to calm down and educate yourself at least a little about contracts. In this chapter, we'll help you understand what a publishing contract is all about, and give you guidance in knowing what to expect, and what to ask for.

You may not be able actually to demand much, especially the first time around, but you need to understand what you are signing. So read on, and ask questions of your editor if you need to.

How You Will Hear

The beginnings of the process can be shrouded in mists of procedure, so we'll shed some light there first. If an editor is interested in a manuscript—perhaps after

Vocabulary List

To **acquire** a manuscript an editor receives approval from the company, and then negotiates a contract with an author. Your manuscript is now (in a sense) the property of the company. The editor has made an **acquisition.**

corresponding with you about it and getting you to revise it, perhaps on first reading—he or she must get some kind of approval from the company to *acquire* it. At a minimum, this usually means getting several higher-ups to read it, and to OK the *acquisition* in a meeting known variously as publishing meeting or acquisition meeting. Financial analysis of the expected costs and possible profits may be required too, perhaps in great detail, perhaps just as rough estimates.

Without the formal approval of the publishing committee, no editor can offer you a contract (unless he or she works at a small house, and makes the decisions alone, or works at an unusually old-fashioned publisher that grants editors complete autonomy.) Approval in hand, the editor makes the call, and murmurs that phrase that will make you feel weak in the knees, "We want to offer you a contract."

Quiz—What Do You Know?

Contracts are complicated and full of terms most people just don't know. To help you assess where you start in learning about contracts, we've put together this short quiz. Write down whether you think each statement is true or false, then check the answers and see where you stand.

1. Copyright refers to the copy you as an author write.
2. A royalty is a special bonus payment you get for winning a literary prize.
3. Subsidiary rights are the rights of subsidiaries, or divisions, of a publisher to publish your work.
4. Joint accounting is a clause you want in a contract—it means you and the publisher jointly track sales of a book.
5. An important negotiating tactic is to decide what you want before you start to talk, and then walk away if you don't get it.

And the answers are …. These are all false, though for different reasons.

1. Copyright is the right to make copies of an original work.
2. A royalty is a percentage you are paid out of the money a publisher receives for the sale of a book.
3. These rights are actually the rights that a publisher sells to other companies, to make a special edition or some other use of your work.

4. You don't want this in your contract. You'll find out why below.

5. This kind of stance can be counterproductive. It's always possible to learn that you don't need what you thought you did, or that a compromise will get you something you hadn't even thought about. Negotiating a contract involves give and take.

How did you do? If you got all of these right, you may not need to read this chapter. Otherwise, read on!

Hand It Over

Contracts exist in publishing for a very simple reason. You, as the writer, have a property. It's not something physical like a house or a piece of art, but you can sell it, or sell the rights to make use of it. In short, you can sell the right to copy it—that's your copyright. (We'll look more deeply into copyright in the next chapter.) A publisher can do many different things with a manuscript, from publishing it once in a magazine or publishing it in many different ways over a period of many years. But first, the publisher must establish its right to use the property.

It does that with a contract. The core of a publishing contract is the transfer of an author's rights in a manuscript to a company that (we hope) has the resources to use those rights in ways that you could not. In return, you get some form of compensation.

What You Gotta Do

Of course, you aren't just handing in a final exam and going on vacation. Publishers usually ask you to do more than that, and they'll spell out just what that is in the contract.

You'll be expected to revise to suit their standards. This can be sticky! What if they want you to make changes that you don't want to make? The contract may allow them to make them. Most publishers try not to make significant changes without consulting with an author, but just about all publishers put language in their *standard contracts* that allows them to decide on their own when a manuscript is ready to be published.

You'll also be expected to meet the publisher's deadlines. This may involve not only finishing the manuscript itself on time, but also handling edits and other materials sent for checking at later stages.

Vocabulary List

A publisher's **standard contract** covers all the items they think they need in a contract, which won't all just be to their benefit—some items will be there because everyone will expect them. The terms in this contract are sometimes referred to as "boilerplate," implying they're just stamped on, like a plate on a boiler.

179

You may also be asked to allow the publisher to use your likeness (a photo!), your name, and information about you in promoting the book. Unless you are publicity-shy, you should have no objection to this. Publishers generally do not require that you actively promote your book, though they may encourage you to.

What Publishers Do

In return for your labor, and for the use of your creative efforts, publishers will do as little as possible other than publish the book. Publishing is a business, after all. On the other hand, you can expect certain things, or publishers couldn't stay in business.

Generally, a publisher will:

➤ Pay you royalties on sales of the book, usually twice a year, and usually some money up front. Sometimes, you get a fee only (an arrangement known as work-for-hire).

➤ Pay you a share of any proceeds from selling the right to do something with it, such as make a book club edition or a filmstrip.

➤ Agree to consult with you while the book is being developed.

➤ Send you free copies of the book on publication and allow you to buy more at a discount.

➤ Copyright the text of the book in your name.

In practice, a publisher may do more than this, such as send copies of reviews and consult with you even when not required, but they'll try to keep their contractual obligations to a minimum.

You should be able to find clauses covering the areas we've touched on in just about any contract. If you don't, or you don't understand what they say, ask. There's more to be said about the key areas, so let's keep moving.

Class Rules

Make sure that you understand all of the commitments you are making when you sign a contract. Can you meet the deadlines? Provide the materials you are required to? If you aren't sure, discuss your concern with your editor. It's better to know now than later, when you suddenly find you can't deliver.

Your Allowance

As a writer, you live by the income produced by your writing. Well, maybe not—many writers live on the salary of some other job. But you certainly want to make a living from your writing, and so the payment you receive for a book may be the most important part of any publishing contract.

Vocabulary List

A **royalty** is money paid to an author, based on a certain percentage of the price of the book times the number of copies sold. It may be based on **list price** (or retail price), the price marked on the book, or **net price,** the amount of money the publisher receives for the book. So that an author will not have to wait until publication to be paid, a publisher usually pays an **advance** on the royalties, but the author must wait for the advance to be recouped before seeing more income.

How you get paid depends upon the publisher. Traditional trade publishers have long paid *royalties* based on the *list price* of a book. Typically, the royalty is 8 percent to 10 percent for a hardcover novel or other work you create yourself, and half that for a picture book, because you split the royalties with an illustrator. Newer publishers, or publishers in other markets, often pay royalties based on *net price,* which is the amount of money they actually receive when they sell the book; these are often 10 percent to 15 percent, again split if an illustrator is involved. The percentage may be higher, but keep in mind that a publisher may sell a book to bookstores and wholesalers at a discount of 50 percent off list price, so figure out what you will make per copy sold, and ask your editor about their usual discount. Contracts usually specify a paperback royalty, usually lower than the hardcover, and may go into other kinds of books as well, such as board books and big books.

If you are paid royalties, there is usually an *advance.* This is money paid in anticipation of the money that will be earned from the book. For example, you might receive a $3,000 advance for a novel, on which you will receive a 10 percent list royalty. If the book sells for a list price of $16, you get $1.60 per book, and you will start getting paid that after your advance *earns out,* which in this

Vocabulary List

An advance **earns out** when the amount earned in royalties equals the amount paid out in the advance. For example, if you were paid a $3,000 advance on a picture book, and are receiving a 5 percent list royalty on a list price of $15, the book will earn out after 4,000 copies are sold. Up until that point, the money earned is charged against the advance. From that point on, you will be paid any royalties the book earns.

case will be after the book sells fewer than 2,000 copies. In this case, you can realistically hope to receive more money in the future.

Sometimes, your advance is all you receive. If a publisher pays a $3,000 advance on a picture book manuscript, and you are being paid a 5 percent *net* royalty on a $16 book, you might get 5 percent of $8, or 40¢ per book, and 12,000 copies of the book would have to be sold before you received any more income. It's possible your book would never reach that level.

We give these examples partly to demonstrate that the other option, being paid a fee for a book—with no hope of receiving future royalties—is not always a bad idea. Everyone wants royalties, but in some cases you might consider taking a fee. It may be the only option, for some publishers, and you may not do any worse financially. If you do take a fee, check and see if the book is still being copyrighted in your name. Mass market publishers, in particular, use work-for-hire contracts that put you in an employee role, and allow them to copyright the book in their names. This is OK if you are doing contract labor, writing stories about a TV character according to the publisher's detailed guidelines; it's not OK if you have created a truly original work. You want the world to know that you created that work, and you want to have the rights to it when the book goes out of print.

Can You Keep a Secret?

Most publishers pay royalties twice a year, based on the number of copies sold in a six-month period. For January to June, for example, you might get paid in September. Why the delay? Publishers aren't just holding your money—they're waiting to be paid themselves, because booksellers can take months to pay, and they are waiting for returns (unsold books that are returned to the publisher). Returns sometimes come back in such numbers that a book has negative sales in a selling period. Dealing with the flow of books and money is one of the bigger challenges facing publishers.

As with any allowance, timing is important. You don't get royalties until the book comes out. Some publishers pay an advance on the signing of the contract, which isn't just good for you—it also helps them to lock you in. If you want to get out of such a contract, you'll have to repay that money. A payment may be made on delivery of a partial manuscript. Many publishers pay part or all of the advance when the manuscript is approved by them, which may require considerable work on your part. And some publishers pay part of the advance on publication. This isn't as bad as it sounds— that's still better than waiting to be paid royalties. Depending on the publisher, and the type of book, advances for first-time authors range from nothing to perhaps $5,000. Be sure you understand what you need to do to be paid your advance, or the different parts of your advance, and when it should happen.

Subsidiary Rights

As we will explain in more detail in the next chapter, your creation of an original work means that you have the right to dispose of a bundle of different ways in which your work can be used. The publisher will directly use the right to publish a book, but most publishers also want to acquire what are known as subsidiary rights—the other things that you can do with a manuscript. Generally, you'll split the income from the agreements a publisher makes in this area with them and the illustrator, typically half to the publisher, with the rest shared between you and the illustrator. If the agreement is for your text only, you usually get 50 percent. You can ask for a better split, but you might not get it. There are many different kinds of subsidiary agreements a publisher might make. We'll cover the most common ones.

Some subsidiary agreements are for other kinds of books. Until recently, many publishers sold the right to make a paperback of a book they were publishing in hardcover. Now, most publish their own paperbacks. But books are also sold by book clubs, by school book fairs, and by publishers in other countries, perhaps in translation, perhaps in English. Publishers usually work pretty hard to sell rights in these areas.

Magazine rights are licensed under the names of first serial (before publication) and second serial (after publication). Many publishers are generous with the proceeds from the first serial rights, on the grounds that a magazine article based on your book that came out before publication would do a lot to publicize the book. They might pay an author 80 percent of the proceeds if a sale was made for "first serial." That's not a given, but might be worth asking for.

The use of excerpts from your text or even the whole text in a larger collection falls under the umbrella of permissions. With interest in use of trade books in the classroom well established, this is perhaps the most reliable area for a subsidiary rights sale, as textbook publishers seek out material, sometimes years after publication of the original book.

The text of your book can also be enhanced in various ways, ranging from filmstrips and videotapes to plays, films, or even television shows. Don't count on sales in this area, but if they come, they can be lucrative.

And then we get to the tricky area of electronic rights. With hardly a week going by without news of some new format or initiative in the electronic

Class Rules

If you don't have an agent, don't make a fuss about "giving" the publisher the right to do something with your subsidiary rights. Do confirm that the publisher has staff whose job it is to sell them. As an individual, in almost all cases you would find it almost impossible to do anything with any rights you did keep. Let the publisher sell them: 50 percent of something is more than 100 percent of nothing.

book arena, it's no wonder that this is source of great contention between authors and publishers. Publishers want to establish clear rights to publish or sell rights in this area, while preserving the usual splits. Authors are leery of handing over rights, when they see a possible gold rush in the future. The situation is still in flux, but don't expect to be able to insist on special deals. Publishers will drop a deal with many authors rather than give in on what they have set up as their standard in this area.

If you're just getting started as an author, look at subsidiary rights as the icing on the cake. For your first book, you can't expect much in the way of income in this area, and so seeking changes to the standard language may not be a good use of your energy. Understand what this is all about, but don't make it a big issue.

Legal Language

Get past the things you must do and the payments and splits you can expect from a publisher, and you come to a tedious and sizable part of the contract—the legal language. Typical contracts range from six pages to 25 or so. The difference is largely due to a thicket of clauses designed to guard a publisher against some pretty unlikely bad outcomes. Should you be concerned about these clauses? Well, are you concerned about being struck by lightning? No? That's about how concerned you should be about many of these, because that's about how likely some of these are to be activated— they may have gotten into the contract due to things that happened to the publisher's adult division (or even their TV or Internet division), or due to some reading in contract manuals that someone in the contract department did on a quiet day.

What should you expect? That really varies. Typical clauses include:

➤ A guarantee that you actually control the rights that you are handing over—that you haven't already sold them.

➤ A warranty that you aren't infringing anyone else's copyright or saying anything libelous or otherwise illegal.

➤ What the publisher can do in the event of legal action against you and the publisher.

➤ How and in what circumstances the contract can be terminated or canceled.

➤ What happens when the book goes out of print.

➤ What happens if the book isn't published in a timely way.

Can You Keep a Secret?

Need help figuring all of this out? Lawyers specializing in book contracts exist, but they are expensive. Instead of an agent or lawyer, published authors should consider joining the Author's Guild (see Appendix B, "Resources"). Members can get the services of the staff lawyers in deciphering a contract.

Should you understand these clauses? Absolutely. Just don't expect to be able to change them, with the possible exception of the last two mentioned. Unlike some of the stuff we discussed earlier, these clauses are usually not ones your editor has any authority to change.

Ch-Ch-Ch-Changes

So what can you change? How much you can change in the terms that are offered to you depends (to be blunt) entirely on your leverage. If you're a first-time author, you have very little. If you have something of a track record, or have been lucky enough to have acquired an agent, you may have more leverage. But there will still be a limit as to how far a publisher will go. A publisher also may not see any need to make changes. They may already have offered you terms they believe to be reasonable, taking into account what their competitors do and what their own pay scale is from beginners to top-level authors.

Regardless of just how much leverage you have, you won't get more by acting outraged or being demanding. Be firm, but polite and professional, and be ready to suggest or listen to alternatives. This approach, even in a negotiation in which you get little of what you want, will earn you the respect of the publisher, increasing the chances of improvements the next time around.

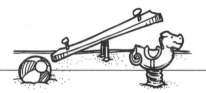

Stories from the Playground

Agent Sandy Ferguson Fuller has this to say about negotiations: "Don't try to tinker too much with advance amounts but do insist on reasonable royalty rates. With a standard trade book, definitely try to negotiate a royalty-based vs. flat-fee agreement, even if you must waive any advance and agree to a sub-standard royalty.

"Be sure that the various deadlines are reasonable. Don't be unreasonable in your dealings with a publisher—but don't be intimidated either. If a contract isn't equitable or negotiations turn sour, turn away—believe in your work, take a risk, persevere—you will find a better deal!"

Here are some goodies to ask for, beyond the obvious idea of a larger advance, or more free copies of your book. In the long run, you may be able to get what's called an escalator clause, which increases the royalty once a certain number of books are sold. You can ask for a pass-through clause, which passes through your share of large subsidiary rights sales (if your advance has earned out) when the money is received, so that you don't have to wait for the next royalty statement. Ask for a higher royalty on "special sales," deals made for large quantities of the book at a high discount, for which you usually receive less than your usual royalty. Keep asking.

As well as asking for goodies, watch out for no-nos. Object to your royalty being reduced on small printings of the book (losing an increase in royalty from an escalator clause isn't so bad, so long as it doesn't go lower than it was to start with). Avoid joint accounting, a clever setup that ties together your advance with those of other books, so that all of them have to earn out their advances before you see royalties. And do make sure that the book is copyrighted in your name, not the publisher's name. You do not want to actually give up ownership of the copyright—you just want to let the publisher use it.

Literary agent Sandy Fuller has a somewhat different idea from ours of what's important in a contract. So might you—and you should think about what that is. But no matter what you want, do not walk out if you don't get it. Try instead to do better. Even a publisher that won't make any changes at all to a contract may be worth working with, for now, but go into all your negotiations with the attitude that the best contract is one with which both sides are happy. Be willing to compromise and to listen, and expect to be listened to and compromised with. If, time after time, you're unhappy with what you've got when the negotiations are over, either you're working with the wrong publisher, or your expectations are just too high. Find out by talking to other authors in a similar situation. Then, move on, or adjust.

The Least You Need to Know

➤ Contracts in publishing involve a creator (author or illustrator) handing over the right to publish a work in return for some kind of compensation.

➤ Publishers usually pay royalties to an author and will make other commitments in a contract, such as providing free copies to the author.

➤ Publishers don't just hope to publish a work—they hope to sell its subsidiary rights, and a large part of a contract will spell out just what's involved.

➤ Much of a contract is made up of legal language you probably can't change, but should still try to understand.

➤ Ask for what you think you want in a contract, but be ready to compromise.

Chapter 20

They Might Take My Idea! Copyright Basics

In This Chapter

➤ What a copyright is and why publishers copyright your work

➤ How unpublished works are protected

➤ All about "ideas" and why they are *not* protected

➤ How folktales fit into the copyright world

➤ Why you really don't need to worry about a publisher stealing your work

➤ Avoiding plagiarism—intentional or otherwise

Invariably, we've all done it: worried about someone stealing our fabulous idea for a book. After all, few people surge with the genius necessary to come up with such a fine idea for a children's book! *Au contraire*—many people do. But that's OK because ideas themselves aren't worth much on their own, at least under copyright law. Your actual created work, written down on paper, is worth far more. By putting an idea into written form you can protect not only the work but also that original idea. So let's take a look now at the protection of your created work—your idea put into a form. And let's also see why a publisher stands little to gain from "stealing" your proposal or manuscript and much to lose.

A Tale of Two Writers' Ideas

Come on, tell the truth. You remain just a little shy of sharing your idea for a children's book with anyone because you fear whomever you tell your tale to will move with it and "steal" your idea! Right? Hey, it happens to the best of us—especially when unpublished and wanting desperately to write a book. But there's a difference between an unpublished work and an "idea" for a book. Consider the following two aspiring writers with whom coauthor Lynne recently came in contact—teacher A and teacher B.

Knowing that Lynne has published several books and numerous magazine articles, two teaching colleagues approached her about wanting to write a book, each looking for a little advice. So Lynne, wanting to help them and looking forward to gauging whether the book concept was interesting and worthy of forwarding to her agent as a favor to the colleagues, asked them both, "What's your idea?" Teacher A—the journalism instructor at the school and a published newspaper reporter—candidly talked about his book series idea. Teacher B, however, got a funny look on her face, paused, and said, "Well, I want to tell you but I'm afraid you'll steal my idea!" Can you all say "Paranoia"? After reassurance from the writer that her "idea" was safe, that writers—real writers with their own talent—don't make a habit of "stealing" the ideas of others, the colleague was coaxed into letting go and telling about the book concept. Unfortunately, however, this paranoia about "thievery" amid unpublished writers remains prevalent.

Here's the lowdown: Ideas are not protected by copyright laws. An idea is an idea is an idea (with apologies to Gertrude Stein), and that's all it is. You may be cursing the copyright office right now, but hold on. Think about it. There are very few original ideas. It's what you do with the ideas that matters. Most authors will agree.

Take heart—it's all just a common beginner's mistake. In fact, one of the most frequent questions coauthor Harold receives on his Web site and at conferences when he speaks is, "How do I stop someone from taking my really wonderful idea?" His response? "Well, you can't!" But what you can protect is *"original expression"*—your idea put into final form. In other words, you can protect something you've actually written.

Let's take an example, so we all get this concept perfectly clear. Gail Greatidea comes up with a great idea

Class Rules

Many writers remain under the mistaken assumption that they must file with the copyright office before using the copyright symbol of their work, thereby giving notification to others of their rights as the creator of the work. In actuality, the use of a copyright notice *does not* require advance permission from or registration with the U.S. Copyright Office.

Vocabulary List

Your ideas become "**original expression**," and thus protected by the copyright laws of the United States and many other countries, when you take those ideas and actually create something—a book, a story, a sculpture, a symphony—from your idea that is completely true to you and absolutely original.

for a children's book about a girl and her horse. She tells her buddy, Claire Klepto, about the promising story line sitting in the recesses of her imagination. Now that Gail's spilled the beans to Claire, Claire can use the idea and Gail has no recourse. But if Gail writes down her horsey tale—complete with the details of the singing ducks and talking trees—and then sees her story three years from now with the author as "Claire Klepto," Gail can come with the full power of copyright law behind her and lunge at Claire's throat (legally speaking, of course)! And that's "original expression."

You may be asking, "Why does my idea need to 'take form' in order to be deemed original expression?" Well, again, most story ideas are *not* original. In fact, think of any famous story, boil it down to its "core idea," and it may not seem so original. Take *Where the Wild Things Are*. It's about a child and monsters. How many stories out there are about children and imaginary monsters? How many stories are there about a child and his or her first pet? A first day at school? Dealing with a new sibling? Dozens for each type, right? There just aren't that many different story types. Does this mean that everyone is stealing from an original story? Nope. What makes the difference in the idea remains the originality employed by the author about the idea once it's put to paper and actually created.

Class Rules

Remember: The more original and less "generic" your work is, the easier it becomes to protect the work. The more distinct, the better. Literally the first thing any writer should do is develop an idea into something unique and put pen to paper. Otherwise your idea remains "unprotected."

"Mommy, What's a Copyright and Where Does It Come From?"

Which leads us to how a writer protects a creation taken form: with a copyright. Our forefathers realized how we feel about our creative endeavors and thus responded in the Constitution (Article 1, Section 8) as to why we copyright, saying, "To promote the Progress of Science and Useful arts by securing for limited Times to Authors and Inventors the exclusive Right to their respective Writings and Discoveries." This part of the Constitution protects what is known as "intellectual property," and is put into effect through the laws of copyright, trademark, and patents. Most countries have similar laws. Today we flock to the U.S. Copyright Office to ensure our artistic creations remain *our* artistic creations.

In a nutshell, copyright law protects original expression. So what does that mean to a writer? Title 17, U.S. Code, provides protection to the authors of "original works of authorship." Meanwhile, Section 106 of the Copyright Act provides the possessor of the copyright several unalienable rights in respect to the copyrighted work. Basically, the copyrighter holds the power over the reproduction, distribution, sale, and

Vocabulary List

When a manufacturer or dealer distinguishes a product from competitors by a specific design, word, or letter, the registration that protects the company's representation is called a **trademark.**

performance of the work. So, anyone wanting to use your work must have your permission, and if you require it, must pay you for it. And that is the basis of publishing as a business. You, the writer, grant a publisher the right to use your copyrighted work, in return for a payment.

Before we get any further, however, we want to point out that trade publishing is built on copyright—creative and individual expression. Much of mass market publishing is built on another kind of "intellectual property," in this case *trademarks*. The stories in many mass market books, though they may be copyrighted, aren't selling because they are blindingly original. They sell because the consumer recognizes the trademark, either the publisher's own, like Golden Books, or something from another medium, like Disney or Pokémon or even Cheerios.

Stories from the Playground

Want a few good reasons why the publisher puts the little copyright symbol on your work? First, immediately the public is informed of the copyright protection—"Back off! It's our author's work!" Next, if the work carries proper notice and someone uses the material or steals it, there is no way that the thief can claim "innocent infringement." What is innocent infringement? When the party who used the creative property of another claims to have not realized the work held copyrighted status. That's important because if the infringement isn't innocent then the infringer is liable for extra damages.

Safe, So Far

Now that we've established that copyright laws protect your written creation—not your mere idea—what do you do about it? First, you need not register your work with the copyright office before sending it to the publisher for consideration. In fact, doing so will mark you as an amateur. If the publisher picks your work for publication, the house will automatically file for the copyright for you. Just denote somewhere on your manuscript, "copyright" and your name and the date. There. Your work is now protected under copyright laws!

Some have suggested that to prove the date when you did this, you can mail a copy of the manuscript to yourself, and keep it unopened. The postmark establishes the date on which the manuscript took final form. This may not be accepted in a legal setting, however. It's best just to limit the distribution of the manuscript. Do send it to individual publishers. Don't post it on the World Wide Web—that's a form of publication.

Can You Keep a Secret?

If you're interested in finding out more about copyright rules and regulations, hop on-line and navigate your way to http://lcweb.loc.gov/copyright/. The U.S. Copyright Office provides everything from general information to publications to legislation affecting copyright laws—all on-line.

The Trouble with Folktales

Working with other people's original expression can by tricky, and yet many children's books are essentially retellings of existing stories. These differ in the details from the source, but have more in common than the bare idea. This particularly comes up as a problem with folktales.

Vocabulary List

Creative work that is not protected by copyright is in the **public domain.** The author of that work is not entitled to any payment if someone else uses it, and does not even have to be asked for permission. In a sense, it is the collective property of the public, while copyrighted work is still the property of the author.

You may want to tailor a folktale you heard as a child or came across in your travels or research; what do you do? After all, you know you never possessed the "original" idea. The good news is that, in many cases, the story is in the *public domain,* meaning that it is not protected by copyright law and may be used by other authors in any way they choose without permission. Copyright does not last forever. Anything published 75 years ago is almost certain to be in the public domain, and many other works may be as well.

Since many folktales follow oral tradition, they've been around for decades—even centuries. You may retell the story, essentially, with your own style and interpretation and copyright your version. But here's a warning! An old folktale, or the version you know, may have been published only recently. This is an active field and new versions of folktales from all over the world are coming out all the time. Even if you don't quote from it, if you use the plot and descriptive details you may be violating someone's copyright.

Class Rules

Using someone else's work as a source for your own telling of a foltake (or tall tale, a biography, or work of history) is OK, provided that you've used at least three sources and that you explain how you used them in an acknowledgement or author's note.

So check carefully. Was your source published in a collection a long time ago? You're in the clear. Can you find multiple sources for it, even if they are recent? That's OK, too. Cite all of them in your notes for the book, and don't rely heavily on one of them, and go ahead and tell that story. Just like writers of historical fiction must check their sources, you—the reteller of a folktale—must check your sources, acknowledge them, and make sure that you aren't relying on someone else's copyrighted work as your sole source.

Just because a story is in the public domain, or you've been able to find several different versions of it, you should still do some careful work before using it. Do you know the culture from which it derives, or in which you want to set it? If you don't, you may create an inauthentic story, with details or a plot turn or a moral that no member of that culture would create. Also, do you understand how folktales work? As Aaron Shepard, a successful folktale reteller, says, "If you want to retell folktales successfully, it's not enough to be familiar with just the tale you want to retell. You have to know folklore in general. Otherwise, there's not much chance you'll handle it right." In fact, Shepard continues, confirming, "Usually this means knowing folklore better than most editors."

"Dummy! Dumb-Dumb!" Why Stealing Is Stupid!

Right now, you may still have concerns about sending your manuscript off to a publisher and having the publishing house steal your work, right? Stop worrying. We're here to tell you why stealing—by the publisher, by you, by anyone writing a book—is just plain stupid.

To start with, copyright laws protect writers. In order to steal your creation, the thief will literally need to lift a chunk of your creation. Both recognizable and blatant—the thief will get caught. In the form of a children's picture book, the thief would literally need to steal the whole darn tale! Even taking extended passages from a book, or paraphrasing them in detail, is a copyright violation, and the victim, or their publisher, could go to court and win.

Publishers in particular have very little if anything to gain from "stealing" your idea or manuscript, yet have much to lose. Think about it. Imagine you send a manuscript to a publisher. They advise you, "Sorry, not for us." Then three years later, you see your story, word for word, on the shelves at the local bookstore with the illustrator as the author, too. A nightmare, but not likely to happen. Why would a publisher do that? The gains for the publisher would be minimal—perhaps a couple thousand dollars in payment to you. That's it! But the loss could be monumental if this kind of deception came out. The publisher would lose its good name—and that's enormously important to the company. Other authors, writers, illustrators, distributors, sales forces, editors, production managers—everyone in the business—need to trust the publisher in order for the books to hit the shelves and the publisher to make money. It's really not in a publisher's best interest to steal and tarnish a good reputation.

On a final note, stealing is a pain in the butt! Publishers receive too many great stories from respected writers to need to connive to thwart the success of an unknown, previously unpublished writer by taking the writer's work and not pursuing a contract with them. Most publishing houses run on a schedule like a newsroom—harried and frantic. No one has time to steal your story. Of course, as we've all heard, stealing is said to happen in other parts of the media world, notably in the film industry. What's the difference? The big difference is that films often get go-aheads on the basis of an idea, with the screenplay worked and reworked to the point that no one author can claim it as their own (and since the studio owns the copyright, that's beside the point anyway.) Thankfully, children's publishing—and most adult publishing—operates with more respect for the creator.

Plagiarism, Intentional and Otherwise

What about when you, the writer, mess up and take someone else's words as your own? Well, sometimes the use of another's words within your work falls under what's called *"fair use."* Under "fair use" you can have a quotation from someone else to add flavor to your piece, or to support your argument, or for whatever reason, without asking permission. But when the use of someone else's words does not fall under fair use, then you are guilty of *plagiarism*.

For example, let's say you're writing a young adult novel set in the 1960s and want to include a line from a newspaper article or another book to further illustrate your theme or point. Generally speaking, that's OK. That's "fair use." We can do this—take a few lines here and there—without asking permission of the author because we're taking just a few lines from a really big creation and we're citing it! Yep, you need to give credit where credit is due. In this book, for example, we've quoted facts from various articles—but we've cited the source of the information.

Now, what about a song lyric? Perhaps in that same young adult novel about the sixties you want to title a chapter with the line from a Rolling Stones song. Only one line, right? It must fall under "fair use." *Not!* It's probable that you'll need to pay the American Society of Composers, Authors and Publishers (ASCAP) for the use. Why?

193

Vocabulary List

Copyright law allows an exception to the protection of copyrighted material. Under **fair use,** a modest quantity of a copyrighted work can be quoted in another work without permission or payment, provided that the use is acknowledged. If a writer instead presents that work as his or her own, that's a case of **plagiarism.**

Because if you quote one line from a song that only encompasses, say, 20 lines, you've quoted a pretty big percentage of the creation.

If you do need to quote from someone else, say in a biography, go ahead and do it, but seek your publisher's advice as to which quotations fall under fair use guidelines and which require permission. In a work of fiction, it's probably better to stay away from using copyrighted material until you understand the boundaries of fair use. Do you *have* to use that line from the Rolling Stones in your novel? Probably not, so for now, do without it.

The good news about copyright law is that it protects *you* and your writing. Provided that you follow some common sense guidelines, as we've outlined here, you're unlikely to run into any problems with it.

The Least You Need to Know

➤ Ideas cannot be copyrighted or protected, but work put into a final form can.

➤ You don't need to actually register your unpublished work with the U.S. Copyright Office in order to maintain protection of your work. Writing "copyright" and your name and date on your manuscript will suffice.

➤ If you plan to retell folktales, check your sources. Make sure the story falls within public domain or has multiple sources before proceeding with a manuscript.

➤ Don't fret about a publisher stealing your story; publishers stand to lose more (their good reputation) than they stand to gain (a few measly bucks) from taking your work.

➤ Until you understand "fair use" law, look to your publisher for guidance in using copyrighted material.

Chapter 21

Make It Better

In This Chapter

➤ Why revision is important

➤ How editing helps with revision

➤ Different kinds of editing

➤ How to work productively with an editor

Once your book is under contract, and sometimes before that, an editor is going to want to revise your manuscript. Don't be embarrassed—it's not because you're a novice or a bad writer. Editing and revising are central to producing quality books. Ironically, the writing that seems the most effortless is probably writing that has been sweated over the most. Here we're going to explain the different ways in which editors may work with you to make your writing better, and give you some hints on how you can work with them more productively.

The Revision Process

Writing is *revising* and rewriting. Just about any writer will agree with that. The first words that you put down on the page will not be the ones you end up with. Some writers revise well on their own, and turn in manuscripts that need minimal editing. Others prefer to work with editors, often through multiple *drafts*. And others go through some of both, which can lead to box after box of revisions of a novel taking up space in their garages (these do make for good visuals on school visits, though).

The Best Part

Revision sounds like a lot of work, and it can be. True writers savor it, however. They know that getting something down on paper is the hard part. Then you can play. The pressure's reduced, if not gone. Once you have something to work with, you can tinker and think and try different ideas. It can only get better (or so you need to tell yourself).

So revision is not only important—it's the best part of writing. But don't take our word for it. Jane Yolen, author of many picture books, novels, and books of poetry, points out that revision is what helps you actually recapture some semblance of that first, dazzling vision, which you then lost when you tried to get it down on paper.

Vocabulary List

To **revise** literally means to "re-see"; strive to see your writing afresh when you make changes. Each new version of a manuscript is called a **draft.** Your first draft is just that; a rough draft is one that needs polishing; and a final draft is the one you hope doesn't need to be revised again.

Author Larry Dane Brimner agrees, saying that in writing, "the real excitement comes from wordplay. I simply enjoy writing a sentence and then seeing if I can make it sharper or clearer or more beautifully expressed. For me, the enjoyment and art of writing is in rewriting."

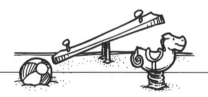

Stories from the Playground

Jane Yolen says this about revision: "The words in my head were splendid, of course. Once on the page they needed enormous reshaping. Isaac Asimov is reputed to have said that he never revised anything. Then he must have done all that work in his head. I have never written a sentence that couldn't be improved. Even my book *Owl Moon*, which I once heard described by Bill Martin—the dean of children's literature—as 'the perfect picture book, not a word wrong,' could do with some reworking. When I read it to kids, I revise on the fly."

On Your Own

Much of your revision you'll handle on your own, and as you become a more experienced writer you'll become increasingly able to polish your own work without help from others. Take this as far as you can, making sure to cover the different kinds of editing we will describe later in this chapter, because the more finished your manuscript is when you submit it, the more likely it is that an editor will be interested in it, and the more rapidly it may go through the publication process. Manuscripts that need a lot of work won't be tackled until the editor has time to deal with them, and will end up on a list far in the future.

Writer and teacher Barbara Seuling says that she revises many times: "I revise a gazillion times, and I love the process because I seem to get better in layers. I really do "re-see" each time. I find it invaluable." You don't have to revise quite so many times, of course, but go as far as you can on your own.

With Your Editor

Take advantage of working with an editor. Every writer, no matter how experienced, can use the help of editors when revising. An editor comes to your writing with a fresh perspective. We aren't going to claim it's an objective perspective, just a different one, and perhaps one more akin to that of a reader reacting to your work the first time. Editors do much more than correct your spelling. In some ways, an editor is a very experienced reader, someone who can be conscious of her own intuitive responses to your work. They'll notice gaps, and incomplete characterizations, and statements that are vague or awkward. They'll point out problems, and maybe even suggest solutions.

Ideally, when you and an editor are working on a revision, you'll form a partnership with the goal of producing the best possible finished piece.

Can You Keep a Secret?

Good editing can make a huge difference to your work. Don't lose a golden opportunity by refusing to listen to it. As Barbara Seuling says in *How to Write a Children's Book:* "Editors often see more clearly than the writer, who is close to his work, and they can point out areas for improvement .... If you are rigid about your work, unwilling to change words and sentences and paragraphs, and even characters, you may be sacrificing the success of the total book for the sake of a few well-crafted words."

The Writer's Reference Bookshelf

When you're revising, you'll find that there are certain books you'll want to have available for reference. Some are standard across the industry. Some are of greater use for writers of fiction or of nonfiction. As you develop as a writer, others will become your trusted companions, so build on the following list as you see fit (see the expanded version of Appendix B online at Harold's web site for publication details and more information: www.underdown.org/ciglinks.htm):

➤ *Bartlett's Familiar Quotations*

➤ *Brewer's Dictionary of 20th Century Phrase and Fable*

➤ *The Chicago Manual of Style, 14th Edition*

➤ *The Concise Columbia Encyclopedia*

➤ *Dictionary of American Slang*

➤ *Dictionary of Modern American Usage*

➤ *Information Please Almanac* or another standard almanac

➤ *Roget's International Thesaurus*

➤ *Webster's Third New International Dictionary*

But It's My Story!

A trap all writers fall into at some time or another is to fall in love with their own writing, and to believe that it is perfect, that not one word should be added or taken away from this divine state. You've labored over the work, you've revised, you've listened to your writer's group. It can be tempting to believe that you can't possibly improve it anymore. This is almost certainly not true.

You do not need to take the editor's suggestions literally, on the other hand. It's possible that a problem she points out can be solved by making changes she hasn't actually suggested. For example, if an editor comments that a quiet character acts uncharacteristically noisy at one point in a story, the problem might not be with that incident. You intended that character to act that way, and you need him to. So you don't want to change that, but you've discovered something. Even though you intended all along to create a character that gets rowdy in certain circumstances, you neglected to establish that earlier on in the story. So this editor's comment on one spot in the story, if you have listened to it carefully, could lead to changes in entirely different places.

Get Me Rewrite!

Once you get started with revision, don't expect an editor to exclaim over the perfection of your manuscript while making only minor spelling corrections. That's not what an editor does. Unless your manuscript is in unusually good shape, you can expect editing at three different levels: the overall structure of the manuscript, the flow of the sentences and paragraphs, and, almost as an afterthought, corrections of spelling, grammar, and the like.

Hard work? Yes. Serious writers welcome it.

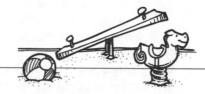

Stories from the Playground

Barbara Seuling notes that she much prefers editors who have something to say to her: "I've had editors who took my manuscripts and never touched a word, or gave me any feedback. I didn't trust them. I've heard other writers say the same thing. You feel like you can't trust that someone will be there to catch you if you fall. We all need editors. Then there's the other kind of editor that makes you just about fall in love—who takes every word and every line seriously, and gets into the mind and heart of what you have tried to do and helps you to achieve it."

Structural Editing

Some manuscripts require changes in the way that they are put together. They may need to have characters dropped or added, they may need an additional chapter, or they may need to be reorganized. All of these kinds of changes fall into category of what we call structural, or developmental, editing. To do it, your editor may write you a letter, or she may just call you and ask questions, perhaps along the lines of …

➤ "What happens to William in the second half of the book? He drops out of the narrative."

➤ "Have you considered dropping the first chapter and starting in the middle of things with the second?"

➤ "Could you go into more depth on how jet engines work?"

➤ "In the conflict between Sue and Naomi, do you need all four arguments?"

➤ "What if this were told in the first person?"

➤ "Could you show us in what ways Paul is dependent on his father, instead of just telling us he is?"

We could go on and on, but we think you get the idea. Think these kinds of questions over carefully, and if you make changes in response to them, think again. Have your changes affected the book in such a way that you need to make additional changes? If you think they do, don't be afraid to make them, or at least to discuss them with your editor.

Even short picture-book length manuscripts can need structural editing. Harold was working on the manuscript of Larry Pringle's *Bats: Strange and Wonderful* when he noticed that a few lines that were a couple of paragraphs into the manuscript would actually work better as opening lines. He suggested this, Larry moved them and reworked a bit to make them even better, and now that book has an opening that has been singled out for praise by reviewers. Author and editor worked together well in this case. Try to do the same.

Do this stage of revision as thoughtfully as you can. All editors respect writers who respond well to revision suggestions.

Line Editing

Once the manuscript is in good shape, it still needs polishing. A careful editor will go through it line by line, with the aim of sharpening descriptions, getting rid of passive constructions, cutting out run-on sentences, and generally making it more of a pleasure to read.

During this stage, your editor is likely to use some strange-looking marks and symbols. Mostly these are the standard marks that *copy editors* and *proofreaders* use. You'll see more of them later in the process, when the manuscript is actually copyedited. During editing, your editor will tend to use these marks, since she is familiar with them. You'll see marks in the margin of the manuscript, and right on the text. There aren't that many, and you'll find them useful yourself. We're putting a table of the most commonly used ones here, but you can find a guide to all of the copyediting symbols in standard writing reference works like *The Chicago Manual of Style*.

Soon after this stage, you can expect your editor to declare herself finished with the manuscript. You aren't. The copy editor still has to read it. And you'll then get another chance to learn copyediting symbols.

Common Editing Marks		
What they'll write	**What it means**	**The result**
(cap) new york city	capitalize these	New York City
(lc) Please STOP shouting	lowercase these	Please stop shouting
(lc) TOO MUCH NOISE	lowercase all of them	too much noise
It was dark and stormy	run them together	It was dark and stormy
Up in the the air	delete this	Up in the air
A drink of water (tall)	insert something	A tall drink of water
dirty laundry	put in a space	dirty laundry
(break) Four score and seven	start a new line	Four score and seven
(tr) cats dogs and	transpose these	cats and dogs
The end	insert a period	The end.
Planes, trains and	insert a comma	Planes, trains, and
To sleep perchance to	insert a semicolon	To sleep; perchance to
Bring to an end	insert a colon	Bring to an end:
write off	insert a hyphen	write-off
(stet) Don't touch that!	ignore the mark	Don't touch that!

Here are some common editing marks and what they mean.

Fact Checking

For nonfiction manuscripts, and perhaps for historical fiction and folktales as well, many publishers will want to assure themselves that the research you've done is sound. In classic fact checking, the fact checker will work through your manuscript fact by identifiable fact, checking each in the sources you used and in others he locates.

Some manuscripts don't lend themselves well to that approach. If you've written historical fiction set in seventeenth-century England, the publisher will seek out a historian of the period. Or if you've done a poetic piece describing the ebb and flow of life in a small salt marsh on the coast of Oregon, your editor might want to send it to a marine biologist with knowledge of that area. In either case, the fact checker will comment on his overall impressions, but not necessarily check every fact.

Your editor will pass on comments to you, in some cases reviewing them first, though in other cases not. This may seem like a burden to you, but it can also be a great opportunity, a final check that may well turn up a note-taking mistake or a distortion that you meant to be a simplification.

Ask for It!

Working with an editor isn't all highfalutin discussions about theme, plot, and turns of phrase, of course. Your editor, as you'll see in detail in the next chapter, is a busy person, probably juggling dozens of books and other responsibilities. Some editors are more active than others, too. So if you need something from her, you may need to ask for it, and you may need to ask for it repeatedly. Don't be bashful about this, but don't be obnoxious either. Just be politely persistent.

Editing

One of the shameful results of the increased amount of work an individual editor is expected to do is that some books don't get the editing they need. The situation in children's books is not yet as bad as in adult publishing, where we've heard that at many publishers manuscripts come in, get a quick copyedit, and go straight into production. But editing, like writing, requires a kind of relaxed concentration, and long stretches of time. Both of these are hard to find in a typical office. Some editors find they can only edit effectively if they take a day to work at home.

What with the increasing workloads expected of editors, in some cases, if an editor thinks there isn't much wrong with a manuscript, and if he's got a lot of other things to do, he may be tempted to move it along without editing. If you think that this is happening, don't hesitate to express concern. If there's something that's nagging you about your manuscript, tell your editor, and ask him what he thinks. Don't accept reassurances—tell him that's not what you want. Tell him you want his expertise, and be as specific as you can be about what you think the problem is.

Class Rules

When in doubt, communicate. If you want to know what your editor thinks, ask her. If you need two more weeks to finish the manuscript, say so. If you don't understand what an editor wants you to do, ask her to clarify. Editors are not telepathic, even though a good one may seem to understand what you are trying to do with a manuscript better than you do yourself.

My Paper's Late

Most likely you will be working toward a deadline as you revise, or perhaps for the actual delivery of a manuscript that was signed up on the basis of a proposal. That deadline is there for two reasons: to help the publisher maintain a stable program of so many books per year, yes, but also to help you finish. Deadlines are a useful spur. Are they absolute? No. We all miss deadlines, but we need them; very few books would get published without them. If you can't meet a deadline, ask for a new one. And try not to agree to a deadline you know you won't be able to meet.

No Guilt Trips, Please

In all your dealings with your editor, be professional. Nothing turns editors off faster than a writer who complains constantly of overwork or tries to wheedle payment of an advance before it is due.

The Care and Feeding of an Editor

Your relationship with your editor will go far beyond the editing of an actual manuscript. Editors hope that another manuscript is coming. And you also want to work with them on other ones. So let a relationship develop. Discuss ideas with your editor. Let her know that you're interested in hearing her suggestions for subjects for future books. Get to know her interests. You've got a lot in common. Make this a friendly relationship and you'll find that it becomes a more productive one.

Every relationship you'll have with an editor will be different, as noted by Pam Muñoz Ryan, author of picture books and novels:

"Over the years I've had 15 different editors. And like any 15 different friends I might have, each relationship has been different. Some have been simple affiliations where both of us seem to play our author and editor roles rather specifically with formal direction letters and no friendly chit chat. The books ended up being OK. Other relationships have been more personal, collaborative, and sometimes even fun. Those books were more successful. A few of my author-editor liaisons have been disasters and didn't work at all and I and my manuscript became the bridesmaid of another editor and sometimes another. When that happened, I rarely got bridal treatment, nor did the book. Those titles usually ended up in the mediocre category. But I have been lucky enough to have had a few pairings that were epiphanies, where I had the opportunity to work with brilliant editors who were prophetic and inspiring. It is no surprise that those titles have won the most awards and are my best sellers."

Like Pam, if you stick with children's publishing you'll have a variety of experiences, but make the best of whatever situation you're in, pull what you can from an editor with whom you may not be getting along, and make the book be the best you can make it. And of course, enjoy the experience, when you and the editor "click."

Can You Keep a Secret?

Once you start working with an editor she usually won't expect you to follow all the submission "rules." Got an idea for a story? Call her up instead of querying her, and discuss it. Send her a few rough chapters and see what she thinks instead of waiting to finish a manuscript. Editors want to be involved in your work. Let them be. If they're too busy at some point, they'll let you know.

The Least You Need to Know

➤ Many writers think revision is the most enjoyable part of writing, and it's certainly the most important.

➤ Don't resist editing of your work. It will make it better.

➤ Structural editing, line editing, and fact checking are three different kinds of editing.

➤ Be sure to ask for editing if you feel your manuscript is being rushed through.

➤ Feel free to build a personal relationship with your editor, and make the most of it if it's a good one.

Chapter 22

My Editor Doesn't Understand Me

> **In This Chapter**
>
> ➤ Some insight into "what editors are really like"
>
> ➤ The backgrounds of typical editors
>
> ➤ Editors' interests
>
> ➤ Profiles of several editors at different levels at different publishers

Now that you know a little bit about how you'll work with an editor, the question remains: What are editors like? Since writers typically don't get to know their editors very well at first, perhaps not meeting them in person until one or more books are out, it's easy to have all kinds of notions about them. In this chapter, we'll make some sweeping generalizations about editors, but ones that in our experience are accurate. Then we'll provide detailed profiles of several editors, showing what they do and how they got where they are today.

What Are Editors Like?

While attending and speaking at writer's conferences over the past several years, Harold has heard some wildly differing ideas about what children's book editors are like. (Since he's male and 90 percent of editors are women, he confounds one of the assumptions right from the start.) To some, editors seem to be nurturing-mother archetypes, lovers of books, committed both to the very best for children and to careful grooming of writers to be the best they can be. Others see them as scary intellectual gods or goddesses who expect you to understand the difference between metonymy and metaphor. Still others see editors as skilled hacks dedicated to the smooth functioning of corporate machines. Some truth resides in all of these imaginings, but it's a bit more complex than it appears to be at first.

The New York Ivory Tower

Editors have some typical characteristics. One is that they are still mostly based in New York. Publishers exist all across North America, but since the large publishers are mostly in New York, the bulk of publishing professionals reside there, too. Harold has observed that editors are college-educated, with degrees from Ivy League colleges or similar small, liberal arts colleges. Editors generally come from the middle class or above, and don't go into publishing to make money. In fact, as assistants they often need partial support from their families until they reach a level where they can actually live on their salaries. Children's book editors are mostly white; though people of color are working their way up in the field, editing is still less integrated than most professions. Children's book editors are mostly young, in their 20s and 30s, until they reach the senior level. This is a job in which people move up or out. In short, editors don't "look like America," and may not look much like the writers with whom they work. Whether this has good or bad consequences is open to debate.

People Who Love Books

Why do people become children's book editors? For the most part, it's not because editors love children, or at least not in the way that teachers or pediatric nurses do.

Can You Keep a Secret?

Nervous about holding up your end of the conversation if you meet an editor at a conference? Don't be. Just ask about his favorite books as a child. He'll happily tell you, probably ask you about yours, and if the two of you somehow finish discussing those, just ask what he's enjoyed reading recently.

Editors may not actually have children; some of the great editors in children's publishing, such as Ursula Nordstrom and Margaret K. McElderry, never did. Editors did love books when they were children, and still do.

Their love of books is a sizable part of the reason why editors do what they do. They feel that they have a sense of what children will respond to in a book, because the editors themselves still react in the same way. And they want to be part of making more books like the ones they love. Editing is a great way to do this, because one's income is more regular than that of a writer, and one can be involved in so many more books at once. Some editors write on the side, but many do not—their creative side is entirely fulfilled by editing. The opportunity to work with creative people like writers and artists is also part of the attraction.

Outside of work, editors are a diverse group. Many do read books other than the ones they are working on, and not just children's books. Some read serious adult literature, some mysteries, some romance novels. But editors don't spend their entire lives reading. Editors may pursue outdoor sports, from softball to cross-country skiing, or belong to a choir, or quilt or do woodworking. For the most part, editors don't dress in black turtlenecks and go to smoky bars where they can discuss Sartre. So, yes, editors may live in New York but you'll find that their interests are as varied as anybody's.

Cogs in a Machine

Editors love children's books, like writers, and like working with them (or most of them, anyway). But let's face it, you don't pay their salaries, or at least not yet. The publishing company for which they work does, and they would not be doing a good job if they didn't put the interests of that company first. That doesn't mean that they'll always agree with their immediate boss. In some cases, they will argue that doing something that in the short term seems to go against the publisher's interests, such as paying a writer a larger advance, may work in the publisher's favor in the long term, by making that writer feel more loyal.

It's unrealistic, however, to expect editors to always side with you or with difficult but exciting books. They know that they must produce books that make money for their publisher, or lose their job (or, in the case of a smaller company, risk the publisher going out of business). They probably understand that side of the business all too well, and that will mean that there will be times when they don't publish a manuscript they love, because they know it will lose money. Sometimes they will take risks, and that will be more possible at some publishers than at others, but not at every opportunity. They can't.

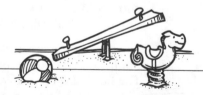

Stories from the Playground

Increasingly, editors work from home. Melanie Kroupa publishes her books at New York City's Farrar, Straus and Giroux while working nearly 200 miles away outside Boston. Many know that other well-known editors do the same, but may not know that editing is routinely becoming a satellite task, as publishing follows the trend in other industries. For example, Dana Rau worked at Children's Press as an associate editor on their early reader books. Wanting to spend some more time at home with her young son, she left—and now edits from 20 to 30 books a year, on top of writing projects which include both early readers and nonfiction.

We all would like to believe that children's publishing is different from other businesses. During the 1990s, we all learned that it isn't, when every publisher of any size laid off staff, closed imprints, or merged with another publisher, or did all of those. The business, at least in New York, is more corporate than it used to be, and editors must be able to navigate those new seas. Editors can no longer just be passionate advocates of books for children. They must also be corporate infighters. We hope you find an editor who balances those two characteristics creatively.

Vocabulary List

A **novelty book** is any book with features added to it beyond the binding and pages: foldout, die-cut holes, lift-the-flap, pop-ups, or sound chips. Novelty books are similar to but different from **book plus** products, which are books packaged with something else, such as a plush toy. Both are mainstays of mass-market publishers.

Class Rules

Mass-market publishers like Cartwheel are not a good place to send manuscripts. If you want to work with them, you'll do best to check their guidelines, which will ask that you send them such materials as samples of your work and your resumé.

Mass-Market Books for the Very Young—Bernette Ford

Bernette Ford is the editorial director of Cartwheel Books at Scholastic, a position she's held since she founded the imprint in the late 1980s. Cartwheel publishes about 100 books per year, for babies up to seven-year-olds. A sizable number of these—35 to 40—are original paperbacks for three- to six-year-olds, including books for the "Hello Reader" program. About half are board books and *novelty books*. She also does some individual hardcover titles without jackets, such as the "I Spy" books and Robert Munsch titles, including *Aaron's Hair* and *We Share Everything!* And at the top end of her list are gift books for the hardcover market, such as *A Child Is Born,* by Grace Maccarone, and books Bernette feels strongly about, such as Miles Pinkney's *Shades of Black.*

As you might guess from the kinds of books Cartwheel publishes, its books sell mainly in the mass market. The bulk of their sales are to the big bookstore chains or to retailers such as Wal-Mart and Sears. Like other mass-market publishers, many of Cartwheel's books are produced on assignment, by writers whose work and resumés are kept on file, while others are created in-house or by packagers.

Scholastic started Cartwheel specifically to have a mass-market presence, and hired Bernette from Random House, where she had been working in their well-known mass market division. At the time, Golden, Random House, and Grosset were the primary mass-market publishers for children. Now all of the big publishing houses have their own mass-market divisions, and Landolls (a major new mass-market publisher) has appeared, and the market is more competitive. It has also become more dominated by books tied to TV, movie, or other licenses, and at the same time less distinct from the trade market. There are now higher-quality mass-market books, and many mass-market books are versions of existing trade books—board books in particular are likely to be versions of hardcover picture books, rather than original creations.

Bernette enjoys the challenges of this market, and the shaping of each season's list from its beginnings to the point when she can look at it in the catalog and say, "That's a strong list." Fourteen full-time staff work with her to produce the list, along with a few regular freelance designers. Of course, since Cartwheel is a pretty large imprint and is also part of a large and successful publishing company, she must spend perhaps three-quarters of her time in meetings, and often finds that she must take time to read manuscripts at home. But Bernette Ford's work at Cartwheel Books shows just how much impact one individual can have in developing an imprint, even one publishing for the more price-driven mass market.

Successful at a Smaller Publisher—Regina Griffin

Regina Griffin came to Holiday House, the oldest children's book–only publisher in the United States, from the trade division at Scholastic. The company is celebrated as a publisher of quality hardcovers, publishing a little more than 60 books a year, two-thirds of them being picture books, both fiction and nonfiction. The rest of the list consists of novels, mostly middle-grade level, and some older nonfiction. Their market is the reverse of Cartwheel's, as they make 80 percent of their sales to the libraries and schools market. Though Holiday House would like to increase their sales in bookstores, they have been able to rely on this market due to their reputation for quality. There are advantages to publishing for it, too; most notably, they don't get unsold books returned to them.

Since Holiday House is an independent company, owned and run since the 1960s by John and Kate Briggs, Regina does not have to spend much of her time in meetings. She has a staff of only six, and must do without the corporate structure of a larger publisher; corporations may add paperwork and meetings to an editor's time, but they also take care of some tasks. As a result, she has to wear more than one hat, so her responsibilities as subsidiary rights manager (she is the one who licenses their books to book clubs, to audio and film companies, and the like), as managing editor, and as contracts manager cut into her editorial time. She gets much of her work done on the 30 titles or so for which she is personally responsible during regular hours. But she has to spend about 15 hours each week at home reading manuscripts.

Almost all the books that Holiday House publishes come in as submissions, either from one of the regulars on their list or from someone just getting started. Holiday House is known for its loyalty to its authors and illustrators, and so it comes as something of a surprise to learn that they make room for new talent. Perhaps a third of the titles on a list have a first- or second-time author or illustrator. To acquire one of these books, Regina simply has to decide that she cares enough about it to want to publish it, and then let John know about it. In many ways, Holiday House still does things the old-fashioned way, and Regina enjoys this, getting to work with straight-forward people who care first about books.

Hearing about Regina's love of the independence of Holiday House, you might be surprised to learn that when she arrived there in 1995 her experiences had been mostly at larger publishers. When she was getting started, she had worked as an editorial assistant and for an agent, developed feature films for Disney, and handled some production responsibilities at Stewart, Tabori, and Chang, a midsized independent publisher. At Scholastic, she started out by working as an editor for young adult paperbacks, especially those with movie tie-ins. Gradually she also started to work on younger paperback, general fiction, and hardcover books. Her experience with contracts and rights and production was just the mix needed for her to head the list at Holiday House, and to begin, cautiously, to innovate.

Successful at a Larger Publisher—Kate Jackson

As Associate Publisher and Editor-in-Chief of HarperCollins Children's Books, Kate Morgan Jackson oversees four imprints: HC Children's Books itself (hardcover books), HarperFestival (novelty), and HarperTrophy and the children's part of Avon (both paperbacks). The heads of the more personal imprints—Joanna Cotler Books, Laura Geringer Books, and Susan Hirschman at Greenwillow—report directly to the publisher, Susan Katz. These seven imprints together publish over 500 titles annually, some of them paperbacks of previously published hardcovers. They publish more or less equal amounts of novels, picture books, and "other," which includes novelty books, audio cassettes, boxed sets, and the like. This is a diverse program, with different imprints concentrating on different parts of the market, from bookstores to price clubs.

With such a large program to oversee, meetings make up a large part of Kate's day. These include acquisition, editorial, marketing, and business strategy planning meetings, as well as individual meetings with the editorial directors of the imprints. She does still make some time each day for editorial work, and personally publishes five to ten picture books per year. She feels that although she does less hands-on work than she did when she worked as an editor, she is still very much involved in shaping books—and the shape of HarperCollins's list.

As is the case at most large publishers like HarperCollins, most of their titles come in from authors and illustrators with whom they are already working or who have a track record elsewhere, or from authors with agents. They are also moving into the "brand" market, seeing brand names on books as a necessary way of getting the attention of booksellers and of children.

Some brands are of their own creation. HarperCollins has a rich and deep backlist, stretching back to the time of legendary editor Ursula Nordstrom, and recently supplemented by the acquisition of William Morrow's children's imprints, so they have less need than some publishers to create new programs from the ground up. Instead, they can mine their backlist; we note that Kate was personally involved in developing one such initiative, the "Little House on the Prairie" program, an extensive line you may have seen in the bookstores, including picture books and paper dolls derived from the famous novels.

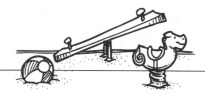

Stories from the Playground

Though the higher one goes in a publishing company, the more administrative work one does, people in managerial positions in children's publishing are still very much involved in creating books. As Kate Jackson says of her job, "I love the fundamental result of what I do—helping to create, and helping others to create, good book for kids. I feel strongly that what I do and what my team does makes a difference in the world. I love being around the creativity of the authors, the artists, the editors, the designers. I love being able to help shape and guide the direction of where this company and our list is going."

To reach her current position, Kate moved up within HarperCollins, where she arrived in 1991 after beginning her career at two college publishers. She feels very pleased to be where she is, and comments that although the company has changed and expanded from the company it was when Ursula Nordstrom was the head of the children's department, "our heart and soul is still the unmatchable backlist of books, authors, and artists that she cultivated." So HarperCollins may be a corporate publisher, but such labels miss the day-to-day reality of a place where every new person is assigned to read *Dear Genius,* the collected letters of Ursula Nordstrom, and where "her name is invoked on a regular basis in regard to what she did and what she would have thought and said." There's hope for children's publishing so long as such editors are remembered.

Getting Started—Jennifer Greene

Though we've kept saying that a lot has changed in children's publishing, we discovered when we talked to Jennifer Greene, an associate editor at Clarion Books, that at

211

least at some companies things are still done the traditional way. She knew when she left college that she wanted to work in children's publishing, but her first two jobs were with companies doing books for adults. Her break came when she took a course in children's book publishing at New York University with Virginia Duncan, who told her about an opening at Clarion. She has been with Clarion ever since.

Can You Keep a Secret?

Don't let this get out to just anyone, but we're encouraged to have discovered that a number of publishers still work by having editors sign up the books in which they believe. That's how it works at Holiday House, Clarion, and Margaret K. McElderry Books, and we suspect it's true in other places as well.

The day-to-day details of Jennifer's job are encouraging to the many who bemoan the loss of proper mentoring in publishing. Clarion is carefully set up to have senior and junior editors working together. Jennifer serves as what is known as a backup editor on some titles, working with that editor so that she will see how they handle things, perhaps take care of some tasks, and know exactly what is happening with those books. When she started, that's almost all she did. Now, she also edits five or six books each year, some of which she acquired, and some of which she had been backup editor for and inherited when the editor left.

Jennifer gets to work on a variety of books, as Clarion publishes a mix of picture books, fiction, and older nonfiction. They are particularly well known for their historical fiction and their biographies. Like Holiday House, their sales are primarily to the school and library market, though they are selling more to bookstores. Clarion's books regularly receive respected awards and their authors stay with them. Their system seems to work.

The Clarion way of doing things also means a lack of meetings. Jennifer does have meetings, but only productive ones, such as working with the art director, or a weekly session when the staff gets together and reads the slush. There's a minimum of paperwork, and Clarion doesn't even have publishing meetings. If she wants to acquire a title, she discusses it with other editors, and then gets an OK from Dinah Stevenson, the head of the imprint.

In this idyllic setting, she finds time to write thoughtful rejection letters. She loves finding new people, and has pulled manuscripts right out of the slush. Her hope is that she and the authors she discovers are setting off on their careers together. She also loves developing picture books, a deeply collaborative process involving her and the art director as well as the writer and illustrator, and working through the process that leads from the words to the pictures. Her only lament is that she wishes she could respond immediately to submissions, but she has too much to do. At least what she's doing is all satisfying. May there always be places like Clarion.

Fifty Years Later—Margaret K. McElderry

Having said repeatedly that so much has changed in children's publishing, we now must say that some things, happily, remain the same. One is that Margaret K. McElderry continues to edit children's books. She may be the last of the generation of editors with a background as a librarian, having started her career in publishing as Editor of Children's Books at Harcourt, Brace in 1945. Margaret now edits mostly at home while Emma Dryden oversees the Margaret K. McElderry imprint at Simon & Schuster.

Margaret K. McElderry Books today is a small imprint within a large company, publishing 25 or so books per year. Margaret personally edits five to eight of them, and Emma most of the rest. The list is about half picture books, some of them imported, and almost half middle grade and young adult fiction, with a few poetry and nonfiction titles. Like Holiday House, they publish primarily for the school and library market and for the independent bookstores. Margaret comments that she continues to publish the books she cares about, unaffected by the wider trends in the children's book market.

What has Margaret always published? She's known as an editor who did a lot to bring in books from foreign publishers, starting with German, Swiss, and Scandinavian authors in translation—such works as Margot Benary-Isbert's *The Ark*. She's brought in authors from Britain and Australia, including Mary Norton, Margaret Mahy, Lucy Boston, and Patricia Wrightson. She is also known for working with and developing writers and illustrators such as Irene Haas, Carol Fenner, Sarah Ellis, Eloise McGraw, Louise Borden, and X. J. Kennedy. Though she didn't say this to us, books she has edited have won just about every award there is to win, from Caldecotts and Newberys on down.

Class Rules

Margaret K. McElderry's tip for writers is a simple one: "Read, read, read."

How is it that she's been left alone to publish what she wants to? Perhaps it's because what she publishes so often seems to be what children want to read, and librarians want to buy. Or as she comments wryly, "It doesn't hurt to have a book that sells awfully well every once in a while." And so she has continued to do what she has always done, though perhaps now more very young picture books, reflecting the greater demand for them today. In her new role, she concentrates on editing, and leaves the administrative work to Emma, who reports that she, like every other editor at a corporate publisher we talked to, spends a good bit of her work day in meetings. Margaret gets to do what she likes best, working with "unusual and interesting people." In her long career, she's always felt that "it's a privilege to work with authors and artists." That humility and her life-long love of books help to explain how she's been able to help so many people create their best work.

In Good Hands?

So there you are, a peek into the lives of some editors from trade and mass-market publishing. We hope you'll agree that as long as such people are involved in children's books, there's hope that books children will love will still find a place at publishing companies, and that these portraits gave you a better sense of the person behind the name in the market guide.

The Least You Need to Know

➤ Children's book editors typically come from white, middle-class, college-educated backgrounds.

➤ Editors share a love of books, regardless of the level at which they work.

➤ Editors at independent publishers and smaller imprints get to spend more time editing.

➤ Administrative duties at larger publishers can take up much of an editor's time, but editors still find time to edit.

➤ Margaret K. McElderry, still active after a 50-year career in children's publishing, is one of the great editors of our time.

What If I Don't Like the Pictures?

You already know that manuscripts don't need to be sent to publishers with illustrations, notes for an illustrator, or suggested illustrators. What happens once you start working with a publisher on your soon-to-be book? What does a publisher expect you to do? What will a publisher allow you to do? In this chapter, we'll tell you all about the writer's involvement (or lack of it) in the illustration process.

After the Manuscript Is Done

Your book isn't finished when the manuscript is done. If it's a picture book, it will be illustrated throughout. If it's a novel, it will need a jacket illustration, and perhaps some small "spot" illustrations. Other books get illustrations too—you'll see a hen's tooth before you see a children's book without an illustration, even if it's only on the cover.

Only in the nonfiction world can you expect to have much say in that process. This can be hard to take. You see the story as yours, and so you want the book to follow your vision. Keep in mind that the story started out as yours, but turning it into a book has become a true team effort. As picture book author Tony Johnston comments, "You have to trust whoever's at the other end." The publisher coordinates this, and pays the bills. In the end, with so much of the time and expense of creating a book being the responsibility of the publisher, it's no wonder that the publisher wants to be the one deciding who illustrates a book. And after all, they've probably got more experience than you do in making that kind of decision.

Class Rules

You probably expect a lot of the illustrator of your book. They expect the same of you. Experienced illustrator Megan Halsey says this about the manuscripts she likes the best: "Most good manuscripts have crisp, clear visuals that I see in my mind's eye while I read. I look for an element of fun, a good story, and tantalizing visuals to illustrate." Illustrators build on what's already there.

Generally, publishers believe that your work stops once you have finished revising the manuscript. You have been creative with your words, and now someone else will be creative with images. You can ask to see sketches or copies of the finished art, but don't insist upon it, or you will either end up frustrated or without a contract. Even authors with "pull"—successful, experienced authors—usually don't get to do more than consult on the art. They can't insist on changes.

Of course, keeping artist and author separate isn't done just because it allows artistic freedom to the illustrator. It's also easier and less time-consuming for the publisher, because there are fewer people involved. In any case, it's a reality.

Do you just need to grit your teeth and bear it? No. You might well be able to be involved. You might be asked to get involved. Just don't expect too much.

Finding a Good Match

The process begins when the publisher—either the editor or the art director—chooses and hires the illustrator. How much you are involved depends on the publisher, and to some extent on the editor. Mass market publishers, which usually have accelerated production schedules, may keep you out of the process altogether. An editor at a trade publisher may show you samples of possible artists, but will also remind you that they make the decision.

How much influence can you have on that decision? That depends on your relationship with your editor, your approach, and your leverage. Once an editor shows you samples, she will make an effort to avoid selecting an illustrator whose work you don't like. But if you don't like any of her choices, and suggest alternatives that the editor doesn't like or are unattainable, you may be out of luck. Not liking any of her choices suggests one of two things. Either your tastes are simply different, in which case the editor will go with her taste, or you can't accept any illustrator unless it's someone you have in mind. The editor again may have to act on her own instincts.

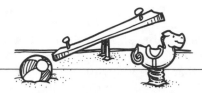

Stories from the Playground

Harold once did take an author's suggestion—because it was so obviously a great match. He was finding an illustrator for Evelyn Coleman's *The Foot Warmer and the Crow*, a powerful folktale–like story about a man escaping from slavery, and a difficult book to match up with an illustrator. He showed samples to Evelyn of the experienced picture-book illustrator he felt was the best possible choice. She asked Harold to consider Daniel Minter, an unknown artist. He reluctantly let her send him a package of samples. When Harold opened it, he knew that the strong forms on Daniel's brightly painted carved panels were just right for the book.

If do you have very specific preferences, try to express them in a way that leaves your editor some room to move. Maybe you've imagined your story all along with the dignified oil paintings of Allen Say. You can suggest that style to your editor, or comment that you've always liked his work. You may not know about them, but there are dozens of artists working in a style more or less like his. Your editor can find them, if she agrees with your suggestion. She has heavy books that showcase the work of many illustrators, and drawers full of samples.

Stories from the Playground

"In most cases, you have little or no say on the art, even if you are shown samples as a courtesy. In general, this makes good sense, since most authors think they know more about art than they do. Picture book writers must keep in mind that a picture book is a *collaboration* between writer and illustrator. However, you might ask to check the artist's preliminary sketches for consistency with your text." So says Aaron Shepard, picture book author and folktale reteller, in *The Business of Writing for Children*.

But she may not agree. Different kinds of stories call for different kinds of illustration. A light, fun story might call for loose, cartoony illustrations done in watercolor, while a serious, dramatic story might call for realistic oil or acrylic paintings. Just what to do with a story may start as a gut reaction based on experience, and an editor might want to go for a style that contrasts with the tone of your story. It's up to her, and if you are involved you should only try to engage with her on her terms.

Put your two cents-worth in, in as cheerful and positive a manner as possible. Suggest alternatives rather than vetoing what's presented. Discuss, don't demand. And if in the end the illustrator isn't to your liking, try to keep an open mind. You might be surprised by the final result, and there's a long way to go yet.

Can I See Those?

Some publishers give very specific instructions to the illustrator at every stage of the process. Others let them develop their own ideas. First, the illustrator breaks up the text and plans the sequence of illustrations. The illustrator then will explore different alternatives to a particular illustration. He may toss off 20 or 30 versions, in the form of *thumbnails,* small, very loose sketches, which help him explore possibilities. As Jeff Hopkins, an up-and-coming illustrator, puts it, "It's like brainstorming on a page." Once he's more or less settled on one, he'll rough out what he is doing with each page of the book, and may submit this preliminary work to the publisher, again in the form of thumbnails.

You will probably not see the thumbnails. Since they are done mainly to look at different compositions or to see how the book will work as a whole, they can be very crude. Should a character appear in a particular pose? What are the scenes to show so that the book has a good pacing and illustration and text appear in balance on the pages? Visual pacing and page turns at the right moments in the story come in at this stage.

You may get to see the actual sketches, and some illustrators go straight to them anyway. These might look very finished, or they might look very rough—different illustrators use this stage differently. So if you do see them, do not focus on the apparent quality of the art. Folks at the publisher can take care of that, and it will change from sketch to finish. You should be checking to see that the characters and setting match up with what you said in your words, or at least that they don't contradict it. If your story has a historical setting, are the sketches accurate with the period dress and architecture? Above all, do not complain if the illustrator has done something different from what you expected. The illustrations need to work on their own terms.

Vocabulary List

Editors or art directors often ask an artist to send them **thumbnails.** Artists use these rough thumbnail-sized sketches to try out ideas and develop the layout and pacing of a book before moving on to full-size sketches. See examples of both kinds online at www.underdown.org/cig_correct.htm.

But Her Hair Is Brown!

You also may not see the final art, but it doesn't hurt to ask. You won't see the art itself, but color copies or printouts of in-house scans. Now is not the time to ask for lots of changes, but you are another pair of eyes, and you are familiar with your manuscript (we hope) so you might catch some direct contradiction between the art and the text that no one else has.

Sometimes you won't see it at all. By the time the art comes in, the season in which the publisher wants to book to appear is fast approaching. Usually, time is short. As a result, some companies that showed you the sketches may not show you the final art. And you really may not need to see it. If there were problems, you should have pointed them out in the sketches, or if the sketches weren't clear, alerted your editor to issues she should watch for when the art came in. Now is not the time to start over.

With some kinds of publishers, mass market in particular, you may have no idea what is happening with the illustrations until you see finished books. The publisher just doesn't allow for the extra time that would be needed to show you what's happening, and to respond to any concerns you might have. This can be frustrating if you saw your characters as people and they've ended up as animals, or vice versa, or the art style is radically different from what you imagined. But this happens a lot. It's not just you being exploited or ignored! Don't take it personally. Take another look and see if you can get used to it, even appreciate it.

Many books only have an illustration on the cover, or perhaps the cover and some small illustrations scattered through the book. Some companies see jackets as being part of the marketing of the book. So they'll be more concerned with making an attractive cover than with making it accurately reflect what's in the book. The illustrator may not even read the entire book—or even be given it. Sometimes the illustrator gets detailed instructions from the art director, and a summary of the book.

You can ask to see this art, and you'll get to see it sometimes. Again, it depends on the company. As with picture books, you can serve as another pair of eyes. Harold remembers a novel whose main character wore glasses, for which the jacket artist did a nice piece showing her, but without glasses. The author caught that.

Can You Keep a Secret?

These illustrators' Web sites have sections that explain the stages in the illustration process and show examples:

Theresa Brandon at www.theresabrandon.com/

Michael Irvin at www.geocities.com/~mirvin1129/index.html

Buck Lewis at www.buck-lewis.com

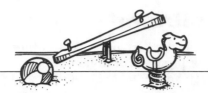

Stories from the Playground

Harold remembers witnessing a publisher's worst nightmare—a delayed book and extra money spent that will never be made back—caused by an author who had the power to approve the illustrator's work. Harold won't mention any names, but this book had three illustrators, one of whom completed illustrations for the book before the author vetoed them. For the publishing staff working on the book, this was particularly frustrating because those illustrations seemed to be exactly what the author had wanted. Publishers will often drop a project rather than grant an author this kind of power.

Helping Out with Nonfiction

As you know, nonfiction can be done a little differently than fiction is. If your nonfiction book is being illustrated, you won't be asked to go out and find photographs for the illustrations. But you may still be asked to help out, or even required to do so. There's a logic to this. While doing your research, you've probably come across good sources for the illustrator to use, whether they are pictures of animals or period costumes. Why make the illustrator find them all over again? And if you haven't found good visual references, maybe they don't exist. The publisher needs to know this, and you may need to rewrite your text so that it doesn't depend on illustrations that can't be done.

You may also have personal knowledge or experience on which you've based your book, and this can help with the illustrations too. Sneed Collard, the author of *Forest in the Clouds,* didn't read other books to write this picture book about a visit to a high-altitude "cloud forest" in the mountains of Costa Rica. He went there. And he took pictures. When the illustrator, Michael Rothman, was ready to get to work, Sneed passed on several dozen slides to him. Michael also did his own research in published sources, but those slides were a useful part of his references.

Letting Go

The illustrator makes a picture book what it is, and is important to other kinds of books as well. Once you've done the best you can with your manuscript, you need to let them do their thing.

Illustration is an act of interpretation, and there are many ways to interpret even the simplest of statements. If you'd like to see this in action, get your hands on *Mary Had a Little Lamb* as illustrated in three different ways: by Tomie dePaola in simple, bold paintings; by Bruce McMillan in bright color photographs; and by Salley Mavor in three-dimensional fabric art. If you can't find these books, ask a children's librarian if she can show you a folktale for which they have different picture-book versions. Examine the different versions. You may well prefer one, but can you really say that one is right, and one is wrong?

The same thing applies with your own book. If six different editors looked at it and chose the best possible illustrator for it, you'd end up with six different illustrators. And at least some of them would have very different styles. All of them will add things that you wouldn't have imagined.

Sometimes you may even be asked to adjust details of the story to fit in with something an illustrator wants to do. Don't reject such a request without first seriously considering it. If the changes don't affect the story itself, why not accept them? The illustrator almost entirely must conform to your world, but if a few changes will allow the two of you together to present a more seamless whole, why shouldn't you consider them? We've said it before, and we'll say it again, children's books are collaborative efforts. Be a team player, let go of your ego, and strive to make the book be the best it can possibly be.

Class Rules

You may be involved in the different stages of the illustration of your book, or you may not be. Don't make the mistake of making a fuss if you aren't, or of championing your ideas as to how your writing should be illustrated. Express your point of view and move on. The publisher may know more than you do about what's good for your book visually; even if the publisher is wrong, it has a contractual right to do what it is doing.

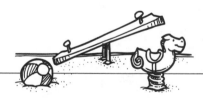

Stories from the Playground

Illustrators may bring not only their interpretation of a manuscript, but might add purely visual elements to the story. Tony Johnston's *The Quilt Story* includes a family that goes West in the nineteenth century. Tomie dePaola, the illustrator, put a cat in every picture until the point in the story when the family actually left. He knew from his own research that families heading West didn't take their pets. A reader may or may not notice that detail, but it's there, adding another level to the story.

Let the magic of illustration happen. Time after time, Harold hears from authors, when a book is done, how pleased and surprised they are with the illustrations, and what they've added to the book. The authors might have had something in mind for the illustrations; they've ended up with more than that. The illustration process does not always go well, but most times, it does. Play your part in it as best you can, and watch the magic happen.

The Least You Need to Know

➤ Editors may or may not involve you in choosing an illustrator for your book. If they do, be professional and reasonable.

➤ Illustrators usually do thumbnails and sketches before moving on to do finished art.

➤ If you get to see sketches, comment on how they match up with your text. Don't be an art critic.

➤ By the time finished art is done, you, your editor, and the art director should have found any problems. If you see the final art, don't bring up new issues.

➤ You might be asked to provide reference materials for an illustrator of a non-fiction book.

➤ Illustration can be magic! Let the magic happen to your book.

Chapter 24

The Rest of the Process

In This Chapter

➤ Who does what after you turn in your manuscript

➤ The process that turns your manuscript into a finished, sellable masterpiece

➤ Why it takes so long—book production, step by step

➤ The difference between writing a book and publishing a book

Once you hand over your manuscript, you move from writing alone to working with a team of individuals all geared toward producing the best book possible. You may think that the text from your book miraculously appears in perfect book form down the road, but it doesn't; a host of magicians work wonders. From here on out, your book becomes a collaborative effort. In the next months, there will be many others involved in designing, manufacturing, marketing, and producing your book. You most likely won't work directly with any of them, but they play a valuable part in the success of your book.

Your Editor ... and Beyond

In other kinds of publishing, there are often two editors involved with a book. One, the acquisitions editor, acquires the book, and the other, the development editor, does most of the actual editing. This division does not exist in most branches of children's publishing. Instead, one editor handles both (as well as other) functions. Most likely you'll be working with this same person until the point at which the manuscript goes

Vocabulary List

Galleys are long pages of type, not set up into the actual book pages. **Page proofs** are set up like a book. **Blues** or bluelines are used to check the final film of the book. **Color proofs** are a check on color for picture books.

to the copy editor. Edits could be substantial or minimal, depending on many variables (as we describe in Chapter 21, "Make It Better").

Then others start to get involved. Once the substantial editing is done, a copy edit occurs. After or at the same time as the copy edit, design and illustration begin. All the while, a managing editor keeps track of the schedule and the materials for your book. Finally, a production manager gets involved in planning work with a printer. Then *galleys* or final *page proofs,* which you may see, arrive. The final checks on the book are *blues* (for novels and such) or *color proofs* (for picture books), which you probably won't see. And lastly, the printer prints and binds the book. Voilá! That's the cycle of production on your book, in broad outline.

Here Some Copy; There Some Copy; Everywhere Copy, Copy!

Once the manuscript needs no further editing (in the judgment of the editor!) it moves to the copy editor. You may be thinking, "Yuck, another person messing with my words." But don't think like that. The copy editor gives your book polish—and makes you look even better as an author. The copy editor may seem picky and overbearing, asking a whole lot of questions and making changes to your sentence structure, spelling, use of capitalization, grammar, and other details. The copy editor might even question your choice of words. He or she asks all the questions and fixes any errors for your benefit, however.

The copy editor also makes sure your manuscript conforms to your publisher's "house style," which may address such matters as when numbers should be spelled out and when they should be written as numerals. The copy editor makes sure you've spelled or capitalized a name the same way throughout, double-checks the front and back matter, confirms the accuracy of names, and generally focuses on all the little things that are easy to forget or overlook.

So, although you need to check your manuscript thoroughly and turn in the best book possible, rejoice in the meticulous, keen eyes of a copy editor, which provide a further, objective check. Not many people in this world maintain the patience or mind-set to accomplish this task. Bow down before the copy editor and praise him or her. The copy editor just may prove your best buddy on the team! And in the end, if the copy editor suggests a change you don't like, you don't have to go along with it; provided that you have a reason for wanting to do it your way and your editor agrees, you can overrule the copy editor.

Some publishing houses keep a staff of copy editors; other houses hire freelance copy editors. Sometimes, picture books get copy edited in house, while longer nonfiction and novels go to freelancers. Either way, your book receives very focused scrutiny. Your copy editor is an important member of the team working on your book, though you will almost certainly have no direct contact with him or her. Instead, your editor will send you the copy edited manuscript, with handwritten notes and Post-it tags. You address the comments and questions and return the manuscript with revisions—also written on the manuscript or on Post-it tags—to your editor. If you have questions or concerns about the copy editor's suggestions, discuss them with your editor. Ultimately, it's your editor who has the final say and must be satisfied, though she will defer to the copy editor on many issues.

Class Rules

If the copy editor is making changes with which you don't agree, you can say so—but you better have a reason. Needing to have your characters use slang so that you can capture the flavor of their speech is a good reason. Thinking it "looks better" to spell out all numbers below 100 when the publisher prefers to stop at 10 is not.

High-Fashion Time: Designers

The "look" of your book comes from the conceptualization of the designer and, if there is one, the illustrator. The designer brings the text of your book alive with the cover design, the width of the margins, the regular typeface, the display type (the type used for titles and headers)—everything. Especially in children's books, the tasks of the designer vary greatly. There remains a huge difference between designing, say, a novel and a picture book. But in a nutshell, the art director, who oversees the designer, and the designer or designers of the publishing house, create the actual design. They decide how all the various elements of a book (the ones we reviewed in Chapter 7, "What's in a Book? A Guided Tour") will look on the printed page.

Usually the designer suggests several design possibilities. The editor, illustrator, and sometimes you sit down and choose the actual design. Today, the designer will implement that design using a computer program such as QuarkXPress. In the past, he or she would take the typeset pages or galleys from the printer and paste them onto thin cardboard, often called "mechanicals," to show how the pages would look.

If there are illustrations, they are incorporated into the design. Some publishers have high-tech scanning equipment in-house that allows the designer to generate electronic images from the original illustrations. Other publishers outsource this task to companies that specialize in fine resolution scanning. When this is the case, the designer prepares the original art for scanning. When the scanned images come back, the designer incorporates them into the layout.

Just the Facts, Ma'am

The fact checker—like the copy editor—looks closely at the text, possibly the illustrations as well, to detect any discrepancies that may exist. So this happens later in the process. Unlike the copy editor, the fact checker isn't concerned about grammar. He or she focuses specifically on factual information. Fact checkers play a role in nonfiction, but may also be called in on historical fiction. Are the names, dates, and places accurate? Are there any anachronisms? Are there any contradictions? Did this person really say that? Is the information up to date? So many questions, so little time. The fact checker then tracks down the answers to ensure your book does not carry any mistakes or omissions!

100-Proof

Haven't enough people looked closely at the book? Well, no. The proofreader takes the typeset pages and checks to make sure that the book as typeset actually follows your manuscript and all the little changes made to it in the copy editing stage. She also looks—another pair of eyes!—for obvious or glaring mistakes before the book is shipped off to the printer for manufacturing. Look upon your proofreader at the last person in the line to make sure all is well. Sometimes everyone from you to the editor to the copy editor can miss something, and the new set of eyes of the proofreader catches it.

Lights! Camera! Action! The Production Manager

While the proofers, designers, checkers, and editors are working their magic, the production manager is scrambling to put the vision of your book into tangible form and still keep costs within budget. The production manager decides what printer will print your book—and when. The production manager literally finds and buys the paper on which your book is printed. Children's books oftentimes incorporate interesting design elements—like the sparkles on the rainbow fish in *The Rainbow Fish*. A production manager was the person who found the paper, the sparkles, and the printer to produce the book—all while keeping the costs within budget.

When the book is all done—with a complete design, all elements in place, from the art on the front of the jacket to the bar code on the back—the editor or designer hands it to the production manager. He or she sends it to the printer, and coordinates the rest of the process. The printer takes the files from the production manager and makes film from them, following the design and making sure that illustrations appear where they should. But checking that isn't just up to the printer. The publisher may have already produced proofs for checking, but the printer will do it again. First come "blues," a blue-colored printing from the film, which are checked by the publisher. If the book has color art, the printer may also produce color proofs, showing what the art will really look like. Usually there isn't time for an author to see these so just your editor and the designer review them—and then the book is printed, and bound, and shipped. It will probably take a few weeks (if printed in North America) or a couple of months (if printed abroad) to make it to the publisher's warehouse, but it's on its way.

Can You Keep a Secret?

Don't complain to your editor if the grade of paper or type of binding for your book isn't what you envisioned. Paper and binding costs are a major part of the cost of a book. A production manager may search far and wide to find the grade of paper necessary for a high-quality, glossy picture book, but not be able to get it at the right price. Cost and quality always have to be juggled.

Why do publishers take the time to send books overseas to be printed? In a word: cost. Printing a full-color book isn't cheap, but it's less expensive in Hong Kong and other parts of the Far East, due to lower wages (and, so we're told, less strict safety regulations). When perhaps twenty cents per copy can make the difference between making or losing money on a picture book, the opportunity to save that much or more by printing overseas is hard to pass up.

So That's Why It Takes So Long!

Considering the process, no wonder it can take up to three years from the time an editor buys your book until the book hits shelves! Especially with picture books, where an illustrator may take up to a year to create the panels, don't expect your book to make it into stores with any great speed. Your editors will give you timelines for the production of your book. Be patient—the wait is worth it. When a book follows the correct process thoroughly and meticulously, the end result will be better. Better to take three years for a beautifully produced, well-selling picture book than a year for a slipshod, weak, and cheap book that no one wants to buy, right?

You can expect …

➤ Several months in the editing stage, once your editor gets to the book.

➤ A couple of months for copy editing.

➤ A year or more for illustration and design.

➤ A few more months for proofreading and fact checking (if it's needed).

➤ Several months for layout and printing and shipping.

That's a long time, though it can be shorter if your book is not a picture book—and it can be even longer if the publisher's schedule is full. But at least when your book is done you can go find it in the stores, right? Not exactly. The publisher first wants to get it to reviewers and show it to booksellers, as we will explain in the following chapters. So it's a few months more waiting while that happens. And *then* your book will be on the market. Woo-hoo!

The Least You Need to Know

➤ Where your writing was a solo process, you now belong to a team of individuals all working toward a common goal: the production of your book.

➤ Although the people working on your book may make changes, try not to take the changes personally. The editors are there to make your book the best it can be.

➤ Several people—the copy editor, fact checker, and proofreader—will check and recheck everything in your book. Get used to the constant queries.

➤ The designer and the production manager are the people who create the final look and feel of a book.

➤ Understand that producing a children's book may take up to three years from start to finish (beyond the time you took to write it). Be patient.

Part 5
My Book Is Published! Now What?

On that happy day when your children's book is published, you might think that your troubles are over. Well, not quite, because it still has to be marketed and publicized. We'll explain what your publisher probably will do, might do, and almost certainly won't do. If you want to play a role, we'll give you tips on how to do that productively, from doing your own publicity to putting on bookstore events and doing school visits.

Though they may not come with your first book, we'll tell you about some of the awards and other forms of recognition you can expect, and give you some guidance on building your career. You want to publish other books, you'll need to figure out what to do when your book goes out of print, and how to bring in income between royalty checks. If you haven't already, take yourself seriously.

Chapter 25

What Are You Doing for Me?

In This Chapter

➤ The scoop on publisher's catalogs and what they do for the sale of the book

➤ Who reviews your book and why it matters

➤ The difference between periodicals that might discuss your new book—from newspapers to magazines, from local to national

➤ How bookstores handle your book's arrival

➤ The long-shot publicity machines your publisher may approach before the book hits the shelves

---

After you've spent all your time on the creation of your baby—your book!—and after the publisher has spent all that money and time on the actual production of your book, you may expect that it's show time for the publisher in ye olde publicity mill. Well, yes and no. There are certainly standard things a publisher may do to market your book to the public. But many writers assume that the publisher will launch a major publicity campaign and dole out the big bucks to get the word out about your book. In this chapter, we'll give you the lowdown on what you realistically can expect the publisher to do in the marketing of your book.

I'm in the Catalog!

The first place you might find proof-positive that your book really, really, *really* will someday arrive at stores across the nation is in the publisher's catalog. Until you see your book listed with a description (and perhaps even a photo of the cover) within the

Vocabulary List

The **pub date** of a book is the official (and somewhat arbitrary) date when a publisher says it will be available in stores. Reviews of the book are often timed to come out before the pub. date—but the book itself may have already left the publisher's warehouse weeks earlier, or may have been delayed.

pages of a publisher's catalog, your book just isn't real—especially since, as we've mentioned, a children's book can take up to three years to produce. Savor that first recognition you have that, "My goodness! I'm actually an author. That's my book!"

For their part, publishers produce catalogs to showcase all of their new offerings each season as well as their strong backlist titles. You should expect your publisher to list your book in the catalog that most closely aligns with the arrival of your book—the publication date of your book. For example, let's say that your book has a *pub date* of March 2003. You might expect the publisher to print the offering in its Fall/Winter 2002–2003 catalog, if it releases three catalogs per year. If it does two, then it will be in the Spring 2003 catalog (the other season being the Fall).

Catalogs are produced for a variety of people. Sales representatives within the publishing house use them when they go on sales calls to promote new books at bookstores, conferences, and other venues. The publicity department may send catalogs to contacts within the publishing journalistic community or to book reviewers. And if a person calls the company and asks for a catalog, more than likely the publishing house will send one out. The publisher's catalog is the first step in getting the news out that your book is available.

Vocabulary List

Publishers may produce an advance version, also called **bound galleys** (from the old term for the long pages created when a book was typeset, before it was laid out in pages). This version, typically unedited and usually without artwork, is sent to reviewers who will write about the book before its arrival in stores.

The Big Mouths

In addition to listing your book in the catalog, most publishers send out advance copies (if it's a picture book) or *bound galleys* (if it's a novel or longer nonfiction) of your book to major reviewers. "OK," you may say, "but who are they?" Certain publications always receive lists and advance copies of your book. These reviewers and publications are the driving force in many ways for the sales of books, especially to libraries. Some of the places your publisher will send notification and a copy of your book are …

➤ *Publishers Weekly.* The review section of *Publishers Weekly* is called "Forecasts." You'll get more booksellers reading this than the others.

➤ *Booklist.* The publication of the American Library Association. Thoughtful, respected reviews.

➤ *School Library Journal. SLJ* reviews the most books per year, though the quality of their reviews varies.

➤ *Kirkus Reviews.* Slightly more selective then *SLJ* and more literary in approach.

➤ *The Horn Book Magazine* and *The Horn Book Guide.* Strictly children's literature. *The Horn Book Magazine* comes out every other month and doesn't have space for many reviews. The *Guide* comes out twice a year with more reviews.

These trade publications exist to report on the upcoming titles and the publishing industry. Booksellers as well as librarians read them. Sometimes, Hollywood producers and directors read them to gain rights to books they think will make good films.

The publisher wants these trade journals to review and write about your book, thereby generating sales. Think about it. These publications are the trade journals of the industry. If you're a corporate pilot in charge of procuring planes for the corporation, you probably read *Business Aviation* magazine. Well, book people read *Publishers Weekly* (*PW* for those in the know), *Booklist, Library Journal, Kirkus Reviews,* and *Horn Book.* In some cases, these magazines put a star or a pointer before reviews of particularly recommended books—if you get stars from more than one magazine, your book will do well.

The Other Mouths

But hold on there a minute—the big mouths aren't the only ones available to blab about your book. In many cases, a publisher will send a galley or an announcement to other publications and people and alert them, too. This isn't to say that a full-scale publicity offense will happen, but perhaps there'll be a little skirmish. To win such a skirmish, a publisher may target local or specialized publications—and you shouldn't hesitate to make suggestions to your publisher's marketing department. If your publisher feels it's worthwhile, they'll send information and maybe a copy of your book to these places.

Class Rules

Don't depend upon your publisher to send review copies of your book to multiple media outlets—especially local papers and magazines. Check first with your publicist to find out if there are plans to blitz your hometown or appropriate national publications. If not, feel free to send a news release and a copy of the book yourself.

Can You Keep a Secret?

What does catalog copy look like and what does it include? Typically, the catalog entry of your book will include all the necessary items that someone or some business might need to buy your book. These include items like ...

➤ A picture of the cover of your book.

➤ The title.

➤ The author's and illustrator's names.

➤ A brief description.

➤ Biographies of the author and illustrator.

➤ The publication date.

➤ The ISBN—International Standard Book Number.

➤ The price.

➤ The trim size.

➤ Recommended age level.

Elsewhere, the catalog will offer instructions on how to order the book, which might differ depending upon who you are—a single customer versus a bookstore.

Local Yokels

What's the appeal of local publications, those papers and media outlets in your own backyard? They look for the local hook of any story. You possess, for example, a better chance of garnering publicity from the *Sacramento Bee* if you live in Sacramento than if you don't.

Though it costs money for a publisher to send out review copies of books, your publisher may want to grab this natural publicity opportunity and send copies with a release to the local reviewers of children's books. The best thing you can do is provide your publisher with a list of all the local outlets—television stations, radio stations, newspaper columnists, and regional magazines—with a contact name, the address, and a phone number. Then sit back and (you hope) watch the interviews and reviews

234

roll in. The more organized publishers will request this information from you. Provide it whether you are asked or not.

Mommy Says I'm Special!

In addition to targeting local publications for review, sometimes a publisher will target specialty publications. For example, let's say you write a nonfiction book about gardening for children. Your publisher may want to send copies of the book to national, glossy women's magazines that include sections on activities with children—such as *Ladies Home Journal* or *McCall's*. Many parenting magazines might like to focus on the book or include the title in a roundup of gardening books for kids in a spring issue of the respective magazine. And don't forget the gardening magazines.

You get the point. Technically, these magazines are not child-focused. The connection between your book and the magazine may not be obvious. But for the publicity manager, the link may prove fantastic for the marketing machine.

For your part, if you believe you know of some unique ways to position your book in various specialty publications, share them with your publisher. And again, make a list with all the contact information for the marketing or publicity representative.

I'm in the Newspaper!

Up until now, we've been talking about your publisher sending out review copies of your book to prominent reviewers and targeted publications. But oftentimes, a publisher formulates a kind of secondary list of people and publications to which only a *press release* or a catalog and request for review copies goes out. There may be hundreds of names on such a list.

As an example, let's say that your publicity manager knows of a freelance journalist who frequently writes about children's books. This freelancer may exist on a press release only—if the freelancer gains an interest in the book from the press release, then he or she can fill out a review copy request and receive a review copy. Many times, the publisher keeps reviewers from smaller media markets on this list. Though *The New York Times* may receive the galley of your cool picture book, *The Seattle Times* may receive only the press release. Then if the *The Seattle Times* shows an interest, of course the publisher will send a copy of the book!

Vocabulary List

A **press release** alerts the media to the publication of a title. Beyond providing an overview of the title, a release may "tie-in" to an event or a news angle—depending upon the book—to garner further interest from the media. Press releases list pertinent information, too, like whom to contact for a review copy and the cost of the book.

Not on the Shelf But in the Store

Publishers sometimes send advance copies of books to bookstores. Generally, bound galleys are too expensive to produce many of; only if there are enough galleys left after the "big mouth" reviewers get theirs will the publisher forward copies to bookstores. Or if the publisher is trying especially hard to generate interest in a book, they may print more up. If this is done, select bookstores receive the copies. You may be wondering why these are sent at all, especially when the store can't even sell the book, as final copies may not be available yet. Quite simply, the mailing allows the booksellers to read the book and generate a buzz about the title. For this reason, in children's publishing, an edgy, hip young-adult galley is more likely to reach a bookseller than a picture book galley is.

Another reason to send booksellers advance copies, of course, is to excite the manager about ordering copies and talking up the book to customers once it arrives. The more prominent the title is in the bookseller's mind, the better chance that bookseller will tell customers about the book.

Can You Keep a Secret?

Want to increase your chances of having a producer for a national talk show choose your book as a focus for the show? Provide your publicist with 1) suggested show topics and 2) suggested interview questions. By doing this, you save the publicist time and make the producer's job easier.

Going Long and Deep

What author doesn't think of it—sitting on *Oprah* chatting with the queen of talk about a book? Come on—we all fantasize about that sort of huge publicity hit! We're reasonably certain that visions of *Oprah* float in your head. Not to shatter your Oprah or other talk show dreams, but publishers rarely send review copies of a title to a major talk show unless the book holds some kind of universal appeal (to adults) or news hook. Moreover, what publicists know is that the producers of these shows rarely handpick a book—especially a children's book—for discussion on a show. It's the author or the author's story that does it. So if you are Jamie Lee Curtis hawking your children's tale, you have an edge.

Nevertheless, sometimes your publisher will find a reason or hook to send Oprah your book. And sometimes you can help them out with suggestions. If you feel strongly about it, and provided that you keep your publisher informed, you might even launch your own campaign. Lori Mitchell, author/illustrator of *Different Just Like Me*, got her book onto *Oprah* and *Maury Povich*, as well as local television. For more information about her book, which will help you figure out what helped it get on TV, visit the Web site at www.differentjustlikeme.cc. This won't work for everyone, and it's a long shot at the best of times, but efforts in this area do pay off.

Publicity efforts are labor-intensive. You can count on some basics but if you want something unusual to happen, you may have to do it yourself.

The Least You Need to Know

➤ You can expect a basic publicity effort from your publisher to promote you and your book.

➤ Nearly all publishers send prepublication review copies of books to prominent review magazines, such as *Publishers Weekly, Booklist, School Library Journal,* and *Kirkus Reviews.*

➤ In addition to sending galleys to the major reviewers, a publisher may send them to local media outlets on your behalf, or to specialty publications, and will probably do a mailing to a secondary tier.

➤ Bookstores sometimes also receive advance copies of your book to generate a buzz about the title with booksellers.

➤ Don't count on your publisher automatically sending your book to national talk shows such as *Oprah.*

Chapter 26

Fun Stuff and Bragging

In This Chapter

➤ Great freebies—but someone has to pay for them

➤ How publishers get creative with marketing

➤ The difference between a publisher's ads and co-op ads

➤ Ways in which publishers help bookstores market your book

➤ Why marketing does not necessarily make for a best-seller

In the last chapter, we discussed what you can expect the publisher to do on your behalf in the publicity and book review arena. In this chapter, we'll look at some things that the publisher may or may not do for you, depending upon the book. We'll also get into how ads are used in publishing and what it *doesn't* take to make a best-seller.

Freebies

You may have many ideas about how to market your book—how to showcase it at libraries, bookstores, and schools, and freebies that are given out to generate interest in your awesome book. When you think of freebies, think of bookmarks with the cover of the book on one side and a brief overview on the other; posters of the cover of the book; or postcards, again displaying the cover and sent out as a notice of the impending release of your book.

First, the bad news: Publishers rarely go deep into their pockets for this sort of free stuff—free for the customer, that is—because the cost often outweighs the benefits of added sales.

Next, the good news: Sometimes a publisher does produce such give-aways to help market your book. In fact, when a publisher creates and produces a freebie, it does so to generate name recognition instead of sales.

X Marks the Spot

Bookmarks are probably one of the most common freebies that a publisher will produce. A publisher may produce bookmarks for bookstores, where they can be used as mini-advertisements, either stuffed in the bags at the checkout or put on a display table for customers to take. Sometimes the publisher will produce bookmarks for teachers and classroom use. Let's say that you will be giving a reading of your picture book to several classes of second-graders. If your publisher has created bookmarks promoting your book, you'll be able to give them out to keep you and your work in front of the teachers and the children.

Put That Up!

Because posters are so expensive, publishers usually produce them only for "long-term" authors and their titles. A publisher might produce a poster, say, for a book with longevity like *Where the Wild Things Are* or *Rainbow Fish*. The poster is then used by bookstores in window displays, in libraries for decoration, and in schools to promote reading. Publishers give these posters out to booksellers, librarians, and teachers at conventions, and also mail them out on request.

Occasionally a publisher may produce a poster for a book that isn't by an author it has been working with over many books and years. This standout title may possess a lot of buzz or be one for which the publisher hopes to create buzz. In either of these cases, the decision to create a poster is made by the publisher's marketing department well before the book is published. You'll find that you won't be able to lobby for it. If it happens, accept it as the gift that it is.

Postcards from the Edge

Postcards are another way the publisher may generate interest in your book. They're a great way to invite people to an event surrounding your book. You may think this is an ideal way to provide the media and your pals information about your next local event, but find your publisher unwilling to foot the tab for the creation of the postcards. You may be able to make a deal with the publisher: You agree to buy the postcards if the publisher pays the postage bill.

Do-It-Yourself

If you find that your publisher won't budge on any of these marketing materials, you may want to produce some yourself. Bear in mind that endeavors like event kits and postcards require time and money. The efforts may not yield desired results.

Creative Genius

Publishers don't limit their marketing ideas to postcards and posters. In fact, publicity and marketing departments spend hours and days thinking up interesting ways to promote your book—as inexpensively as possible. At Charlesbridge, for example, they sent out lunch bags to elementary school teachers with cartoon bugs printed on them and the title of the book *Bugs for Lunch*. The paper bags proved inexpensive to produce and, thus, worthwhile for the publisher to manufacture.

Some publishers create complete party kits for the booksellers to run story hours by. Or displays to showcase the book at the checkout stands of the stores—called dumps!

For Teacher's Eyes Only

Since children's book publishing often maintains an educational focus, naturally publishers strive to gain the attention of teachers. Just as helping the producer with story ideas linked to your title may provide you a publicity hit, creating materials aligned with a title that will help the teacher in lesson planning will win you advocates. Consider the teacher who comes across a kit for a book published about rain forests and he just happens to have planned on delivering a unit on rain forests. The kit includes a taped conversation with the author, and suggested review questions, handouts, and project ideas—all based upon rain forests and the book.

Buying Ads

Publishers think carefully before investing in advertisements—basically because there remain so many better income-generating marketing ideas than buying an ad. When they do buy ads, they'll buy them for their own reasons, so don't try to lobby for them. Nevertheless, ads sometimes work. Let's look at when or why a publisher might buy an ad.

Class Rules

Before devoting yourself to postcard production and bookmark creation, consider how long it will take to complete whatever publicity feat you're choosing to accomplish. Then, factor in how much money you stand to make and whether your project is worthwhile.

Can You Keep a Secret?

Many publishers just don't bother creating teacher's guides for one book. Instead, the publisher links several books by theme or content or author and produces one teacher's guide for several books. The same goes for marketing flyers. A publisher may list several holiday books, for example, on one glossy flyer and publicize all of them for the cost of one leaflet.

The Bookstore

Bookstore managers, owners, and large chain buyers read *Publishers Weekly* (PW) religiously. Many purchases occur because of a review or ad seen in this trade publication. A marketing manager might be more inclined to drop the bank on an ad in a publication that reaches such incredible numbers of professionals in the publishing arena.

But hold on! We are not saying that a children's book publisher will buy an ad for a single juvenile title as a standard procedure. Within the children's publishing world, ads are targeted according to special issues. Let's say *Publishers Weekly*'s editorial calendar calls for a children's book focus (as it does twice a year, when the new season's books are highlighted). Knowing that the magazine will devote page upon page to children's books may incline the publishing house to display some strong, upcoming titles in an ad in the special issue, or perhaps to list all their new titles in one comprehensive ad.

Another ad trick children's book publishers use is purchasing an advertisement featuring several books. Let's go back to the holiday theme. If a publisher decides to promote several Christmas, Kwanzaa, and Hanukkah books, the house may place an ad for all the titles within the pages of *Publishers Weekly*. Now buying an ad in *PW* becomes a very targeted—and cost-effective—way to reach numerous booksellers simultaneously.

Publishers hope that these strategically placed ads bring increased revenue and sales.

The Library

Libraries buy books. And if your book appears to be a title that librarians may snatch up and buy—perhaps an exciting nonfiction title—your publisher may place an ad in *Booklist* or *School Library Journal* to draw attention to the book amid all the other titles out there and get it noticed. Even after publication, if a book gets a starred review, or gets named to an award list, a publisher may take out an ad to point that out to that audience.

The Consumer

You've seen the ads for adult novels in the margins of magazines, but what about children's books or young adult literature? Quite simply, a publisher may—again if applicable and thoughtfully targeted—purchase an ad in a consumer magazine to promote your book. Let's say that the publishing house acquired the rights to all novels based upon a popular teen television series. The show tears up the ratings every week. To piggyback on the success of the show, the publisher may decide to place an ad in a magazine such as *Seventeen,* a consumer publication. The ad targets the youth who actually read the novels.

Or a publisher may buy an ad in a consumer publication such as *USA Today* or a national magazine if a celebrity is associated with the title. Perhaps the celebrity is making an appearance in an area. The publisher may take the opportunity to place an ad in the local edition of *USA Today,* for example, to further position the book.

A publisher probably will not buy an ad in *The New York Times* or some other newspaper your friends read, because the cost is so high, and the ad will not reach enough people who might actually buy the book. Don't feel bad if you don't get an ad in such a newspaper. An ad is an investment, and it has to have a good return.

The Teacher

And again, since many teachers use books as resources or tools in their classroom, children's book publishers may focus an ad campaign on teacher's journals and trade publications. Let's say you just wrote a great easy-reader book—it's imaginative, fun to read, and everyone at the publishing house seems to think it's the coolest book with built-in teacher appeal to hit the shelves in a decade. Well, then, an ad may find its way into a teacher's magazine or journal.

Do you see the point? Advertisements are rarely placed, but when they are the marketing department thinks about the most appropriate venue—then targets it with an ad.

Ground–Level Marketing

We've talked about some pretty big ways to market—ads, freebies, teacher's kits—but there remain other smaller ways to get your book out there, too.

Did Hennie Pennie Live in a Chicken Coop or a Co-Op?

Let's say you book yourself to read your latest picture book at Barnes & Noble during story time the following month. Wouldn't it be nice to place an ad in the local paper advising the public of your reading? Yes, it would and may be possible for the bookstore to place that ad through the use of *co-op money*. In this situation, the bookstore and the publisher share the cost of an ad—cooperatively.

Vocabulary List

Publishers will reimburse bookstores for the costs of ads, events, or displays through **co-op money.** The bookseller usually is limited to a percentage of their actual sales of the publisher's books; if they sold $2,000 worth of books the previous month, they may be able to spend $100 in co-op money.

Bookstore Giveaways

Sometimes a publisher will initiate contests on a smaller scale to generate interest in a particular title or titles. The contest may focus on either the consumer or the bookseller. A bookstore may compete, for instance, in a "Best Window Display Showcasing *If You Give a Moose a Muffin*" contest. The publisher appoints a winner who receives a prize, like a trip or a certificate. Consumer-oriented contests may include drawings for books during story time or discounts on certain titles.

Yet several more ways to draw attention to your title and market it to the public!

Making a Best-Seller

You should know that marketing often makes for arbitrary results. You may think that if your book is good enough, and if your publisher will just buy that ad in *PW,* your book will make it to *The New York Times* best-seller list. Unfortunately, what makes a best-seller is often a tie to a celebrity or a tie-in to some sort of entertainment.

In fact, go check out *PW*'s list of top-selling children's books for the previous year. You'll find that in virtually all cases, the best-sellers were linked to a television show, a movie, or a famous person. Just look at the success of the *Blue's Clues* books. These simple paperback books continue to fly off the shelves because the show is so popular with children.

Stories from the Playground

We analyzed the *Publishers Weekly* list of the top 20 best-selling new hardcover books in 1999. Two were Harry Potter books. Ten were connected to a TV show or a movie. One was connected to a well-known consumer product (Cheerios). Three were by or connected to celebrities. Three were by famous children's authors or illustrators. Only one— *The Dance,* by Richard Paul Evans—could be said to have been turned into a best-seller by the publisher's promotional efforts. In this case, the publisher seemed to have pushed the book for its strong appeal to adults.

Please don't think that we're saying your book will never sit among these best-sellers; it may, but that takes time, and a certain amount of luck. But on the flip side, if your children's book never sees *The New York Times* book review or best-selling lists, don't despair. Steady sales and full speed ahead. Please know you can still be a successful, best-selling children's book author without any of your friends and family realizing it and without seeing your name next to J. K. Rowling. In fact, many children's book authors forge a highly successful career without ever seeing their titles on a best-seller list. Getting there requires hard work and longevity in the business. Don't settle for one book. Just keep cranking out the masterpieces that children love.

The Least You Need to Know

➤ Many great marketing ideas exist—such as bookstore party kits and bookmarks—but it's questionable whether they actually increase sales.

➤ Advertisements can be expensive, so publishers specifically target particular publications for optimal exposure.

➤ In children's book publishing, rarely will you find an ad for just one book. Instead, publishers cluster several like-themed titles into one advertisement.

➤ Though most everyone maintains aspirations of having a best-selling book, best-sellers are typically connected to celebrities, TV shows, or movies, when it comes to children's books.

Chapter 27

Hey, Listen to Me!

In This Chapter

➤ How to prepare your publicity campaign

➤ How to improve your chances that the publisher will take notice of your marketing ideas

➤ How to formulate an angle to generate interest in your book

➤ Ways to approach and target different media outlets

As an author, you may want to go above and beyond what the publisher offers in the way of publicity. You may hold a million and one publicity and marketing ideas that you'd like to see implemented. On the flip side, you may not possess a clue how to generate a buzz about your book. In this chapter, we'll show you how to nudge the publisher into doing the little extras, and how to do your own publicity, if you feel you need to do the little extras yourself.

Nudge, Don't Push

There is a fine line between bugging and harassing the publisher with your ideas and contributing constructively to the marketing and publicity of your book. If you do have ideas, we recommend approaching the publisher in a professional manner. The publicist for your book will want to know of any ideas you have regarding the publicity for your book. In fact, when coauthor Lynne worked as a publicist, she would ask the authors to prepare a list of their publicity ideas. Marketing departments may also send a detailed questionnaire. If you get one, fill it out thoroughly. It will be the basis of publicity materials about you and your book.

Once you offer your ideas, let go! Publicists, like your editors, live a harried and hectic workday. When she was a publicist, it wasn't unusual for coauthor Lynne to receive 10 calls or more an hour. The last thing your publicist wants to hear is your voice three out of the 10 calls each hour. Instead, politely extend your list of publicity ideas and wait to hear from the publicist. A follow-up call about two weeks after submitting your ideas, however, is OK.

Coauthor Harold recalls a story from an author at a conference who thought that planetariums might be really great places to publicize her children's book about stars and constellations. The author went down to her local library and researched all the planetariums and natural history museums in the nation—about 2,000 in all. She took the list to her publisher, who put together a pamphlet about her book (and a few others) and sent out a mailing to all the establishments on her list. The mailing proved incredibly successful for the publisher and the sale of the book.

Class Rules

Publicists know that the best resource in a book's publicity campaign is the author. Oftentimes, the author taps into a creative tie to the book that yields a huge response from the public. It behooves you and the publicist to work in unison. So get to know your publicist and give him or her your ideas—just don't bother the publicist with a million phone calls to share trivial ideas.

Simply, the author provided the publishing house with the tools necessary to complete the marketing idea. Though the endeavor took hours for the author—researching all the addresses and locations of planetariums and natural history museums, the work paid off.

Now let's pretend that the author made the suggestion of sending a pamphlet to planetariums, but didn't pursue it any further. Would the publicist have had time to sit down in the library and research the mailing list? No way. By going that extra mile for the publicist, the author helped the marketing idea come to fruition.

Likewise, let's pretend the author told the publicist the great idea, did not create the list, then called the publicist every day to see if a marketing pamphlet had been designed and sent out. Yikes! Rude, rude, rude. More than likely, the publicist would have erased the messages on voice mail with the initial recognition of the person behind the voice. Don't let this happen to you, so nudge, don't push, and be ready to roll up your sleeves and help!

Lend a Helping Pen

Want to know a great way to move along a productive publicity campaign? Offer to write the press materials for the publicist. Consider this: A publicist will not have unlimited time to devote to your book, and may only be able to send it to a standard review list. If you want a wider campaign in such a case, offer to help. If you create the materials for the press kit, the time spared the publicist creating the items can then be used in follow-up calls or other marketing-related endeavors for the title.

Follow these steps when approaching your publicist or marketing manager about your ideas. Make an initial phone call and politely say, "Hi, I'm _____, the author of _____. I'd like to help you in any way I can and actually have some publicity ideas. Where might I send them?" If you feel comfortable offering to write the press materials, do it. Put together a packet of *clips,* your ideas, and any press materials you have written and mail them to the publicist. Remember to type! Keep in mind that you can use the materials if the publicist doesn't. Wait a few weeks before calling. Give the publicist a chance to look over the materials. Don't bug the publicist. If it appears that your ideas will not be implemented, start using them yourself if you have the time.

Class Rules

If you prepare elements for a press kit, save everything to a computer disk. This way, your publicist will be able to quickly make corrections or edit the documents. Otherwise, someone will need to retype each piece into the computer.

The following are several items that may go in a *press kit:*

➤ **A press release/new book release.** This announces the publication of your book, briefly describes it, and contains contact information. If something about the book holds a topical element, weave that into the release. For example, let's say your children's book is about atomic energy and scientists just found a way to harness atomic energy to cure cancer! The release can touch on the newsworthy aspect of your book.

➤ **An author biography.** This is typically one page detailing the life and writing career of the author. Who better to write this than you?

Vocabulary List

A **press kit** is a folder of materials about your book sent to the media—newspapers, radio and television stations, journalists, magazines—to alert these outlets to your book's release. The best press kits link the book with a newsworthy item or a hook.

Vocabulary List

A **clip** is a copy of an article that you've either written or has been written about you or your book.

➤ **Clippings from previous articles written about your book or you.** The press kit may contain the clip from a review in a magazine such as *Booklist* or *Publishers Weekly*—especially if your book received an outstanding review.

➤ **A minifeature.** Written like an article, it actually contains much of the same information as the press release, just in a different format. Since it's actually an article, publications may publish it directly. For example, if your kit includes a short feature detailing your struggle to rebuild your home after a fire, which resulted in a children's book about fire protection, your local paper—which doesn't always have the reporter to spare—may use your feature.

➤ **Suggested show or event ideas.** If your book can spawn a demonstration that might prove of interest to a talk show, such as a morning show, you may list the ideas together. For example, your book shows kids how to care for pets. You may write a suggested show topic, detailing the devastating effect of animal neglect and offering ways to help kids really care for their pet and ensure a safe and long life for the kittens and puppies.

➤ **Suggested interview questions.** Again, if a journalist becomes intrigued by your book, the more work you can have ready for the journalist the better chance the writer will do the story.

So check to see if your work will be used. Then do what you can and offer it all to the publicist. In fact, just send a letter with a computer disk on which you've saved all the documents and let the publicist know that she should feel free to use any, all, or none of the materials. You can't imagine how much the publicist will love you!

"I Did It My Way"

Frank Sinatra crooned it in his tune "My Way." Once you learn where your publicist's efforts end, you then need to decide how much of "your way" needs to be implemented. Essentially, how much time and energy do you want to devote to publicizing and fueling sales of your book? If you want to self-publicize, take a look at what you need to do.

In the end, you may decide to let go of your book to the marketing department in a similar way to letting go of it to the illustrator. They know their business, and even if they don't do everything you'd like them to, they will do what in their judgment is likely to pay off. So self-publicize by all means, but don't feel that what you do will make or break your book.

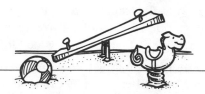

Stories from the Playground

Don't get too caught up in your campaign. Bruce Balan offers this comment: "I spent many years becoming quite well-versed in self-promotion. I've been interviewed by scores of magazines, radio programs, and newspapers. I've created brochures, flyers, and review sheets. I've sent mailings to bookstores. I've spent money to hire a publicist. I've thrown publication parties. I've traveled to, and spoken at, conferences, trade shows, schools, and seminars. And I've come to a few conclusions:

➤ If your publisher is not supportive of your book, it probably doesn't matter what you do.

➤ Even if your publisher is supportive of your book, there are no guarantees of success.

➤ The authors I most admire are those who write well. Not those who promote well."

You Gotta Have an Angle

In order to publicize a book, even a children's book, you need an angle. You need to make your book stand out in a crowd of hundreds of titles—both in the stores and for the media. We devote an entire chapter to book events in stores (see Chapter 28, "Bookstore Business"), so let's look at the media here. First of all, the media offers readers and viewers information. In the case of television, the reporters also need to show something. Conversations with authors are okay, but it's usually better if you can "do" something. In order for a news station to generate a story, some news angle should exist. So your first step in publicizing your title is conceptualizing a hook or an angle. Consider these two hooks for some "pretend" books—both a nonfiction and fictional book:

➤ You've written a how-to garden and plant book for kids. A huge storm sweeps through your town. Gardens are destroyed and trees felled. Your angle is the rebuilding of gardens, teaching kids how to help in the recovery process!

➤ Your picture book details the story of a little boy moving from the neighborhood he's lived in from birth to a new neighborhood across the nation and his integration into a new school. Find out the statistics on children changing schools and the psychological impact. Offer tips in your press packet for acclimating to a new school. Hook adults into buying the book to help their children; the media will want to offer this "good" information to parents.

➤ You've written a multicultural picture book based on an experience you had with your Polish grandfather. You possess a natural "hook" within all the Polish American clubs across the nation. Because a subgroup is represented, you can sell books to those with the same ethnic background.

So let your imagination go wild! How can you hook people to find interest in your book?

Local Yokels, Redux

Your first stop on the self-publicizing train is your local media. Because you live someplace and wrote a book, you're news. If you live in a town or out in the country, try the local papers, radio stations, and TV stations. If you live in a big city, don't expect the major newspapers to be interested (though it certainly doesn't hurt to try *The New York Times* or the *Chicago Tribune* or the *San Francisco Chronicle*). Go for the neighborhood papers, the local cable TV show, and so on. Where do you get your local news? Go there! Take those releases you've written and fire them off to the local media.

Moving on Up!

Once you've sent your releases and kits off to the local media, concentrate on bigger media outlets—but in many cases only if you can accommodate an interview or plan on traveling in the area. Let's look a little more closely at your publicity options.

Newspapers

Any paper outside of your area will want one of two things—a news link or that you will be appearing in their town. Contact the feature editor if the angle you have involves a trend or a newsworthy attribute. Contact the children's book review editor if you plan on a signing or an appearance someplace.

Radio

Radio programs are great for calling you and conducting live or taped interviews over the phone. Find a media directory in your local library and go through the listing of shows by content. If your children's book focuses on sports fitness for children, then pitch yourself as an interview on the morning sports show. Producers of talk radio are constantly scrambling to fill the airtime with interesting and informational interviews. Don't limit yourself to approaching only the book shows. Generally, these shows deal with weighty adult books anyway.

Television

Again, are you in town for an appearance? Television programs need to show their viewers something—you! And moreover, you should have some informational or newsworthy hook for the appearance. We've given several examples of hooks tied to specific book subjects, but you can make yourself the hook. For example, until he got to be known as an illustrator, David Wisniewski got more attention from having gone to clown school than from having created a beautiful book.

Self-publicizing can be a full-time job, or you might decide to skip it completely. Whichever direction you go in is up to you, but do consider your options.

Class Rules

Author tours are expensive, and children's publishers don't pay for them. Unless you possess money to blow, don't put yourself on a six-city tour across the nation. Certainly, if business takes you to Boston for a week and time permits, contact the media about appearances. Otherwise, save the travel for a vacation some place fun!

The Least You Need to Know

➤ Offer your publicity ideas to the marketing and publicity departments of your publishing house—but do it gently.

➤ Any materials that you can put together to help your publicist and the book's publicity are much appreciated. Moreover, you can use them for self-publicizing your book.

➤ Don't devote all your time to the success of your book through diligent marketing and publicity—write more books!

➤ Conceptualize "hooks" for your book to generate interest in different media outlets and make your book stand out over all the others on the market.

Chapter 28

Bookstore Business

In This Chapter

➤ Why and how bookstore events fuel sales

➤ Whom to approach about an event/book signing

➤ What sort of events work best and bring in the crowds

➤ What your part as an author is in the event

➤ Ways to fuel sales of your book the day of the event

Whether you plan to drive all over the continent or stay locally to publicize your book, you won't want to miss out on the bookstore connection. The fierce competition between megachains like Barnes & Noble and Borders against the independent stores actually benefits you and your book. How? Each establishment is continually looking for great ways to draw in customers. The latest trend in bookstore community relations is the book "event."

In this chapter, we'll show you how to navigate your way to the right person to book the event, what type of events draw in the crowds, and how you can help fuel sales of your book at the event. Get ready because we're having a party!

A Tale of Two (or More) Bookstores

Once upon a time, the quaint bookstore up the street ruled the literary roost. People came from all over the neighborhood to buy the latest best-selling fiction title or charming child's picture book. But today, more and more independent bookstores are giving way to *superstores* stocked with more than 100,000 titles dispersed into myriad departments. *You've Got Mail,* the romantic comedy starring Meg Ryan and Tom Hanks, showcased a love relationship between an independent children's bookstore owner (Ryan) and corporate bookstore chain entrepreneur (Hanks). In the real world, you know who the big companies are: Barnes & Noble, Borders, Tower, Crown. Just in

Vocabulary List

In the book business, a **super-store** is a large store typically encompassing more than 100,000 titles. Some superstores even sell other products besides books, such as CDs, stationery, and toys. Two chains known for their superstores are Barnes & Noble and Borders Books and Music.

the small city where Lynne resides, two Borders and one Barnes & Noble vie for customers. A few miles away in another suburb a Tower and Barnes & Noble sit within a block of each other. Now factor in the smaller bookstore chains and the independents stores; with so many choices, competition rages to draw in and retain customers.

One of the great ways these bookstores contribute to the community and then bring in a loyal buying base is through the efforts of community relations departments. Today, even bookstores possess a public relations person in each location. The PR manager of a bookstore chain may address the media over a controversial title, but more common duties include planning events around books and author book signings. Essentially, the community relations manager churns out a monthly calendar of events—everything from weekly story times to monthly book club meetings to author signings and informational seminars. By hosting these "free and open-to-the-public" events, the stores draw in more customers, thereby selling more books—more of your book! The best events—those that bring in the customers—are the parties and seminars. And nowhere are the book parties happier, bigger, or more fun than in the children's departments.

Kids love books, and love socializing at events that deal with their favorite book. Can you remember your own fascination with the "Little House on the Prairie" series or the Hardy Boys books? Wouldn't you just loved to have spent an evening once a month dressing up like Laura Ingalls, reading passages from *Little House in the Big Woods,* and learning how to make a treat that Laura probably made more than 100 years ago? Little girls today can enjoy activities like these by participating in numerous American Girl Clubs run out of bookstore chains. Beyond the clubs for kids based on series like "Animorphs" and "American Girls," bookstores offer pint-sized consumers and their parents other opportunities to love (and buy) books. From story time hours to character costume parties to parent/child book clubs, bookstores around the globe are clamoring for ways to excite children to read and their parents to purchase.

Thus, a great opportunity arises for you to self-publicize your book. And the best part? You can either hit only the local stores or travel as far and wide as you please. But having an event surrounding your book at one or several bookstores isn't necessarily easy. More likely than not, calling and asking a befuddled floor sales clerk about a book signing won't result in an event. You need a plan to get in good with the store manager and/or community relations coordinator/manager.

Target-Rich Environment

Let's say your book, *Giggles and Grins,* a pop-up book of funny faces and jokes, just shipped hot off the presses to bookstores everywhere. And in your hometown, three bookstores exist as possible event targets. The first thing you must do—before pitching a giggly-good event—is find out if the bookstore even offers customers a *calendar of events.* The smaller mall stores, for instance, don't have the room or staff to host events. Call the store first and ask an employee whether or not the store hosts book-related events. If they don't, don't bother the staffer anymore. Move on. If the representative says yes, ask who the events contact is.

First Contact

As we mentioned earlier, many bookstores now employ a person to handle all book-related events and community interaction, a community relations coordinator (CRC) or a community relations manager (CRM). Coauthor Lynne actually worked several years for a major super-bookstore as a CRM. In her role, she oversaw the public relations campaigns of up to four stores in the district. "I scrambled monthly to find good, quality, interesting, and unique events to book—especially in the children's departments," she says. These employees—typically with a title acknowledging the community or marketing—are your point of contact to publicize your book in a bookstore and are actively looking for authors like you to host events and fill the dates on their calendars. When you call the store, ask if there is an employee who handles author relations and author events. Then ask the employee to put you through to the CRC's direct line or ask to leave a message. If the store you're hoping to book an event in does not employ a special community relations representative, then you'll want to speak directly to the store manager.

Vocabulary List

Bookstores that showcase author signings, story times for children, book clubs, and other author-related events out of the store typically print a monthly calendar that details each event, including the date and time. A paragraph description gives customers a clear idea of what to expect. These flyers are usually called **calendar of events** or the **event calendar.**

Class Rules

Don't book a party or gathering in two competitive bookstores around the same time. You glut the market of interest in your book and the event. Pick your favorite store first and give it first priority. Then, later on down the road, book another event at the competition. There will be less confusion and more trust in you as an author by the stores.

Leave a Message at the Tone

Chances are pretty good that you'll get a direct number for the community relations coordinator. Chances are equally as good that you'll need to leave a message. Because of the sheer number of calls this employee receives—everyone from schools asking for donations to authors wanting to book an event—the CRC frequents the phone line and is also often out in the community working, too. Jenn Pfeiffer, a former CRM for Barnes & Noble stores in the San Francisco Bay Area, once lamented the 90 messages she received in the two days during the week that she wasn't working! "I had to check my messages both days and clear off as many as I could each time just to leave space for my mailbox. Otherwise, it would fill too quickly," remembers Pfeiffer.

Because these employees receive an exorbitant number of calls—where the caller typically rambles on and on about his or her business—you really will endear yourself and retain a greater chance of store support for your event if you follow these simple guidelines when making first contact:

➤ Begin your message with your name, preferably spelled, and your phone number. Many times, the CRM will log the calls. Then repeat the number.

➤ Give the title of your book and the ISBN.

➤ Include a time frame in which you'd like an event to occur.

➤ Indicate that you will send a press release about the book and any media clippings (if you have them) and a letter detailing the event you envision.

➤ Send the letter!

➤ Wait patiently to hear from the representative.

If you can include a review copy of your book, do it. If the CRC or CRM decides to schedule an event with you, he or she will need to scan the cover of the book for posters that may be displayed in the store before the reading.

Class Rules

Don't wait to call and attempt to book an event with a bookstore just weeks before your arrival in town. Calendars of events fill up three months or more in advance. The CRC or CRM actually writes the copy for the calendar a month in advance. And then the copy must go to the designer and the printer. Think ahead—at least three months into the future. If you don't, you're likely to hear, "I'm sorry, but my calendar is already full!"

Party Plans

So now you've left a message with the bookstore event representative or store manager. You may hear from him or her before you send more information, but even more likely, the employee wants to see those ideas of yours on paper. It's up to you to sell the store on the event idea. The CRC wants to throw well-attended events that bring in customers. If the event—like a signing of an unknown author—seems unimaginative and certain to fail, the CRC won't book it. Or if they do, you may end up wishing they hadn't.

So put on your creative cap and come up with a plan—several ideas to pitch the store's way for fun events. Your options are only limited by your ingenuity, but you will need to work with the options available in the store. Let's look at the standard event categories that occur in the children's departments of bookstores for which you can design your event:

Class Rules

Book signings, in particular, can prove brutal for authors and bookstore personnel. Unless the author is a celebrity like Will Smith or Arnold Schwarzenegger or a series is beloved (the Harry Potter books are a good example), the public won't show up. The author is left to sit at a table as people nervously walk by. Not an ego boost, for sure!

➤ **Preschool/school-age story times:** Most stores offer story times twice a week or more. Oftentimes, the children's department supervisor or another employee picks picture books at random and reads them during the story hour. Really great story-time facilitators incorporate themes into the hour and sometimes even include finger-play games and singing.

➤ **Series club event:** Kind of like a book club for kids. Groups of devotees to a particular series gather at the store to meet and talk about their favorite books in the cycle. The American Girls Club or Animorph Clubs popping up all over are good examples of this kind of event. Oftentimes, the facilitator of the club will incorporate other works of children's literature into the activities of the evening. For instance, if the American Girls Club focuses on the character living in the 1940s, the leader may showcase a display of old radios from the era and show the girls other books they may like to read to further explore the role of women during World War II.

➤ **Character parties:** Always a favorite event with the little tykes! At these events, your children's beloved storybook characters make an appearance—like Clifford the Big Red Dog, or the Mouse from *If You Give a Mouse a Cookie*. Then several of the stories from that character's repertoire or from the author who created the character are read to the kids. Sometimes treats are passed out, too, to add to the festivities. If your book showcases a noteworthy character, you might want to make your own costume or even puppet likenesses of characters. Along with reading your book to the group, you may host a puppet show!

➤ **Author readings and presentations:** The author of the book reads directly to the kids. Sometimes, like in the case of David Carter, the famed author of those fabulous pop-up bug books, the author treats the kids to a "chalk talk." In a chalk talk, the author/illustrator shows the audience of kids how the ideas become a book. Puppet or props (with practice first!) can also enhance a reading.

➤ **Activity event:** In this type of event an activity focuses on a book. For example, after a story time where *Rainbow Fish* is read, the kids in the audience get materials with which to make their own sparkly rainbow fish. Construction paper, beads, glitter, glue, and paints permeate this type of event.

You Gotta Have a Gimmick

Back to your plan. The CRC or CRM will help you more if you help him more. Meaning: Give him every possible idea you have for an event and offer to help publicize the event, too. Just as when you attempt to garner media coverage, you'll need to go the extra mile here, too. Send the CRC a press kit if you have one. With the press kit, include a cover letter identifying ...

➤ Your name, your book's title, ISBN, and publisher.

➤ Where the publisher can get copies of the book if not distributed through standard means or self-published.

➤ The event you envision.

➤ The dates and times you are available to accommodate and event. (Remember: Think three months or more in advance.)

➤ How you plan to publicize the event and draw in book-buying crowds (see Chapter 27, "Hey, Listen to Me!").

➤ A template for a press release/event announcement to send to calendar editors and various local publications.

Check with the store shortly before the event, to confirm that they have sent out the press kits, and that they are expecting you. The best-laid plans can go wrong! On the day, come early, introduce yourself to the staff, and then introduce yourself to customers. They won't all know about your event, but they might be happy to stay for it.

Do all of this, and you're well on your way to having a real *event*, not just a "book signing" or "reading." Any children's author can tell you stories of going to a bookstore and having exactly three people show up over the course of two hours, or perhaps of being excited to see 25 people come to get a book signed, until they realized that 23 of them were friends they'd begged to come. You want to get people who don't know you to come. Plan and publicize an event, working closely with the bookstore personnel, and you will.

Can You Keep a Secret?

Keep copies of event calendars that list your presentation. Moreover, keep copies of your event proposal letter and press kit that you sent to the CRM. The next time you are looking to self-promote your book through a bookstore, you can reuse your ideas and also provide the new CRM a glimpse into the success of your last event. The calendars also typically list phone numbers for the stores, so the CRM can easily call the store that already hosted an event with you and either find out what worked fabulously or refrain from any mistakes, too.

And afterward, don't forget to write a thank-you note to the CRM. With any luck, they'll remember you warmly, and that can only help when your next book comes out.

The Least You Need to Know

➤ Bookstores, eager to draw in a loyal customer base in the midst of fierce competition, host book signings, and author events regularly.

➤ You can fuel sales of your book by booking an author event in bookstores.

➤ Your point of contact at a bookstore is either the community relations manager/coordinator or the store manager.

➤ Make contact with the community relations employee at least three months in advance of the date you'd like to host an event.

➤ Don't assume that a reading is all that's needed to draw in the kids. Plan either a themed event or an activity to engage the kids and their parents, and publicize your event.

Chapter 29

Back to School

In This Chapter

➤ What a "school visit" is and what it entails

➤ What to expect in payment and fees

➤ How school visits can almost become a full-time job

➤ The benefits of school visits, now and in the future

One of the best opportunities to promote your book is through the educational system. Reading and literacy remain huge focuses within schools—regardless of grade level. Whether you've written a young adult novel or a preschooler picture book, you many want to consider hopping on the school bus and hitting the books! In this chapter, we'll tell you what to do.

School Visit Basics

You remember grade school, middle school, and high school, right? In grade school, do you remember loving the time of day that the teacher read to you—usually after lunch to settle you down, actually! In high school, you read to yourself, guided in the comprehension of the literature by an English teacher—an expert. At either level, you learned to express yourself through writing. You learned history and science and math in other classes. Ask any teacher about his or her field of study, and you're bound to hear a mouthful. Subject-area teachers want to generate excitement about science or math or American history, and English teachers are always looking for ways to ignite a love of reading and writing. One way is through a visit by a successful author.

But you standing in front of the class and saying hello isn't the way to accomplish the task at hand. A teacher or a school will most want you to visit if you produce some sort of learning activity or program. These can take place in classrooms or in larger groups, such as an assembly.

How do these visits come about? When you are just getting started, contacting schools and letting them know you are available may be necessary, as we will explain in more detail later. Publishers also get requests from schools for popular authors and illustrators. Typically, the well-known ones get many more requests than they could possibly fulfill, and in such cases the person in the marketing department who handles school visits will suggest someone else. Let this person know that you are eager to visit schools, and you're on your way. If you develop a good program, and if you have a steady flow of books coming out, soon you'll have more requests than you can handle.

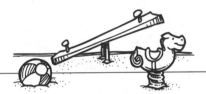

Stories from the Playground

One of the most active authors in visiting schools is Jerry Pallotta, known for such nonfiction picture books in an alphabet format as *The Dinosaur Alphabet Book* and *The Jet Alphabet Book*. He visits 150 schools a year, speaking to teachers as well as to elementary and junior high students. His program features a slide show which he uses to explain the process behind the creation of his books—a focus that ties in nicely to writing and reading programs.

How much time you spend on school visits is partly up to you, and partly up to how much interest there is in the school audience for you and your books. Even if there is a big audience in schools for their books, some authors prefer to save all their time for writing. Others visit a few local schools or scatter visits throughout the year. And a few are able to spend a lot of time on the road, criss-crossing the country, visiting many schools, and making a good income not just from selling their books but from the fees they charge for appearances and presentations.

Yes, you can charge a fee for most kinds of school visits. Many schools have budgets for author visits, and might not take you as seriously if you *don't* charge a fee. Considering the time involved to prepare and travel, even as a beginner you should charge two to three hundred dollars for a one-hour presentation, and several hundred dollars for a full day at a school. Experienced authors charge considerably more. Schools in rural areas or the inner cities may have less money at their disposal, so do waive fees when necessary, but in general, remember that doing a school visit well is hard work, and that the number of books you sell is unlikely to compensate you for your time. You deserve a fee, negotiated in advance, and reimbursement of your travel costs.

The Song-and-Dance Routine

What should you do in a school visit? Depending upon the age level that you'll visit, different sorts of programs apply (for example, whether you'll come in and talk about the writing process or sit down and read your picture book). Myriad ways exist to make a school visit and show off your wares at the same time.

Class Rules

Many school visits are spoiled because the visiting author's books aren't on hand. Make sure your school orders the books *at least* six weeks before the visit, which allows for the all-too-frequent delays in shipping. And check that they have arrived two weeks before, when there's still time for a rush order, not a few days before, when it's too late. Publishers can be slow to ship books, so plan ahead.

And speaking of showing off your wares: Whatever the kind of visit, make sure that the school has arranged to have copies of your book or books on hand. The school may want to have copies for every classroom or child. Or it might set aside time for you to sign them, if they're the kind of books children will want to purchase for themselves. But try not to get involved with hauling books there yourself—that's just extra work. Many publishers will ship books directly to schools at a good discount (allowing the school to sell them at list price and raise funds) and accept the return of unsold books. Or for convenience a school can order your books from a wholesaler, if they come from more than one publisher. Or a local bookstore might set up a table. As we note in the sidebar, whichever option they choose, make sure they allow plenty of lead time.

The Younger Set

If your book falls into the elementary or middle school age category, you will probably make a school visit under one of the following categories:

➤ Rallies

➤ Story times

➤ Class workshop

➤ Storytelling

➤ Carnivals/booths

➤ Parent/teacher fundraisers

Let's explain further.

The Rally

Generally speaking, instead of addressing a class or two or reading your book to several classes, in a rally, you address the whole campus. In order for this to work, your book must possess appeal across all grade levels—from kindergarten to sixth. Or you must have something to talk to the children about in an exciting way that goes across all grade levels. Or you perform something related to your book.

The idea here, however, remains that you are a performance artist engaging a diverse array of kids. As an example, let's say that you are a police officer by trade and you've written a book on safety issues for kids. You may bring your book and talk to a room of kids about safety measures and even demonstrate with audience participants how to escape a possible abduction or what to do if someone tries to harm them.

Story Times and Reading

In this school appearance, you go in to a classroom and read your picture book to the kids. If you've written a young reader or young adult novel, you may read a passage from it. The teacher will introduce you as the writer or author of the book—the person who actually wrote the book! This concept will thrill the kids. You may even want to contact your publisher and see if they produced or will produce any fun items like stickers or coloring books for the children.

Class Workshop

Sometimes, talking about your book is enough. Classes involved in making their own books as part of learning the writing process, for example, may invite you to talk about how your book came about. Children are fascinated by the multiple drafts you go through, intrigued by a copyeditor's marks (so similar to their teacher's comments), and especially interested in materials like color proofs, which you sometimes can get from a publisher after the book has been printed.

Storytelling

This category applies especially to folktale tellers. Storytelling requires a dramatic retelling of the tale. One's voice, mannerisms, and so on are all employed to enhance the story. If you have a flair for the dramatic, this is a great option for you.

Carnivals

Many schools hold carnivals as fundraisers during the year. Always looking for interesting booths, the school may let you set up a reading/book sale booth at the carnival, for a fee or otherwise; here's a case where the school doesn't pay you. The school may require you to donate a percentage of sales.

Can You Keep a Secret?

In a number of states, the state arts commission sponsors grant-based programs to help school districts pay artists such as writers and illustrators to come do programs of varying lengths. Typically the artist registers with the arts commission, which then produces a list for school districts to draw from as needs arise. Contact your state arts commission or education department to find out what opportunities exist.

Parent/Teacher Fundraisers

Just like the carnival, these fundraisers require the author to donate a percentage of sales from the book to the PTA. These events can be a win/win situation. You expose your book to readers, may sell some copies, and the educational system earns a few bucks, too.

Almost Adults

The options for school visits (and increased revenue) also abound at the young adult level—middle school and high school. Here are just a few ideas to play around with:

➤ Lectures

➤ Rallies

➤ Workshops

➤ Reading

➤ Issue/discussion

➤ Storytelling/dramatic performances

Do Lecture Me!

Teachers are always looking for real-life examples for their high school students of English-related professions. Since you are a professional writer once you've published, you then exist as an excellent resource for a teacher—you can guest lecture in the class on everything from writing your book to your career choice.

Rally Up!

Especially if your young adult book deals with significant teenage issues, suddenly you're the expert. Schools may call upon you to speak at school-wide rallies or assemblies on a number of concerns you may have addressed in your novel.

Work? Me, Work?

Yes—in a workshop format. Depending upon your book, you may want to offer students through the district a weekend or Saturday workshop. Perhaps your book deals with horseshoeing. Why not give a seminar or workshop on the "Lost Art of Shoeing a Horse" to all the 4-H students? Or if you've written a novel, you may want to turn your experience into a writing workshop and critique seminar for students. The ideas are limitless; in fact we urge you to brainstorm a few right now.

Debate Team

Another great way to gain exposure of your book is by guest lecturing in a classroom. Let's say your young adult novel develops the theme of realism versus romanticism. You could easily slip into the classroom and give a guest lecture on the theme as it pertains to your novel and many great works of literature. Then invite the students to interpret passages from your book that you've either copied onto separate sheets of paper or read aloud to them. Be prepared—especially at the high school levels—for kids to speak their minds adamantly!

Vocabulary List

Storytelling involves more than reading a book. A storyteller vividly brings the tale alive through interpretation, voice, and dramatics. You watch the book instead of read it when a storyteller becomes involved.

You're Too Old for a Story—NOT!

Finally, high school students relish a really well-told story as much as the next person—the performance art of *storytelling*. Get out your props and enunciate, baby. A skit, a telling of some folklore—these are other ways you can expose your book to the education system. Let's say that you've put your own spin on a relatively new African American folktale. You are also a storyteller by trade. Seek out the teachers and find out whether one class over the other teaches multiculturalism in literature. Then book yourself in the school.

Making Contact

Armed with all of these really cool ideas, now you need to secure a few school visits. We noted earlier in this chapter that you might get referrals from publishers, but you shouldn't count on these. Again, we recommend targeting your local schools—less travel, less of a pain.

Pick an idea, any idea, and make first contact. Call the school and ask the secretary for the principal. Explain to the principal your ideas and let him or her direct you to the next step. This may be to the chairperson of a department, directly to an individual teacher, or to the head of the parent-teacher organization.

Depending upon the principal's response, you may need to do one or more of several things—like prepare a proposal outlining your ideas or drop off a review copy of your book. Whatever the next step is, follow up quickly, and don't forget to ask for suggestions. If you hit if off with one reading teacher, maybe she can suggest friends in other schools, for example.

After your visit, do the same. With a little work you can build up a network of contacts.

On Beyond Schools

Everything we are saying in this chapter focuses on schools, but you can apply this approach to other venues. Libraries also welcome authors, as do local book festivals. You can even do virtual visits, by having an online chat with a classroom of children on the other side of the country, or extend a visit by working with some students on a project to be posted on their school's Web site. Your imagination may be the only limit to the possibilities.

Can You Keep a Secret?

If you are serious about school and other visits, run to your local bookstore and order *Terrific Connections with Authors, Illustrators, and Storytellers*, by Toni Buzzeo and Jane Kurtz (Teacher Ideas Press, 1999). Full of examples of real visits, described by teachers and librarians as well as authors, you'll also find guidance on tailoring your presentation to your audience and on meshing with a curriculum. An indispensable resource.

On the Road

How busy *do* you want to be? You'll have to figure that out for yourself. If your books are the kind that "work" in the schools then you can be very busy with school visits, and doing so will not only sell an existing book but also create an audience for future ones. Imagine that you've successfully visited 100 schools over a three-year period. When a new book comes out, teachers at all of them will be interested in hearing about it, and many of the students will still remember you, too. So make sure that school knows about the new book. And go on the road with a new program.

School visits can become a full-time job, but only if you make it so! Generally speaking, school visits are a great way to gain recognition of your book. But most authors probably won't make an income able to support them on school visits alone. So, take advantage of the benefits of school visits, but not to the detriment of your writing. Continue to write. Ultimately, more books will result in more income.

The Least You Need to Know

➤ Many different ways exist to show off your book at a school visit—including reading the story, giving a presentation, or selling your books as a fundraiser.

➤ Work through the right channel—it might be a teacher, but it might be the school's administration.

➤ School visits can pay very well, but you may need to charge less when getting started or waive your fees with schools that lack the funding.

➤ Regardless, if you roam toward schools often, you can add to the sales of a book significantly.

➤ School visits also help you gain recognition and an audience for future books.

Chapter 30

I Won a Prize!

In This Chapter

➤ What the really big awards are in children's literature

➤ National awards that writers might strive toward achieving

➤ Lists that make a difference in your reputation as a children's book writer

➤ Why state awards mean something

➤ The effects of these awards or recognition

Right now, you may just want to get your gosh-darned book published and don't even fathom the kudos that may befall you, but listen up. Within the children's publishing arena many opportunities exist for authors to achieve recognition and awards. Not that winning a blue ribbon always gains you everything, but it sure can help provide longevity for your career and aspirations. After all, if you win one of the major children's book awards, consider your book a classic with almost guaranteed sales for future generations. Also, publishers will think twice about passing on a second book when your first book received an award like the ALA Coretta Scott King or the National Book Award. In this chapter, we look at the many ways you can achieve recognition and the admiration of your writing colleagues.

The Big Ones—Newbery and Caldecott

Walk into any big bookstore (and certainly smaller ones, too) and you'll likely find an entire bookcase showcasing the Newbery and Caldecott award-winning books. These two awards remain the Academy Awards of the children's book industry. Unlike other children's book awards, which may have little immediate impact on sales, these two also drive publishers back to the printers for tens of thousands of copies. Why? The public recognizes them, and the winners are going to sell. Let's take a close look at each.

Newbery

Each year, the Association for Library Service to Children (ALSC) of the American Library Association (ALA) awards the Newbery Medal to "the most distinguished American children's book" published the previous year. Just a little history here—on June 21, 1921, Frederic G. Melcher proposed the award to a meeting of the Children's Librarians' Section of the ALA and suggested that it be named for the eighteenth-century English bookseller John Newbery.

The Newbery retains special significance over all children's book awards because it was the first children's book award in the world. Although only one book receives the actual medal each year, several noteworthy books, referred to as "honor books" also draw recognition.

Past popular Newbery titles include *The Giver,* by Lois Lowry, *A Wrinkle in Time,* by Madeleine L'Engle, and *Sarah Plain and Tall,* by Patricia MacLachlan.

Can You Keep a Secret?

For a complete listing of all Newbery and Caldecott medalists and honor books, consult *The Newbery and Caldecott Awards: A Guide to the Medal and Honor Books*, published by the ALA. Or on-line, visit these Web sites: www.ala.org/alsc/newbery.html and caldecott.html.

Caldecott

The Newbery Medal certainly paved the way for more recognition of outstanding children's writers. However, the illustrators of children's books found no kudos thrown their way. So in 1937—to give illustrators the honor and encouragement they deserved for bringing tales to life in picture books—a second medal was suggested. The Caldecott Medal, named in honor of nineteenth-century English illustrator Randolph Caldecott, resulted, and is awarded annually by the ALSC, to the artist of the most distinguished American picture book for children (of course, the author deserves some credit too, for creating the text that inspired the illustrations, but it's the illustrator who receives the Caldecott).

Class Rules

In the terms and criteria for the Caldecott Medal, a note exists that reads: "The committee should keep in mind that the award is for distinguished illustrations in a picture book and for excellence of pictorial presentation for children. The award is not for didactic intent or for popularity." Just because a book sells well, doesn't necessarily make it a winner among the experts—keep that in mind for other awards.

Recent winners include Emily Arnold McCully's *Mirette on the High Wire*, David Diaz's illustrations for *Smoky Night*, and Mary Azarian's illustrations for *Snowflake Bentley*. And just like the Newbery Medal, those books not chosen but deemed wonderful anyway earn the title "honor book."

Other National Awards

But just because you don't win a Newbery or Caldecott doesn't mean you'll never receive any recognition for your hard work. Myriad other awards exist to provide credit where credit is due—and offer an alternative list of noteworthy books besides those given kudos as Newbery or Caldecott.

The National Book Awards

First up: the National Book Awards. In 1950, a consortium of book publishing groups sponsored the first annual National Book Awards Ceremony and Dinner in New York City. The goal of the consortium was to enhance the public's awareness of exceptional books written by Americans and increase literacy and the joy of reading. For more than 50 years, the National Book Awards have conferred the preeminent literary prizes each year within four different genres: fiction, nonfiction, poetry, and children's literature. The winners earn "fat bank," a $10,000 cash award, along with a crystal sculpture. The children's book category was recently reinstated after not being included for a number of years.

I Have a Dream: The Coretta Scott King Award

The Coretta Scott King Award honors African American authors and illustrators for outstanding contributions to children's and young adult literature that promote understanding and appreciation of the culture and contribution of all races. Named after the wife of slain civil rights leader Dr. Martin Luther King Jr., the award, beyond honoring her courage and determination to continue his work for peace, also honors the late leader.

In 1999, the Coretta Scott King Award celebrated its 30th anniversary. The winners of this award for the year 2000 were *Bud, Not Buddy,* by Christopher Paul Curtis (Delacorte), also a Newbery winner, and for illustrations, *In the Time of the Drums,* illustrated by Brian Pinkney with text by Kim L. Siegelson (Jump at the Sun/Hyperion Books for Children).

Can You Keep a Secret?

We highly recommend you seek out titles of past winners and peruse them to gain an understanding about the focus on multicultural literature and the world. For a complete listing of all the Coretta Scott King awards since 1970, surf on-line to www.ala.org/srrt/csking/cskawin.html.

Big Award from "Little House" Lady

The ALSC every three years confers the Laura Ingalls Wilder Award to either an author or illustrator whose books, published in the United States, have made, over a period of years, a substantial and lasting contribution to literature for children. Call this a lifetime achievement award.

Few children don't know who Laura Ingalls Wilder was. Her series of books beginning with *The Little House in the Big Woods* provides pertinent historical information, as well as entertainment.

Past recipients of this award include Russell Freedman, Virginia Hamilton, Marcia Brown, Maurice Sendak, and Ruth Sawyer.

Are these the only national awards? Of course not. As you spend more time in this field, you'll learn about others, from the Scott O'Dell Award for the best historical fiction, to the Golden Kite Award, given by the SCBWI to a member, to the Orbis Pictus Award, given by the National Council of Teachers of English to the best nonfiction for children. None of them have the impact of the two biggies, but they'll all help your reputation and may help backlist sales—continued sales over time.

Teen Angst Awards

Up until the 1950s, the concept of the "teenager" barely existed. One moved directly from childhood into the adult world due to the necessities of life. But with U.S.

prosperity and the baby boomers, suddenly teens came of age. Teen angst, rebellion, rock and roll, and even teen entertainment emerged. With the myriad emotions rumbling around within adolescents, it's no wonder this group embraces books that speak to them. Once teenagers were noticed, it wasn't long before the "young adult" book category was invented. And in response to those individuals who really speak clearly to the teen audience two awards stand out: the Margaret A. Edwards Award and the Michael L. Printz Award.

Margaret A. Edwards Award

Established in 1988 and sponsored by *School Library Journal,* this $2,000 award recognizes an author whose work or works provides young adults with a window through which they can view their world and which will help them to grow and to understand themselves and their role in society. Most important, the award recognizes those books that help adolescents become self-aware and address concerns about their relationship within our society.

Stories from the Playground

Who was Margaret A. Edwards? She was an administrator of young adult literature at Enoch Pratt Free Library in Baltimore, Maryland, for more than three decades. Edwards believed in the need to bring young adult literature and library services to young adults and spent her professional career pioneering many programs for her purpose. She also authored *The Fair Garden and the Swarm of Beasts: The Library and the Young Adult*—a work that explains her philosophy for turning young adults into readers.

Past recipients of the award include such authors as S. E. Hinton for works like *The Outsiders* and *Rumble Fish,* and Robert Cormier for *The Chocolate War*.

The Michael L. Printz Award

With the new millennium came a new award that distinguishes the best of the best of young adult literature—with edge. The Michael L. Printz Award honors the highest literary achievement in young adult books for a novel published the preceding year. In 2000, Walter Dean Myers received the award for his book *Monster,* an emotionally charged story of a 16-year-old arrested for murder. Look for upcoming Michael L. Printz Awards. The recipients are certain to push the envelope and speak to young people in a language they understand.

Get on These Lists!

Earning an award such as the ones we've discussed so far probably takes as much luck as skill. Dozens may have a serious chance in any year, but only one or a few are chosen. Needless to say, you may not ever receive a Newbery or Caldecott. But that doesn't mean that you can't see your book on some noteworthy lists, lists that may not have an immediate impact on sales but do add luster to your name and possibly longevity to your book.

ALA Notables

To recognize the best children's books of the year, the ALA doesn't just pick a few select titles for its awards. A committee also compiles the list called "ALA Notable Books for Children," made up of 60 or 70—or perhaps a few more—children's books that the committee considers to be the best of the year. Unlike the procedure with many other awards, the committee discusses the books it is considering in a public meeting, at the ALA's semi-annual conventions. Getting on this list almost certainly means your book will sell better to libraries.

Class Rules

It really is up to you and your publisher to help your book find its way onto lists and to be considered for awards. Each award, medal, and notable list requires a process. An editor or committee needs to see your book to know it exists. Check that your publisher is actively submitting your books to the awards we've mentioned. If not, consider researching the awards yourself and making your own submissions.

Children's Choices

Do you want to get past the gatekeepers and be recognized by children, your true audience? Then being named to the "Children's Choices" list, an annual publication sponsored by the Children's Book Council (CBC) and the International Reading

Association (the organization for reading teachers), may be your highest aspiration. Children all over the country vote on books submitted by publishers, eventually creating a list of about 100 titles. You can see a recent one on-line at www.cbcbooks. org/choices/2000list.htm.

Outstanding Science

Science teachers in the United States recognize the best trade books on science for children in an annual list chosen by a panel named by the National Science Teacher's Association and published with the help of the CBC. More than 100 books on a variety of subjects appear. The list is published every year in *Science for Children*. Copies are available on-line at 199.0.3.5/pubs/sc/ostblist.asp or may be ordered from the CBC for $2.00 and a large SASE with 3 oz. postage.

Notable Social Studies

The National Council for the Social Studies creates a list similar to the science teacher's list, but this time with a focus on social studies. About 150 books come from such areas as biography, contemporary issues, history, and world culture. Published every year in *Social Education,* the list is also available on-line at www.ncss.org/ resources/notable/home.html or by mail from the CBC.

Parents' Choice

The Parent Council reviews books every month and lists recommended learning titles. Nearly 3,000 reviews exist on-line at the council's Web site at www.parentcouncil.com. The council consists of teachers who are parents and emphasizes the value of the book as a learning tool. Making it on the Parent Council's recommended list or re-view category helps you sell more books to parents and teachers.

Wowing Them All Over the Country

In response to literacy problems and to place an emphasis on the benefits of reading, many states now pass out their own awards for outstanding lit-erature for young people. They may be sponsored by local branches of national organizations, by state education departments, or by state organizations.

Can You Keep a Secret?

Starting to feel overwhelmed by all these awards? If you want to learn more, get *Children's Books: Awards and Prizes,* published by the Children's Book Council, from your local library. Or go on-line to this handy index of on-line information on American, Canadian, and other awards: www. ucalgary.ca/~dkbrown/ awards.html.

Books on them may be evaluated by teachers, by librarians, or by children. Authors from all over the country may be eligible, or only state residents. Getting named to one of the lists may not do much for your book. Being on a number of them will, because it makes it more likely that school libraries will purchase it. Some, like the Texas Bluebonnet Award, give a boost in sales just to books nominated, because children all over the state read and vote on the books, and so their schools must have copies on hand. Your publisher should take care of sending your book to the relevant committees. Be pleased if you hear you've been named.

Reading Rainbow

Although technically not an award, receiving play on the PBS series *Reading Rainbow* results in feeling like you've received an award. Only those books with high quality and merit land on *Reading Rainbow*. If your book makes it on a show, you'll experience the benefit of publicity—big time! Thousands upon thousands of viewers—both children and their parents—look to *Reading Rainbow* each weekday and check out the books recommended and read. A spot on the successful literary program for children often results in increased sales and honor. It can't hurt to ask your publicist to send a copy of your book to the producers!

End-of-Year Lists

What is it about us that likes to package things up and box them together at the end of the year? Closure, we guess. Regardless of the reason, your book might place nicely on an "end-of-the-year" list. The most influential of the annual lists of children's books are the *Publishers Weekly* roundup, the *Booklist* "Editor's Picks," and the *Boston Globe/Horn Book* "Best Books of the Year."

We've mentioned just a few of the organizations and magazines that give awards or that create lists of recommended children's books every year. Some will get you more recognition than others. Some will help you reach a specialized audience, while others speak to a national audience. Right now, making sense of them all may be difficult, so keep your eyes open, ask questions if you get an award or are named to a list you've never heard of, and check the resources we list here and in Appendix B, "Resources."

The Least You Need to Know

➤ Many diverse and varied awards exist in the publishing world to give kudos to children's book authors and illustrators.

➤ The original and most esteemed award in the United States for a writer is the Newbery Medal.

➤ The original and most esteemed award in the United States for an illustrator is the Caldecott Medal.

➤ Beyond awards, lists of notable books abound; these lists remain a good way for authors to receive recognition.

➤ In many cases, in order to be considered for all these awards and lists, the publisher must submit information or applications; if your publisher doesn't act, sometimes you can.

Chapter 31

Building a Career

In This Chapter

➤ Some of the challenges you'll face once you get published

➤ How to deal with books going out of print

➤ Ways to make money that aren't completely incompatible with your writing

➤ The importance of continuing to learn and grow

➤ Take yourself seriously, and never forget that you aren't just a writer

Once the first book is published, many writers believe their struggles will be over. They'll have the ear of an editor, and their books will now flow steadily into the publishing pipeline and out into the world. The reality is a bit more complicated than that. In this chapter, we'll reveal some of the challenges that still lie ahead, and point out some possible solutions. It's a big world out there, and we want to give you a few more tools so you can succeed in it.

Becoming a Pro

By the time your first book is published, unless you are very lucky, you will have already spent several years as a children's writer. Inevitably, you've learned a lot, and have absorbed and built upon the advice and information in this book. You are becoming a professional. To be a professional, you need to think strategically about what you do.

Your overall challenge now is to balance writing with the other things you must do to keep your career going. You can't spend all your time promoting your already published books, or bringing in income from other sources. In Part 4, "Working with a Publisher," we covered promoting your book, and later in this chapter, we'll give examples of what you can do to add to your writing income. Don't get carried

Can You Keep a Secret?

Some authors work with more than one publisher to ensure a steady stream of new books. Don't do this unless each will publish a different kind of book, such as picture books at one, chapter books at another. And try not to hop from one publisher to another. Building up a backlist at a publisher will ensure that your books get more support.

away with either of these! You need to be sure to set aside regular writing time, so that your other activities don't prevent you from working on new manuscripts.

You need new manuscripts because you want to have new books coming out regularly. Each new one will help remind readers of your earlier ones, and get them hoping for the next. Ideally, when one book is about to be published, you'll already have others under contract, and be starting to think about still others. Just like a publisher, you need to have a pipeline.

Obstacles

Let's not get carried away. Many authors only dream of having the "problem" of having to balance different demands on their time. After your first book comes out, the next ones aren't necessarily any easier.

The First One's Easy

Everyone is excited by something new and possibly different. Publishers with a book by a first-time author are excited to have discovered fresh talent, reviewers are intrigued, and readers are curious to see if something really unusual has come along. Your book is the new kid on the block who everyone wants to meet. After that first book, reality sets in. If it doesn't do well, by which we mean meet expectations for sales and reviews, the next one will actually be harder. You're already a has-been, even if there was nothing wrong with your effort at all. The publisher might have expected too much. One reviewer might have had a bad day. Or the illustrations you and the editor loved didn't appeal to your readers. And bad luck with a second or third book can have the same effect. Your publisher can decide not to do another book with you.

What to do? First, don't blame yourself if something like this happens. Someone liked your first book enough to invest in publishing it, after all. And work to make your next manuscript irresistible. If your first book isn't out yet, hope that your first few books all do reasonably well. After that, your reputation can stand an off day.

Censorship

It may seem hard to believe, but censorship is an issue in children's books. It's probably more of a constant pressure for textbook publishers, who must produce work that won't offend anyone, but since children's books are sold to schools and libraries, their presence on the shelf or in the classroom can be and is challenged. Most often, fantasy novels get challenged for their magic and witches, and realistic young adult novels get challenged for their language or handling of sex. But just about any book that contains any content that one particular parent doesn't want his or her child exposed to can be challenged, and may actually be taken off the shelves.

Should you be concerned that your career will be damaged by censorship? Probably not, since most trade publishers aren't bothered by a few incidents of this type. But your career can be damaged by self-censorship. Don't anticipate the objections and try to head them off. Children can understand and deal with almost any subject, if it's presented in an appropriate manner for their level of understanding and maturity. So if you want to write about a tricky subject, or even just use realistic dialogue in a family argument, follow your own sense of what's right. If you've gone too far, your publisher will tell you.

Class Rules

What do Captain Underpants, Tiger Eyes, and Harry Potter have in common? They're all characters in books that have been targeted for removal from libraries—books by Dav Pilkey, Judy Blume, and J. K. Rowling. Censorship can affect you. Find out about the extent of the problem and how to deal with it at the Web site of the National Coalition Against Censorship (www.ncac.org/).

Doubts

Perhaps the most difficult challenge to overcome is that posed by your own doubts. You might wonder, "Am I really cut out to be a writer? Did I just have one good idea, and that's it?" You may have lots of new ideas, but not know which to pursue. Or you may feel that you can't generate new ones. Or that you aren't that good after all—that your editor turned your work into what it was. Don't listen to yourself!

Remember that after your first inspiration, it took you a long time, perhaps years, of revision and polishing, before your first book was finished. Why should your next books be any different? Don't be embarrassed to go back to the writing ideas in Chapter 2, "I Don't Know What to Say! And What Comes Next." And do be sure to allow yourself time to write, even if it's only a few minutes to use your journal, or note down a few observations. Keep going back to the well, and sooner or later, the bucket will come up full, and you'll be off, writing again.

An Agent in Your Corner?

To help you with some of these challenges, it might be time to consider an agent. Earlier in this book we pointed out that trying to find an agent before you are published can be a waste of time. Now, though, it will be considerably easier, and an

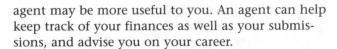

Can You Keep a Secret?

When looking for an agent, ask about fees, about other clients, and if the agent belongs to the Association of Author's Representatives. There are reputable agents who choose not to belong, but the AAR's Canon of Ethics, suggested questions to ask of an agent, and member's list, all on-line at www.publishersweekly. com/aar/, are useful resources.

Vocabulary List

A book is **out of print** (**OP**) when it can no longer be ordered from the publisher, and the publisher does not intend to put it back in print. If a publisher wants to leave its options open, it may declare a book out of stock indefinitely (OSI), meaning it might still decide to print a fresh supply.

agent may be more useful to you. An agent can help keep track of your finances as well as your submissions, and advise you on your career.

If you decide you want to have an agent, use resources such as *Literary Market Place* to locate them, and don't be afraid to ask questions. The Association of Author Representatives has a list of questions you can use, as noted in the sidebar. Find out not only their commission structures but what costs they pass on to you. If they want to charge a reading fee before they'll evaluate your manuscript, run, do not walk, to the nearest exit. Agents can legitimately pass on some expenses, but those charging reading fees are not living on their commissions, which is what you want them to do.

Above all, make sure they are experienced with children's books, because good agents of adult books don't necessarily have a clue as to how to handle children's books. And ask if you can speak to one of their clients. An experienced, confident agent will be happy to provide you with a list of clients.

Books and Their Untimely Deaths

One of the sad facts of life in the publishing world is that books don't stay in print. You want all your books to be available forever, so this can come as a rude shock, especially if it happens only a few years after a book was published, but there are some actions you can take to keep your book available or get it back in print.

Going OP

Publishers keep books "in print," meaning they are available even if you don't see them in every bookstore, only so long. At a point when the cost of keeping books in a warehouse and in the catalog is greater then the income a publisher makes from selling them, or when the cost of reprinting a supply that would take no more than three years to sell is too high, publishers declare a book *out of print* (*OP*). Recently, many publishers have wanted higher sales levels to keep books in print, with the result that books go out of print after only two or three years. This is very frustrating to an author, who suddenly cannot get copies of a book for a school visit or sees backlist sales cut off before they can develop.

Out of print does not mean gone forever, so be ready to take action.

Get Your Books and Your Rights

Don't bother to try to keep your books in print, either by promoting them frantically or lobbying your editor. You probably can't do enough to generate sales to make a difference, and your editor most likely is not involved in OP decisions. In fact, at the larger companies, an inventory manager, who may not even be in the same building, makes the decision in consultation with the marketing department (can they increase sales?) and the production department (can the book be printed cost-effectively?). Your editor may not know that your book is out of print until after the decision has been made and books have been remaindered, or sold off at a discount.

What you can do is let your editor know that you want to hear as soon as possible about any decision to declare your book OP. You need to know so you can buy as many copies of the book as possible before they're all gone. Publishers sell off what's in the warehouse at a greatly reduced price, perhaps not much more than the $2 or so it cost to manufacture it. You may be able to get hundreds of copies. Buy as many as you can afford, and then worry about finding space for them. This is a better dilemma to be in than not hearing until after the books are all gone, as happens all too often.

Get your rights back, too. Once the book is out of print, ask the publisher for a letter formally returning your copyright to you. Even if you are not entitled to this by your contract, ask. If you are entitled to it by your contract, press your case as far as you must. Sometimes, a polite letter from your lawyer will shake this letter loose. Don't accept an OSI status for your book, either. This can be a legitimate designation for a few months, while a publisher waits for orders to come in, but don't let it become a substitute for out of print.

Back from the Dead?

Once you've got your books and your rights, what do you do? You can sell your books on school visits, and make them available through on-line booksellers or specialized services like backinprint.com. This Web site provides a service to Author's Guild members, selling their stock of out of print books and even making print-on-demand copies available.

Putting the book back in print is more difficult. Publishers don't jump at the chance to republish a book another publisher let go. They assume they won't be any better able to reach other customers than the first publisher was. Though a few publishers do re-publish books, the numbers of books that come back to life in this way are small compared to the many hundreds of books that go out of print each year.

Electronic books are another option, though a potentially ephemeral one. Sites like www.mightywords.com, which lists all comers for a fee, can and do decide to clear out materials that aren't selling. You may not stay back in print for long. Companies like ipicturebooks.com, where Harold recently started working, are a better option. At such companies, both in-print and out-of-print picture books are being made available in electronic formats, and the company covers conversion and other costs. Such companies don't take everything they receive. They can't, since they pay the production costs themselves. If e-publishing isn't good enough, then consider self-publishing.

Do-It-Yourself Publishing

When we discussed self-publishing earlier, in Chapter 17, "Deeper into the Maze: Other Kinds of Publishers," we warned you against it. However, once you are published, and provided that you have the time and money to invest, this may be a viable option.

Self-publishing is a lot of work. To do it successfully, you have to act like a publisher, and find people to help with editing, design, and production, then front about $20,000 for a print run of 5,000 books, and then find ways to sell, promote, and distribute. All these things can be done, but to be done well, you have to know how to do them, or be able to hire people who do. It gets a little easier if you have a book that has already been published, and for which you have not only gotten the rights back but have bought or been given the film used to print it. You'll already know about the people who are likely to be interested in your book, and from this book and other experiences you'll have some idea of how to reach them. With the film, which will only need small changes to places like the title and copyright pages, you'll be able to save some money when you go to press.

Self-publish when you can go into it with your eyes wide open, with a carefully thought-out plan, and with the time and the money not only for a first printing but for a second printing before you've sold the first. As Josephine (Joi) Nobisso says of her experiences:

> I'm beginning to get calls from aspiring publishers, as I always did from aspiring writers! Most of these ventures look like vanity to me (meaning, in this case, that these books are being done in vain—no marketing possibilities are built into some of the concepts and/or planned execution of these projects), but I'm quite sure that the route I'm currently taking will soon be a usual one for established and responsible authors who are itching to get pet projects out there and who are willing to do (or to hire out) the promotion to the right markets.

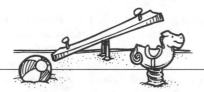

Stories from the Playground

Self-publishing worked for Josephine (Joi) Nobisso. With Gingerbread House, her own company, she began by putting three picture books back into print, and sold a total of 18,000 copies in hard- and softcover in her first season. Lucky? No. She used an experienced printer, did a mailing to children's booksellers, sent out hundreds of review copies, and set up a Web site (www.gingerbreadbooks.com). She presold 3,000 copies of one book to Scholastic Australia and Scholastic New Zealand Book Clubs. She found a "niche" (scrapbook-makers) market for one title, *Grandma's Scrapbook,* and sold 1,500 copies there through a special offer. She sold hundreds more through writing workshops she does in schools. And she also found a distributor who would carry her titles, and it shipped thousands more copies. It was a lot of work, but she'll do it again.

For two more case studies, see "12 Gifts That Keep On Giving" (*Publishers Weekly,* September 25, 2000, pp. 28–29), and "A Self-Published Author Shares His Experience," in the 2000 edition of *Children's Writer's and Illustrator's Market* (pp. 98–99).

What to Do Until You Can Live on Your Royalties

The dream of most children's book authors is to be able to live on the royalty income from their books. In reality, few end up being able to quit their day job or to stop relying on a spouse with a steady income and a health plan. But there are jobs you can take on that are both flexible and relevant to what you want to do, which is write. As you know from Chapter 29, "Back to School," school visits don't just promote your book. They also can be a handy source of income, especially once you have several books on the market. Here we give examples of other kinds of work that can be done on a flexible schedule and at home. You'll undoubtedly find out about other kinds of work you can do just by comparing notes with other writers at conferences.

Packagers

We mentioned packagers in Chapter 11, "Keep 'em Rolling: Series," as a possible home for some kinds of series. They are also a potential source of writing work, perhaps closely related to the work you do. Companies such as Mega-Books, 17th Street Productions, and Parachute Press produce many paperback series for publishers, hiring writers to create the individual books from an outline and a guide to the series often called a "bible." To get this work, you need to have samples to show, and be prepared not to be credited on the cover for your work. Some nonfiction is also produced by packagers, sometimes by one-person operations. Often known as "work-for-hire," you may not get to keep the underlying copyright in such work, but in at least some cases you do get your name on the cover. For just about any type of children's book except the high-end literary titles, you are likely to find a few packagers who specialize in it, if you do your research in the writer's guides.

Writing and Editing

Over the years, as you've gone over manuscripts in critique groups and corrected your writer friends' grammar (while they corrected yours), you will have picked up some general writing and editing skills, which you can use either inside or outside children's publishing. Start by looking locally. Many businesses need help with manuals and press releases and newsletters. Local free papers may expect you to work for free too, but you can gain some writing credits and move on. Magazine and book publishers all need proofreaders and fact checkers, and if you're local, you've got a leg up; you can be a face instead of a voice on the phone, and even come in and work in their offices or pick up and drop off materials.

But there's no reason why you can't look outside your local area. If you are willing to take some time researching writer's sites on the Web that have job listings, you can tap into a national market. Have writing samples and a resumé ready, and if you're looking at specialized jobs, such as proofreading, be prepared to take a test (so learn the proofreading marks).

Can You Keep a Secret?

Helping freelance writers and editors make sense of the job market is the Editorial Freelancers Association. Based in New York, but with national membership, the EFA has a job line, an annual pricing survey, an educational program, and other resources. Find out about them on-line at www.the-efa.org/ or write to them at 71 West 23rd St., New York, NY 10010.

Textbooks and Supplemental Materials

In Chapter 17, we pointed out that some educational publishers acquire manuscripts, either by submission or on commission. These companies also need workbooks and activity books, from straightforward drills to more creative mixes of experiments, arts and crafts projects, and other hands-on activity books. They need stories and activities written to fit a particular theme and format in a textbook, so they work with writers, often as packagers do, on a work-for-hire basis. In the market guides, you'll find companies such as Cottonwood Press, Dandy Lion Publications, Evan-Moor Publishing, SRA McGraw-Hill, and Teacher Created Materials. Look for others, too. Some accept submissions, so you must always check their guidelines.

Teach Writing! You've Learned a Thing or Two

By now, you've learned a good bit about writing from the time you've spent on your own manuscripts. Perhaps you've taken some courses or workshops and felt you could have done better. Well, we're urging you to consider doing just that. Contact local colleges with active adult education departments, and find out if they offer children's writing courses. If they don't suggest that you could offer one, and find out what you would need to do to set one up. You can also set up classes on-line or offer advice and manuscript consulting by mail. You'll need to find ways to let people know about yourself.

Keep Learning

As if you didn't have enough to balance already, we have one more pressing item for your agenda: Don't ever stop learning and growing. Many published writers have told us that although they reach a good level of ability and confidence in what they want to do, they never feel that they can say they have nothing more to learn. You've got to stay excited by what you are doing, if you are going to pass excitement on to your readers. You've got to keep an open mind about everything. Your readers do. So don't stop reading the latest books for children, don't stop debating them with your writer friends, don't stop trying new challenges in your writing, don't stop going to conferences. If you are going to sustain a career, you can't let yourself coast along.

Take Yourself Seriously

As you move forward, believe in yourself and don't let yourself be intimidated, either by an unfamiliar challenge, by a dry spell, or by a publisher. Keep moving, and you'll reach your happy ending. We think a story that Deborah Kogan Ray told us illustrates this point well.

Today, Deborah is an established, well-known illustrator with something like 100 books to her credit. In the 1960s, she was a novice illustrator, taking her portfolio to two publishers on her first trip to New York. Something about her art caught the attention of the legendary Ursula Nordstrom, still head of what was then Harper & Row.

In short order, Deborah had a contract and a problem. She didn't know how to produce preseparated art, which then was standard for picture books. With the help of some very patient design staff, she learned, and she was working away on the finished art for the book when her contract was canceled, with no explanation.

So she sued for the remaining $500 of her $1,000 advance. Harper settled before the case went to trial. Deborah picks up the story:

> I found lots of work with other publishers, but remained *persona non grata* at
> Harper & Row for eight years.

One day, I received a letter and manuscript from an editor named Elizabeth Gordon [at Harper], who was not on their staff when my troubles occurred. She wanted to take me to lunch and asked if I would consider illustrating *I Have a Sister, My Sister Is Deaf.* My immediate question was, "Don't you know that I sued Harper & Row?" She wasn't concerned.

I illustrated the book. It is still in print. The question of what caused Harper to break my first contract has never been answered.

Suing a publishing company is not to be undertaken lightly, of course! But the principle applies in other situations. If you need more space to write in your home, find a way to create it. If you are asked to make substantial revision, and you don't understand why, ask for clarification. If you haven't seen any reviews of your book, even though it's been out for six months, ask why. Take yourself seriously and work to be a partner with your editor and publisher.

That's what Deborah did. She not only won her case, she ended up working with Harper again, and she got something else from the experience: "As to the great settlement from my lawsuit: I took my $500 check and bought my first drawing table. It had a side table, a straight edge, a paper drawer, and big drafting board with a crank to move it up and down. It was the biggest, fanciest drawing table that I could find."

Out into the Big World

Publishing companies can seem like enormous and powerful entities to writers and illustrators. Taking one on like Deborah did seems like a David and Goliath story. But widen the focus a little more. Children's publishing, itself a large and complicated world, is just one part of the publishing industry, which in turn is a pretty small part of any country's economy. We hope you have come to understand it better, but we know that a writer (or an editor, for that matter) is at the mercy of forces beyond one's control. As you travel on in your career as a writer, we hope you'll remember a lesson to be learned from a small boy, named (oddly enough) Harold.

We refer to Harold in *Harold and the Purple Crayon,* by Crockett Johnson (HarperCollins, 1955). This particular Harold has a purple crayon with which he draws what he wants, conjuring up problems at the same time, which he then proceeds to solve. He draws a mountain so he can see where he is, but falls off the other side, and quickly draws a balloon, and on he goes. In the end, he gets to the place he most wants to be. You can read this just as an imaginative adventure, or as a story about dreaming, but we think it also has something to say about how to live in the world.

Harold (the character) doesn't settle for what's in front of him. He creates the world that he wants to live in. When some aspect of it doesn't work out the way that he had hoped, he finds a way to fix it. Harold (the coauthor of this book) often points out at conferences that we can be like this small boy. Like Harold (the character), we can work to make our world be the way we want it to be.

In fact, this is what those of us who care about children's books must do. We are a sizable community—illustrators, writers, editors, librarians, teachers, and, potentially, millions of parents. We all vote. We can lobby our local, state, and national elected officials for better library funding. We can support the use of trade books as well as text books in classrooms when the subject is debated at local school committee meetings. We create books with our purple crayons. But we can do much more. We can and should work to make this a world in which the kinds of books we care about continue to have a place—a larger place than they do now.

This may take a bigger crayon, but it's important not to lose sight of this bigger world, and the impact we can have on it. Use your purple crayon, not only to create your own worlds between the covers of a book, but to make the world we live in a more hospitable place for the books we love and the children who need them.

The Least You Need to Know

➤ Now that you are published, your next challenge is to build a career for yourself.

➤ Books go out of print more quickly nowadays, but there are actions you can take to keep them available.

➤ Working with packagers, educational publishers, doing other freelance editing and writing, and teaching writing are all jobs you can fit in around your writing.

➤ Self-publishing can be an option for you, if you have the time and the money.

➤ Keep learning, take yourself seriously, and never forget that you can have an impact on the world.

Glossary

acquire To make an agreement with an author to publish a book. This is called an *acquisition*.

acquisitions editor The editor who signs a book up, then passes it on to a development editor. These roles are usually combined at children's publishing companies.

advance Money paid by a publisher to an author or illustrator before the book goes on the market, in anticipation of sales. The advance is charged against royalties (see below) and must "earn out" before any royalties are paid.

agent A well-connected professional who places your work with publishers, keeps track of your royalties, and perhaps provides career guidance in return for a percentage of your earnings.

assignment *See* commission.

attachment A way of sending a file over the Internet, accompanying an e-mail. Often used to send documents.

audience The people for whom you are writing. In children's books, this can mean a specific age level.

author's representative *See* agent.

back matter Supplementary material in the back of a book, such as a glossary, recommended reading lists, an index, or information about the book.

backlist Previously published books. A publisher's backlist is an important source of revenue, because backlist sales are more predictable and dependable than frontlist sales.

binding What holds a book together. A trade binding is usually sewn and glued. A library binding is more durable, with cloth reinforcement and often a different sewing method. Paperbacks are usually bound with glue only.

blues or **bluelines**   A printing, in blue only, from the final plates for a book. This is usually seen only by editors and constitutes a final check. If changes are needed, they have to be made to the film, which is expensive.

board books   Short, thick, square-shaped (usually) simple books for infants and toddlers.

body   The main part of the text of a work, not including elements like the table of contents or index.

boilerplate   Standard language in a contract.

book plus   A book packaged with something else, such as a plush toy.

book proposal   Materials sent to a publisher to propose a book, including at least a description of the book or books, sample chapters, and an outline.

chains   Companies that own many individual bookstores. The two biggest in book-selling are Barnes & Noble and Borders. They contrast with the *independents*.

chapter books   Books for older children. They may be illustrated, but tell a story primarily through words.

clips   Samples of one's writing.

colophon   An item in a book's front matter that gives information about how the book was produced, from typefaces to the kind of paint an artist used.

commission   When doing work "on commission" the publisher hires you, tells you what to do, and usually pays a fee instead of royalties.

concept book   A picture book that explores a concept instead of, or perhaps in addition to, telling a story.

conglomerate   A large company with many divisions, increasingly common in children's publishing.

consolidation   The process of combining companies, closing overlapping divisions, and laying off staff.

co-op money   Money a bookseller spends to promote a publisher's books, which is then reimbursed.

copy editor   The person who reviews a manuscript for style, punctuation, spelling, and grammar.

copyright   Literally, the right to create and distribute copies of a creative work. Under copyright law, you hold copyright in a work from the moment you create it.

cover letter   The letter that accompanies your manuscript.

critique   A thoughtful, usually written evaluation of a manuscript, concentrating on problems of structure, tone, characterization, and the like.

development editor The editor who actually edits a book.

development house *See* packager.

draft A version of a manuscript. The *first* draft is the first one written; the *rough* draft is an unpolished version; the *final* draft is the last one.

dummy A manuscript laid out in book form, with sketches of all the illustrations and sample finished pieces.

early or **easy readers** Books written with a controlled vocabulary for children learning to read.

earn out To reach the point when the royalties on a book have paid back the advance paid to the author.

e-book or **ebook** A book that must be read in an electronic format, either on a personal computer or a handheld reader, instead of on paper.

exclusive submission A manuscript sent to only one publisher.

fair use A limited exception to copyright law, allowing others to draw on or use excerpts from a copyrighted work without formal permission.

fairy tale Like a folktale in form, but told specifically for children and involves more literary elements.

fantasy A type of fiction in which the rules of the world are different; animals talk, magic works, and strange creatures exist.

fiction Writing from the imagination, or writing containing elements of imagination, fable, or tale. Also known as "lies," or "something you've made up."

film What most books today are printed from.

flat fee A payment made as the only compensation; the opposite of an advance against royalties.

folktale A story, usually with a message, that has been passed down orally and may appeal to both adults and children.

freelance An independent worker, not on salary, hired instead on a project basis.

front matter The material before the body of a book, including such elements as the title and copyright pages, a table of contents, or an introduction.

frontlist The books a publisher is releasing this year.

galleys Long pages of typeset text, not yet broken out into book pages, not much used today.

glossary You are reading one.

hardcover   A book produced with a hard, stiff outer cover, usually covered by a jacket. The covers are usually made of cardboard, over which is stretched cloth, treated paper, vinyl, or some other plastic.

historical fiction   Fiction in a historical setting, in which the main character, and often many others, are invented, while the setting and other details are based on careful research.

imprint   A part of a publisher with a distinct identity, name, and staff.

independents   Bookstores not owned by large companies, usually free-standing or having only a few branches.

index   An alphabetical list of topics and key words to be found in a book, with their page number locations.

institutional   One of the markets in children's publishing, named for the institutions the books are sold to—schools and libraries.

IRC   Short for International Reply Coupon: good for postage anywhere in the world. Send one or more to a foreign publisher along with a self-addressed envelope for the response.

ISBN   The acronym for *International Standard Book Number*. This number gives the book a unique ID, like your Social Security number, for orders and distribution. The first part of the number identifies the language of publication ("0" for English), and the second part is the publisher's number ("02" in this book identifies Pearson Education).

jacket   Short for *dust jacket,* this is the paper cover on a book. Originally intended to keep it clean, it's now used as a way of catching the eye of the reader.

journal   A blank book to write in whenever you can; not just for recording events, but for exploring ideas and jotting observations.

kill fee   A final payment made to an author or illustrator when a project is cancelled.

layout   The arrangement of all the elements of a book's design, from text paragraphs and illustrations to chapter titles and page numbers.

license   The right to do something. In publishing, the right to publish a book or books, or to something from one book in another product.

line editing   Close, line-by-line editing of a book, concentrating on tone, style, flow, sequencing, clarity, and such matters.

lists   Semi-annual (or more frequent) groups of books produced by a publisher, announced and placed in a catalog together. A publisher's list is simply the books that company produces.

literary agent   *See* agent.

manuscript   A writer's work before it is typeset and printed; originally "hand written," as the word implies, now it is likely to be produced on a word processing program.

mass market   Books sold through general retail outlets, usually with wide appeal and low prices.

midlist   Books with reliable but not outstanding sales.

model release   Written permission for the use of one's likeness in print. Needed if you take someone's picture for a book.

ms./mss.   Short for manuscript or manuscripts.

multiple submission   A manuscript sent to two or more publishers at the same time.

niche publisher   A publisher that specializes in a subject of interest to a small group of people and sells its books nationally, but only in specialized outlets.

nonfiction   Also known as an "informational book," writing in which the author retells the events of history with minimal embellishment, passes on knowledge, or presents activities or experiments.

novelty book   Any book with features added to it beyond the binding and pages; for example, foldout page, die-cut holes, lift-the-flap, pop-ups, or sound chips.

on spec   Work done without a contract, in the hope that one will be forthcoming: "on speculation."

option clause   An item in a contract granting a publisher the right to consider an author's next work.

original expression   What copyright law protects: your own unique way of expressing an idea, telling a story, or creating a work of art.

packager   A company specializing in creating books up to the printing stage or the distribution stage; marketing and distributing the book is handled by the publisher. The packager's name may appear on the copyright page, but the publisher's appears on the spine.

paperback   A binding with a soft cover, usually a light cardboard. A *trade* paperback is usually the same size as a hardcover book, and printed to the same standards. A *mass-market* paperback is usually smaller, designed to fit in a rack, and printed on cheaper paper.

pedantic   Describes a story in which the moral or message the author wants to teach overwhelms the plot.

permissions   Agreements from copyright holders granting the right to reproduce their work.

picture books   Books for younger children, which have pictures on every page, and tell a story through words and pictures.

PP&B   Paper, printing, and binding. The cost of producing a finished book.

press kit   A folder of materials about your book sent to the media to alert them to your book's release.

prewriting   The all-important work a writer does before actually starting to write. This can be as simple as jotting down ideas, as methodical as creating an outline, or as complex as doing character studies.

proofreader   The person who reviews the proofs for errors before it goes to press.

proofs   The typeset pages of a book before it is printed.

pub date   The publication date; the date when a publisher says a book will be available.

public domain   Not copyrighted, either because it never was or because the copyright has expired or lapsed; public domain material can be used without attribution or permission, though good writing practice means making a note of sources.

publishing committee   Also known as the editorial board, this is the group that at some companies approves the acquisition of a book.

OP   Out of print, meaning that the publisher has no copies of a book on hand and does not intend to reprint it.

OSI   Out of stock indefinitely. The publisher has no copies of a book on hand, but may wish to reprint it in the future, and so is not calling it out of print.

query letter   A letter you send to a publisher to ask, or query, if they are interested in seeing the manuscript.

reading fees   Fees charged to read and comment on a manuscript. If charged by an agent to determine if he will represent you, not legitimate.

regional publisher   A publisher who specializes in subjects relevant to a particular part of the country, and sells its books mostly or entirely in that area.

rejection letter   A letter turning down a manuscript. If it is an unsigned photocopy, you've received a standard response. If personalized in any way, take this as a good sign.

remainders   Surplus books sold at a steep discount. A publisher may *remainder* a book and sell off all its stock when putting it out of print, or it may sell only some of its copies to reduce its stock.

response sheet   A feedback device, on which a writer lists certain ideas, devices, or grammatical points for the audience/editor to consider.

response time   The time it takes a publisher to reply to a submission, usually measured in months.

returns   Books sent back to a publisher. Unlike many other businesses, retailers can usually return books for a full refund. Returns often come back several months after a book is published.

revise   Literally to "re-see"; to rewrite, perhaps making extensive changes.

rights   The many different ways a book can be licensed, ranging from book club rights to movie rights and even theme park rights. Also called subsidiary rights.

royalties   Money paid to an author by a publisher on the basis of books sold. It may be a percentage of the *list price,* which is the price for which the book supposedly will be sold to a consumer, or of the *net price,* which is what the publisher actually receives (often 40 percent to 50 percent less than the retail price).

sales rep   Short for *sales representative.* An individual who represents a publisher to a potential customer, such as a bookstore or wholesaler. May be a *house rep,* hired by the publisher; or a *commissioned rep,* independent, and paid a commission for every book sold.

SASE   A self-addressed, stamped envelope, included with all submissions and query letters for return of manuscript or response.

self-publish   An individual doing everything a publisher does, from editing to printing and distribution.

series   A number of books linked in theme, purpose, characters, style, or content, or all of these things, and often given an overall title.

simultaneous submission   *See* multiple submission.

slush pile   All the manuscripts that a publisher has received from writers the publisher doesn't know.

softcover   *See* paperback.

special sales   Sales of a book to nontraditional outlets, such as gift stores, or for use as premiums.

spine   The center panel of the binding of a book, which connects the front and back cover to the pages and faces out when the book is shelved.

structural editing   Editing involving the structure of a manuscript, usually done at an early stage.

submissions   Manuscripts sent to a publisher by an author or agent. They may be *exclusive, multiple,* or *simultaneous.*

subsidiary rights   *See* rights.

subsidy publisher   *See* vanity publisher.

superstore   In bookstores, a large store with 100,000 or more titles, a coffee shop, and other amenities.

tear sheets   Originally samples of an illustrator's work, torn out of a magazine or other source. Now can also be a photocopy of such a sample.

thumbnails   Small, rough sketches done by an artist before full-sized sketches, which may be literally not much bigger than thumbnail size.

trade   The kind of publisher selling books to bookstores, and also to some extent to libraries.

transparencies   Photographs or art on transparent material (like slides) rather than on opaque material.

trim size   The horizontal and vertical dimensions of a book. A book with an 8-by-10-inch trim size is 8 inches across and 10 inches high.

unsolicited submission/manuscript   A manuscript that a publisher did not solicit, or ask for, from an author.

vanity publisher   A company the author pays to publish a book, rather than the other way around. The name comes from the fact that such publishers rely on the vanity of people who want to see their words in print and are willing to pay for this.

work-for-hire   Work done for a publisher to their specifications, usually paid for with a fee and often involving signing over copyright to the publisher.

young adult (YA)   The upper end of the age range covered by children's publishers, possibly starting at age 12. A separate YA category did not exist until the 1960s.

Resources

We could almost fill a book with the books, magazines, organizations, and Web sites we've researched for this guide. Unfortunately, we just can't fit all the good ones here. So here is a highly selected list of some of the best. We've placed more, and Web site links you can click on instead of typing into your browser on Harold Underdown's The Purple Crayon Web site at www.underdown.org/ciglinks.htm.

Books on Writing

There are many how-to books on children's writing. We list only a few here. If none of them sound quite right for you, browse through the selections in a well-stocked bookstore until you find a book that speaks to you.

***A Basic Guide to Writing, Selling, and Promoting Children's Books: Plus Information about Self-publishing,* Betsy B. Lee (Learning Abilities Books, 2000).** Created as a text for writing classes, this book provides basic information. Of special interest to many may be the information on self-publishing; not many books detail the task because of the difficulty. This book does.

***The Business of Writing for Children: An Award-Winning Author's Tips on How to Write, Sell, and Promote Your Children's Books,* Aaron Shepard (Shepard Publications, 2000).** Perhaps not the glossiest or snazziest how-to book on children's writing, but nonetheless a useful how-to guide, especially for picture book and folktale authors, from a successful writer. He also gives sound advice on working with publishers and the process. A thin book, but packed with useful information.

How to Write a Damn Good Novel, How to Write a Damn Good Novel II, **and** *The Key: How to Write Damn Good Fiction Using the Power of Myth*, **James N. Frey (St. Martin's Press, various years).** Great resources for any writer of YA novels in particular, regardless of experience. "These books offer solid, step-by-step advice and are funny and really fun to read," says Laurie Halse Anderson.

Love and Death at the Mall: Teaching and Writing for the Literate Young, **Richard Peck (Delacorte, 1994).** Peck analyzes what young people read and why in his book. The author tackles such notable teen problems of peer pressure and suicide and how social issues relate to the writing to which young readers respond. A good reference if you strive for realism in your writing.

Origins of Story: On Writing for Children, **Barbara Harrison (Editor) and Gregory Maguire (Editor) (Margaret McElderry Books, 1999).** You'll read illuminating and inspiring essays by accomplished children's book writers and illustrators like Maurice Sendak, Gillian Cross, Ursula Le Guin, Madeleine L'Engle, and Susan Cooper. This collection provides writers with an understanding of children's interests and a look at the writer's mind and passion for writing.

A Sense of Wonder: On Reading and Writing Books for Children, **Katherine Paterson (Plume Books, 1995).** Another collection of essays on reading and writing for children; this book looks at the child's imagination. A good reference.

Transcending Boundaries: Writing for a Dual Audience of Children and Adults, **Sandra L. Beckett (Editor) (Garland Publishing, 1999).** Steep in price (over $50 dollars!) and specialized, this book contains a collection of essays on those modern authors who write crossover books, which appeal to both adults and children, like the Harry Potter series. An intriguing but serious book for serious writers as the essays are largely from scholars.

The Way to Write for Children, **Joan Aiken (St. Martin's Press, 1999).** This book gives an overview of what children's books shouldn't do—like prove boring or condescending—but also offers the obligations that children's authors have toward their audience—"to demonstrate that the world is not a simple place." Basically, the book is inspirational.

What's Your Story?: A Young Person's Guide to Writing Fiction, **Marion Dane Bauer (Clarion Books, 1992).** Though this book was written for a young audience, the author, an award-winning children's book novelist, covers many important facets of writing—idea-generation, building characters, plots and themes, mastering grammar, and more. For those looking to hone their writing skills, this sensible and functional book will help.

The Writer's Idea Book, **Jack Heffron (Writer's Digest Books, 2000).** Do you find yourself unable to put words to paper? This book provides prompts to get your creative juices flowing and begin writing. Though not intended specifically for the children's book writer, the over 400 prompts are certain to help those interested in writing for children spawn ideas.

Writing Books for Young People, James Cross Giblin (The Writer, 1990). A how-to by a master of nonfiction.

Writing Hannah: On Writing for Children, by Libby Gleeson (Hale & Iremonger, 1999). Australian author Libby Gleeson shares the writing process within a journal for aspiring writers. A good look at "how-to" write a children's book by watching a children's book writer actually write one.

Young at Heart: A Step-by-Step Way of Writing Children's Stories, Violet Ramos (VR Publications, 1999). A mere 80 pages but this book works like a writing workshop with worksheets to help writers develop key components like characterization, dialogue, and even word choice. Look at this manual as a more programmed, step-by-step approach to begin writing.

Reference Books

Children's Books: Awards and Prizes, Children's Book Council staff (Children's Book Council, 1996). This is an extremely comprehensive guide, and an expensive one. Use it in your library.

Children's Books in Print/Subject Guide to Children's Books in Print (R.R. Bowker, annual). These are a complete and massive reference set. Use them in your library, but for easier and more up-to-date research, learn how to use the advanced search functions on www.amazon.com; you can search by publisher and year of publication, for example.

Children's Writer's & Illustrator's Market, Alice Pope (Editor) (Writer's Digest Books, November 2002). An invaluable annual reference book for writers of children's literature, this compendium lists about 800 publishers, magazines, scriptwriter markets, and many other places that you, the children's writer, can sell and publish your work. A must-have on the desks of those who write or want to write for kids.

Literary Market Place (R.R. Bowker, annual). Use this massive and expensive reference book at your library. It's the yellow pages of publishing and has information and addresses for publishers, packagers, and agents.

The Self-Publishing Manual: How to Write, Print, and Sell Your Own Book, Dan Poynter (Para Publishing, 2000). If you want to self-publish, this is a good resource. Josephine (Joi) Nobisso used it (see Chapter 31, "Building a Career").

Terrific Connections with Authors, Illustrators, and Storytellers: Real Space and Virtual Links, Toni Buzzeo and Jane Kurtz (Teacher Ideas Press, 1999). This is the only book you need if you want to do school and library visits.

Valerie and Walter's Best Books for Children, Valerie V. Lewis and Walter M. Mayes (Avon Books, 1998). A great general guide to books for children, organized by interest and ability level. Use it to become more familiar with the best books of today.

Magazines

Booklist. The most consistently thoughtful and inclusive review magazine. Published monthly, aimed mainly at librarians. Booklist, PO Box 607, Mt. Morris, IL 61054-7564. Phone: 1-888-350-0949; www.ala.org/booklist/

Children's Book Insider. A helpful monthly magazine for writers, and the place where updates to *Children's Writer's and Illustrator's Market* are published. Children's Book Insider, LLC, 901 Columbia Road, Fort Collins, CO 80525-1838; 1-800-807-1916; www.write4kids.com/index.html

The Horn Book Magazine. A literary review magazine for children's books, with in-depth feature articles and regular columns on subjects such as multicultural literature and young adult novels. Published bimonthly, with *The Horn Book Guide* semi-annually. The Horn Book, Inc., 56 Roland Street, Suite 200, Boston MA 02129. Phone: 1-800-325-1170 or 617-628-0225; www.hbook.com/index.shtml

The Lion and the Unicorn. An academic journal on children's literature, and a good place to go for a different (sometimes difficult-to-understand) perspective. The Johns Hopkins University Press, Journals Division, 2715 N. Charles Street, Baltimore, MD 21218. Phone: 1-800-548-1784

Once Upon a Time. A quarterly magazine by and for writers, with an inspirational and supportive focus. For information, write to Audrey B. Baird, Editor, OUAT, 553 Winston Court, St. Paul, MN 55118

School Library Journal. Monthly, reviews the most books, but not always consistently. School Library Journal, PO Box 16388 North Hollywood, CA 91615-6388 USA; 1-800-595-1066 (within the USA); 818-487-4566 (outside the USA); www.slj.com

Organizations

Association of Author's Representatives. To get the AAR's Canon of Ethics, suggested questions to ask of an agent, and member's list, send a $7 check (payable to AAR), and a SASE with 55 cents in postage to Association of Author's Representatives, 10 Astor Place, 3rd fl., New York, NY 10003; www.publishersweekly.com/aar.

The Author's Guild. This national organization is open to published authors for adults and for children. 330 W. 42nd St. 29th fl. New York, NY 10036; 212-563-5904; www.authorsguild.org/.

Canadian Society of Children's Authors, Illustrators, and Performers. CANSCAIP publishes a newsletter and brings those concerned with children's literature together. To apply, contact them at CANSCAIP, 35 Spadina Road, Toronto, Ontario, Canada M5R 2S9; 416-515-1559; www.canscaip.org/.

The Children's Book Council. The trade association for children's publishers creates lots of useful publications. The best may be their list of their members, available for a

6" × 9" SASE with 3 oz. postage and a check for $2.00 from The Children's Book Council, 12 W. 37th Street, 2nd floor, New York, NY 10018-7480. They also have a Web site at www.cbcbooks.org/.

Society of Children's Book Writers and Illustrators. Get access to the SCBWI's newsletter, free publications, reduced rates for conferences by joining. Get an application form from SCBWI, 8271 Beverly Boulevard, Los Angeles, CA 90048; 323-782-1010; www.scbwi.org/.

Web Sites

Bookwire, www.bookwire.com. This is a good place to start for information on publishing, from a business point of view. Leads to articles from *Publishers Weekly* and other magazines.

The Children's Literature Web Guide, www.ucalgary.ca/~dkbrown. Run by a librarian at the University of Calgary, this is the best place to start to find information and other Web sites on children's books and children's publishing.

The Purple Crayon, www.underdown.org. Don't forget Harold's Web site. You'll find articles, interviews, materials from this book, and Harold's own idiosyncratic selections of useful Web sites.

Samples and Examples

Sample Guidelines from a Trade Publisher

Welcome to our warehouse of samples! Here you will find a sample of typical guidelines from a trade publisher, so you'll know what to expect. Actual guidelines vary a lot, so you should still write for guidelines from actual publishers. We've also got samples of different kinds of cover and query letters, and a sample manuscript format. Study these and you can't go wrong (well, you can, but they'll help you make that less likely).

```
                  SUBMISSION GUIDELINES

              for Children's Book Writers

           from a Pretty Good Publisher, Inc.

Pretty Good publishes children's books for the trade market
for children of all ages. We publish both fiction and nonfic-
tion, but do not publish board books, reference books, or ac-
tivity books.

Pretty Good reads all unsolicited manuscripts that we receive,
provided that they are submitted to us on an exclusive basis
through the mail. At present, we do not review or reply to
submissions or queries made by e-mail or fax, in disk form, or
consisting only of Web site addresses.

Manuscripts of fewer than 20 typed pages can be submitted in
their entirety. For longer manuscripts, we prefer to receive a
```

query letter, summary (not an outline), and three sample chapters. Please write "Query" on the envelope, and include a self-addressed stamped envelope (SASE) with your query.

Manuscripts should be typed double-spaced on white paper. We recommend that you make a copy of your manuscript before sending it, as we cannot be responsible for submissions lost in the mail or at our offices. Your name, address, and telephone number should appear on your manuscript as well as in your cover letter. Do not include illustrations.

Please submit your manuscript to the attention of the Trade Editorial Department at the address above.

Enclose a SASE with sufficient postage (not a check or cash) for our response and return of the manuscript, or for response only if the manuscript need not be returned. If you do not enclose a SASE, your manuscript will be discarded.

Please send only one or two manuscripts at a time. We make every effort to respond in three months, but cannot guarantee that we will be able to do so, due to the volume of submissions. For confirmation that your project was received, include a self-addressed stamped postcard.

Before submitting a manuscript to us, we encourage you to review some of our published books in a library or bookstore or to take a look at our Web site (www.prettygoodpublishers.com). If you would like to request a catalog, please send a 9-by-12-inch self-addressed stamped envelope with $1.47 in postage.

Illustration samples should be sent to the attention of the Art Director. We prefer tear sheets or color photocopies. Slides and CD-ROM portfolios may not be reviewed. Samples are not returned; we will contact you if we are interested.

Questions about the status of a manuscript must by made by mail, in an envelope marked "Manuscript Status," with a SASE enclosed. Please do not contact us until at least three months have elapsed and do not contact us by phone.

Comment: Most publishers post their guidelines somewhere on their Web sites, and all will send them to you on receipt of a SASE.

Three Sample Cover Letters for Unpublished Authors

Please use these with caution. We don't present these as perfect examples of the craft of cover-letter writing, but as examples of approaches. You should adapt, improvise, and generally find your own way to best present your unique work.

```
Your Address

Date

Some Editor
Pretty Good Publishers Books for Young Readers
1 Main St.
Anymetropolis, HC 00000

Dear Editor,

When I remembered the time I gave my little sister a bloody
nose in the backyard five minutes after Mom had praised her
report card, I knew that I had the beginnings of a story.
Mom! She's Bothering Me Again! is the story itself.

I hope you'll agree that the humor and drama of it—and the
unsentimental ending—make this a worthy new rendition of a
perennial theme.

In keeping with your company's policy, I have submitted
this manuscript exclusively to you. I look forward to hear-
ing from you soon.

Yours sincerely,


An Eager Author
```

Comment: If you haven't been published, do like this author did and don't apologize (or even mention this fact). You still have relevant personal experience with which to hook an editor. Words like *humor* and *unsentimental* also suggest that you know what you are doing. Above all, keep these letters short and business-like. A cover letter should make an editor want to read your story; now the story just has to live up to what you've promised! If you are writing nonfiction, personal experience is still a great approach, as the next letter demonstrates.

Your Address

Date

A Learned Editor
Informative Books for Young Readers
99 High St.
Middleville, PB 00000

Dear Editor,

You and I know that sharks are far less dangerous to humans than the average SUV. But these primitive yet efficient creatures still excite fascination and fear in adults and children alike.

I drew on my years of experience studying sharks at the Jaws Research Institute and my unquenched enthusiasm for the subject to create Shark!, dramatic nonfiction for a middle-grade audience.

How can this compete with the dozens of books on the subject already on the market? By providing up-to-the-minute information on sharks, told from a first-person perspective by a scientist active in the field.

I've seen the books that Informative publishes and believe that my approach suits your list. I enclose a SASE for my manuscript's return if you do not agree.

With best wishes,

A Shark Scientist

Comments: In this example, our author is a scientist. But you don't have to be an academic expert on a subject to write about it for children. You *do* have to know the latest research and be able to communicate it. First-person experiences are almost always a good way to catch an editor's eye. So is knowledge of what's out on the market, but be succinct, like this writer is. You don't have to describe the competing titles and compare yours to each of them. Knowledge of a company's publishing program is *always* a plus; if can even become the basis of a cover letter, as it is in the next example.

Your Address

Date

Some Editor
Pretty Good Publishers Books for Young Readers
1 Main St.
Anymetropolis, HC 00000

Dear Editor,

My six-year-old son never gets tired of the goofy humor in The Gerbil Looks Unhappy, or the rambunctious antics of Eleanor in your easy-reader series. Thank you for publishing them!

Because PGP Books seems to welcome such wild and wacky stories, I'm hoping that you'll enjoy the enclosed, Where's Davey?, an over-the-top adventure based on the (apparent) disappearance of one of my own children.

In the event that I'm wrong, I enclose a SASE for the return of the manuscript. I hope to hear from you soon.

With best wishes,

A Funny Author

Comments: It impresses an editor if you display familiarity with a publisher's program, especially if you don't just mention such extremely well-known books as *Goodnight Moon* and *Where the Wild Things Are,* as you might if writing to Harper-Collins. This isn't a form of name-dropping! It's also important to say something about the books, and to compare them in approach to your book. Do not focus on the *subject* of the book; it's not too insightful to claim that a publisher who's done one book on dogs will obviously be a good home for another one.

A Sample Cover Letter for Published Authors

The three approaches used above will work well for you too. All you need to do is add a brief paragraph about your writing experience for children. This example simply reworks one of the previous examples.

Your Address

Date

Some Editor
Pretty Good Publishers Books for Young Readers
1 Main St.
Anymetropolis, HC 00000

Dear Editor,

When I remembered the time I gave my little sister a bloody nose in the backyard five minutes after Mom had praised her report card, I knew that I had the beginnings of a story. Mom! She's Bothering Me Again! is the story itself.

I hope you'll agree that the humor and drama of it—and the unsentimental ending—make this a worthy new rendition of a perennial theme.

I'm the author of Wombats and Dodoes (Informative Books) and The Thing in the Closet, just released by Conglommo, Inc. I've also had several stories published in Cricket.

I have submitted this manuscript exclusively to you. I look forward to hearing from you soon.

Yours Sincerely,

An Eager Published Author

Comments: You can mention magazines as well as books, provided that they are nationally distributed, mainstream publications. Books for adults are not relevant. Really!

Two Sample Query Letters

Publishers often require query letters to reduce the volume of their submissions, particularly of longer manuscripts. Here you have to work harder to get their interest; with a shorter manuscript a reader will almost always glance at the manuscript, even if the cover letter is a downer. With a query letter, you have to make her want to request and then read the entire manuscript.

Your Address

Date

A Learned Editor
Informative Books for Young Readers
99 High St.
Middleville, PB 00000

Dear Editor,

You and I know that sharks are far less dangerous to humans than the average SUV. But these primitive yet efficient creatures still excite fascination and fear in adults and children alike.

I drew on my years of experience studying sharks at the Jaws Research Institute and my unquenched enthusiasm for the subject to create Shark!, dramatic nonfiction for a middle-grade audience. Eight compact chapters provide the latest information about the lifecycle, special adaptations, and threats to the survival of the shark. I've also taken an in-depth look at human-shark incidents—and concluded that the shark often is the loser. A guide to shark species, book and Web resources, and a diagram of shark anatomy round out the book.

Through personal contacts, I can also put together a complete set of full-color illustrations, and I enclose a sample of what's available, along with an outline and two chapters. The complete 76-page manuscript is available.

I've researched the market, and I believe that there's no book on this popular subject that not only provides up-to-the-minute information on sharks, but also is told from a first-person perspective by a scientist active in the field. I'm confident this approach will suit your list. I enclose a SASE for your response.

With best wishes,

A Shark Scientist

Comments: Compare this to the earlier cover letter about this hypothetical book. You need to include more information about the manuscript, since it's not in front of the editor. Since this is nonfiction for older readers, and potentially photo-illustrated, the author also lets the editor know that she can help to gather those materials. Another plus is that the entire manuscript is available. Getting a contract offer for just a proposal is a possibility for nonfiction, if you are published, but if you aren't it's better to complete the manuscript before trying to place it.

```
Your Address

Date

Some Editor
Pretty Good Publishers Books for Young Readers
1 Main St.
Anymetropolis, HC 00000

Dear Editor,

Do you remember the bully in eighth grade? Many middle-
schoolers are confronting a contemporary version of that ter-
rifying figure, as Josh does in this passage from my novel,
The Gauntlet:

     "Hey, kid! Think you're cool, don'tcha, all dressed in
     black? How's that black gonna look with some red on it?"

     Josh stopped dead in the hall, looked quickly behind him.
     No one. He'd have to face Steven on his own.

You know these issues. Dealing with difference, and dealing
with the reactions of those angered by it, are major chal-
lenges for our society. We can stand back and talk about
them. But they are all-too-real, concrete problems for my
protagonist, as he navigates the halls of a large public
school.

The sample chapters I enclose will show you that The Gauntlet
is no message-driven polemic, but a gripping story about
Josh. There are many YA novels on this subject, especially
recently, as we struggle to learn from Columbine. But there's
little for the middle-schooler, and I believe there needs to
be. I hope you agree, and I enclose a SASE for your response.

Yours sincerely,


A Determined Author
```

Comments: An actual excerpt from your manuscript, provided it can stand the scrutiny, can be an effective lead-in to a query letter for a fiction manuscript. Our example doesn't hold up—do better! As with the nonfiction query letter, work hard to get across what's unique about your manuscript. Make the editor *want* to read all 100-plus pages of it.

For more examples of cover and query letters, including one amusing look at what not to do, take a look at Jackie Ogburn's "Rites of Submission: Cover Letters and Queries," on-line at www.underdown.org/covlettr.htm.

Sample Manuscript Format

Your name
(optional—word or page count)
Street address
City, state/province, and post code
Telephone number
(optional—e-mail address)

(leave a break of at least four lines)

Your Title

by Your Name

(leave a break of at least four lines)

Start your manuscript here. It should have margins of at least one inch on the sides, top, and bottom. Indent your paragraphs. Double space between lines. Do not be tempted to save on paper by single-spacing a long manuscript. This will make it harder to read, and you want the editor's reading experience to be the best you can make it. For the same reason, use a common, easy-to-read type-face, no matter what your word processor offers.

You can number your pages, starting with the second page, in the upper right hand corner, if your manuscript is longer than a picture book.

You can put "Copyright © (year) by Your Name" on the first page, but this is no longer necessary. Unpublished works are protected by current copyright law, even without it.

For presentation purposes, you can create a separate title page, starting the text on the second page, but this is not necessary for short manuscripts.

Index

D

E

F

331

Y–Z

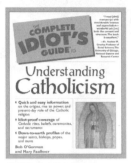

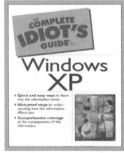